Wyndham Lewis

RELIGION AND MODERNISM

Wyndham Lewis

RELIGION AND MODERNISM

DANIEL SCHENKER

THE UNIVERSITY OF ALABAMA PRESS

Tuscaloosa and London

Portions of an earlier version of chapter 6 of this work appeared in "Favoring the Divine: Wyndham Lewis's *The Human Age," Religion and Literature* 20.2 (summer 1988), and are used here with permission of *Religion and Literature,* University of Notre Dame. The author gratefully acknowledges the following sources of permission to use quotations in this book: the Wyndham Lewis Memorial Trust, a registered charity in the United Kingdom; the estate of Mrs. G. A. Wyndham Lewis; Black Sparrow Press; the Wyndham Lewis Collection, Cornell University Library; New Directions; and Henry Regnery Co., Washington, D.C.

∞

The paper on which this book is printed meets the minimum requirements of American National Standard for Information Science-Permanence of Paper for Printed Library Materials, ANSI Z39.48–1984.

Library of Congress Cataloging-in-Publication Data

Schenker, Daniel, 1955–
Wyndham Lewis, religion and modernism / Daniel Schenker.
    p.   cm.
Includes bibliographical references and index.
ISBN 0-8173-0535-1
    1. Lewis, Wyndham, 1882–1957—Criticism and interpretation. 2. Lewis, Wyndham, 1882–1957—Knowledge—Literature. 3. Criticism—Great Britain—History—20th century. 4. Modernism (Literature)—Great Britain. 5. Lewis, Wyndham, 1882–1957—Religion. 6. Religion in literature.   I. Title.
PR6023.E97Z88   1992
828'.91209—dc20   91-13775

British Library Cataloguing-in-Publication Data available

in memoriam
Abraham Schenker
"They told me, Heraclitus . . ."

Contents

Preface   ix

Abbreviations   xiii

1. Wyndham Lewis in the Modernist Canon:
   Dissent, Division, and Displacement   1

2. In Praise of Life: The Aesthetics of Deadness   19

3. From Morality to Metaphysics: Lewisian Satire   49

4. Religious Sensibilities   94

5. *The Childermass:* Modernist Apocalypse   126

6. *The Human Age:* Favoring the Divine   159

Epilogue   193

Notes   195

Select Bibliography   209

Index   219

Preface

In this study of Wyndham Lewis, I analyze the development of a literary career that spanned almost half a century. Quantity alone has made this a formidable task. Lewis's complete bibliography runs to almost forty full-length books and includes novels, short stories, poems, plays, literary criticism, and social commentary. While a few of these writings hold little interest for contemporary readers (his political tracts of the 1930s, for example), most of the fiction and criticism constitute important contributions to modernism, and so I have touched upon nearly all the major works.

An effective account of Lewis's career must come to terms with one very peculiar feature: its culmination in theological fantasy. Lewis himself hoped that he would be remembered by an unfinished trilogy entitled *The Human Age*, which describes the adventures of a twentieth-century writer who dies and finds himself traveling through Heaven and Hell. This single work occupied, and preoccupied, Lewis for thirty years, from the mid-1920s to his death in 1957. Previous studies of Lewis have tended to step around this work, seeing it as an interesting failure that distracted Lewis from exercising his talents as a satirist and social critic. I have taken the religious concerns of the book more seriously than my predecessors and argue that

The Human Age is the logical outcome of Lewis's uncomfortable relationship with modernity.

In retrospect, we can observe a series of dialectical turns in Lewis's career. Broadly speaking, the young Lewis concerned himself with art as an alternative to, and an escape from, the commercial spirit of the modern age. The outbreak of the First World War showed the impossibility of escape, however, and several months on the front line transformed him into the bitter satirist of the 1920s he called the Enemy. The intractable nature of social and political evil in the 1930s, and the inexorable drift toward the Second World War, increasingly led him to consider values that transcended the accidents of time and space and so drew him toward religion. Of course, living after Darwin and Nietzsche, Lewis could no longer equate religion with simple piety and faith in an all-knowing God; rather, it served him as the repository of the nonhuman, the necessary reminder that man was not the measure of all things. While Lewis is in some respects an idiosyncratic figure, the overall direction of his career is by no means unique. The progression from aesthetic to social to religious concerns that I pursue here finds echoes in the classic Virgilian movement from eclogue to epic, in Kierkegaard's outline of the stages of spiritual development, and in the careers of Lewis's most important contemporaries, Joyce, Pound, and Eliot.

Let me conclude here with a methodological note. Concurrently with his writing, Lewis also produced hundreds of paintings and drawings. While I have chosen not to treat this subject in any detail, I have also not hesitated to discuss Lewis's visual art when I thought it would illuminate points in my argument. This procedure is partly justified by the literary nature of Lewis's art. Although for a variety of reasons he insisted upon the strict separation of the verbal and visual imagination, Lewis's pictures usually have a very readable content; that is, they either tell a story or, like the work of his Italian contemporary Giorgio de Chirico, assert some philosophical point.

Encouragement and assistance for this project has come from a variety of sources. My first acquaintance with Lewis's work came in conversation with Hugh Kenner, who later urged me to undertake this study. Reed Way Dasenbrock has been over the years my principal sounding board for ideas about Lewis. Other thoughtful advice has come from H. E. Francis, Charles G. Smith, and Richard S. Moore. Thomas Fitch of the University of Alabama in Huntsville Library managed to obtain whatever materials I needed through interlibrary loan, and Linda Stevens of the UAH English Department resolved a variety of computer problems. My greatest debt, of course, is to my family: my grandparents, David and Helen Schenker, under whose roof I started this project; my in-laws, Gene and Bonnie Kay, in whose backyard I virtually completed it; and my wife, Amanda J. Kay, who provided invaluable editorial assistance, not to mention love, patience, and understanding.

Daniel Schenker
Lacey's Spring, Alabama

Abbreviations

ABR	*The Art of Being Ruled.* 1926. Ed. Reed Way Dasenbrock. Santa Rosa: Black Sparrow, 1989.
AG	*The Apes of God.* 1930. Santa Barbara: Black Sparrow, 1981.
B1	*BLAST 1.* 1914. Santa Barbara: Black Sparrow, 1981.
B2	*BLAST 2.* 1915. Santa Barbara: Black Sparrow, 1981.
BB	*Blasting and Bombardiering.* 1937. London: John Calder, 1982.
CD	*The Caliph's Design: Architects! Where Is Your Vortex?* 1919. Ed. Paul Edwards. Santa Barbara: Black Sparrow, 1986.
CM	*The Childermass.* 1928. London: John Calder, 1965.
CPP	*Collected Poems and Plays.* Ed. Alan Munton. New York: Persea Books, 1979.
DPDS	*The Diabolical Principle and the Dithyrambic Spectator.* London: Chatto and Windus, 1931.
E	*The Enemy: A Review of Art and Literature.* 1927–29. New York: Kraus Reprint, 1967.
L	*The Letters of Wyndham Lewis.* Ed. W. K. Rose. Norfolk, Conn.: New Directions, 1963.
LF	*The Lion and the Fox: The Rôle of the Hero in the Plays of Shakespeare.* 1927. London: Methuen, 1951.

MDM   *Mrs. Dukes' Million*. Toronto: Coach House, 1977.

MF   *Malign Fiesta*. 1955. London: Calder and Boyars, 1966.

MG   *Monstre Gai*. 1955. London: John Calder, 1965.

MWA   *Men without Art*. 1934. Ed. Seamus Cooney. Santa Rosa: Black
      Sparrow, 1987.

RA   *Rude Assignment*. 1950. Ed. Toby Foshay. Santa Barbara: Black
      Sparrow, 1984.

RFL   *The Revenge for Love*. 1937. Chicago: Henry Regnery, 1952.

RP   *The Red Priest*. London: Methuen, 1956.

SB   *Snooty Baronet*. 1932. Ed. Bernard Lafourcade. Santa Barbara:
      Black Sparrow, 1984.

SC   *Self Condemned*. 1954. Santa Barbara: Black Sparrow, 1983.

SF   *Satire and Fiction*. London: Arthur, 1931.

T   *Tarr*. 1918. Ed. Paul O'Keefe. Santa Rosa: Black Sparrow, 1990.

T2   *Tarr*. 1928. Harmondsworth: Penguin, 1982.

TWM   *Time and Western Man*. 1927. Boston: Beacon, 1957.

WA   *The Writer and the Absolute*. London: Methuen, 1952.

WB   *The Complete Wild Body*. Ed. Bernard Lafourcade. Santa Barbara:
      Black Sparrow, 1982.

Wyndham Lewis

RELIGION AND MODERNISM

1

Wyndham Lewis in the Modernist Canon

Dissent, Division, and Displacement

In a few lines of verse from his satiric self-portrait "If So the Man You Are," Wyndham Lewis described with uncanny accuracy his place in English letters as it stood in 1933 and has continued to the present day:

> I am an "outcast" and a man "maudit."
> But how romantic! Don't you envy me?
> A sort of Villon, bar the gallows: but
> Even there I may be accommodated yet.
> Why yes it's very jolly to be picked
> As the person not so much as to be kicked,
> As the person who de facto *is not there*,
> As the person relegated to the back-stair. (*CPP* 51)

Lewis wrote these lines during a two-and-a-half-year period when he published eight books and an art portfolio but received few of the customary rewards of authorship. Despite his reputation as a serious artist and thinker, his advances from publishers were small, usually in the £150 range, and earnings from his book sales almost never recouped these meager sums.[1] Even more than poverty, though, he resented his exclusion from the public notoriety that had come to other avant-garde artists of his acquaintance. Around 1920, Ezra Pound had written of Wyndham Lewis and James Joyce that "the English prose fiction of my decade is the work of this pair of authors."[2] In 1931, however, when people violated federal laws to obtain copies of *Ulysses*, Lewis's novel *Tarr*, published by Knopf and legally available, sold eleven copies in the United States.[3]

Still, we can discern through the bitterness of his sarcastic comparison with Villon a defiant spirit that tells us just how much Lewis could enjoy the role of outcast and how, paradoxically, it could assuage, if not quite fulfill, the need for recognition. To be kicked means that one is merely a nuisance; to be condemned to virtual nonbeing implies that one represents a formidable threat to the established order. Lewis wanted us to see him (and wanted to see himself) as a one-man memento mori of contemporary culture: invisible to the eye but lurking just beneath the horizon of consciousness, he promises to come flying up the back stair to speak words we would rather not hear about ourselves. On several occasions, Lewis compared himself with Machiavelli as one who explored the unpleasant realities of human nature. Archetypal predecessors in this enterprise might also include Milton's Satan and Byron's Manfred; it was indeed a romantic persona that Lewis had created for himself.

Lewis's insistence on playing the role of adversary or "Enemy," as he liked to call himself, brings us to the major stumbling block in beginning a critical study of his life and work. Simply stated, Lewis created a highly polemical art that forces the reader to be either for him or against him: he opposed his vision of an agonistic relationship between man and the world to what he saw as attempts in every area of modern cultural life to obliterate this necessary opposition, which he once described as "the ancient and valuable iranian principle of duality" (*ABR* 25). He saw himself as a kind of spiritual aristocrat and opposed efforts to resolve conflicts (usually through man's/the self's/the subject's conquest of the world/the other/the object) meant to achieve such utilitarian ends as the greatest good for the greatest number. His uncompromising attitude on this point marks him as a kind of zealot and also connects him with an Old Testament tradition that extends from Amos and Elijah down through such latter-day prophets as William Blake and Friedrich Nietzsche.

Lewis's relatively few critics have tried to see his volatility as both the symptom of, and sometimes even cure for, the ills of modern life. Pound established the pattern for this approach in the essay cited above and published not long after the appearance of Lewis's novel *Tarr*:

The book's interest is not due to the "style" in so far as "style" is generally taken to mean "smoothness of finish," orderly arrangement of sentences, coherence to the Flaubertian method.

It *is* due to the fact that we have a highly-energized mind performing a huge act of scavenging; cleaning up a great lot of rubbish, cultural, Bohemian, romantico-Tennysonish, arty, societish, gutterish.[4]

Three decades later, looking back over Lewis's career in the first comprehensive survey of his work, Hugh Kenner echoed these same sentiments:

Afoot in the void, his savagely energetic intelligence hunting down chimerical images of itself not only enacts in a dream-play the suicide of the West, but demonstrates the ubiquity of the illusions into which more fortunate intelligences have from time to time barely succeeded in not being betrayed. ... If Lewis has stood for intelligence rather than intuition, for creation rather than craftsmanship, for Western Man rather than his daemon the *Zeitgeist*, without ever personifying any of these things quite convincingly, yet even in illustrating the radical incapacity of will alone to do the work of patience, he has discredited the spuriousness we meticulously reward. . . . He is the necessary antidote to everything, from Freud and Lawrence to the cults which have surrounded Eliot and Joyce.[5]

While this approach has successfully brought other dissenting artists into the canon (one thinks immediately of Pound), Lewis remains almost as much an outsider as he has ever been. Neither have two waves of republication (Methuen and Regnery in the mid-1950s, and Black Sparrow in the past decade) brought the revival of interest sought by his admirers. Lewis cannot simply be dismissed as an inept writer; testimonials to his accomplishment come from such contemporaries as Pound, T. S. Eliot, W. B. Yeats, H. G. Wells, Rebecca West, and Ford Madox Ford. What, then, has been the cause of his continuing status as "the least read and most unfamiliar of all the great modernists of his generation"?[6]

Most of us can live with an artist's obnoxious politics, clumsy prose, or immoral conduct if we can identify a sense of unity and purpose in his or her career, directed toward the fulfillment of some recognizable (and forgivable) human need. Wyndham Lewis fails to meet this important criterion, exhibiting, on the contrary, a set of internal divisions that have always made it difficult for readers to "place" him. First, he harbored divided cultural loyalties that affected the substance of his art and politics;

second, he pursued commitments to the practice of what he saw as two diametrically opposed arts; and finally, though not a conventionally religious man, he understood life as a struggle between the human and the divine and tended to side with God against man. Let us briefly consider each of these divisions and its effect upon Lewis's reputation.

For Lewis more than for any of his contemporaries, the three milieus that contributed to the development of twentieth-century modernism—American, British, and Continental—lay almost equal claim to importance in his own artistic development. Certainly other writers of his generation traveled a good deal and spent years in unlikely places under the constraints of self-imposed exile; but Joyce in Trieste, Pound in Rapallo, and Lawrence in Taos, New Mexico, remained quintessentially the Irishman, American, and Englishman each had been born, respectively. Lewis's origins, however, spanned two continents. He had an American father (with a distinguished Civil War record) and an English mother and was born on his family's yacht in the harbor at Amherst, Nova Scotia, on November 18, 1882.[7] (Lewis retained Canadian citizenship for the rest of his life.) In the late 1880s, the family moved to England, but within a few years, his parents separated when his father ran off with one of the maids; Lewis remained in England with his mother. He attended the prestigious Rugby School, but as his abysmal performance there would suggest (he finished twenty-sixth in a class of twenty-six), Lewis seems to have detested English morals and manners from the time he was old enough to have opinions on the subject (perhaps partly on account of his American ancestry). A few years at London's Slade School of Art told him that the English also had little to teach him about aesthetics, and thus he removed himself to Paris and the Continent when barely out of his teens. Here he began to develop his mature style in painting and writing out of French, Italian, and Russian models; he also spent a number of summers in Brittany painting and meditating upon the Celtic inhabitants, whose rather primitive way of life made as deep an impression upon Lewis as the Polynesians had made upon Gauguin. When the allowance from his estranged father ran out and he returned to England in 1912, the English barely recognized him as one of their own; indeed, the early reviewers of *Tarr* (which began serial publication in *The Egoist* in 1916) praised the work for qualities uncharacteristic of most English novels. Rebecca West called it "a beautiful and serious work of art that reminds one of Dostoevsky only because it is too inquisitive about the soul";[8] Ezra Pound also drew the comparison with Dostoevsky after remarking dryly that Lewis was "the rarest of phenomena, an Englishman who has achieved the triumph of being also a European."[9]

The First World War put an end to this early phase of his career just as he had brought out the first issue of the journal *BLAST* and more or less established himself as leader of the English avant-garde. When Lewis returned to the public eye at the end of the war, Continental painting—the cubist and futurist art that had gone by the name "postimpressionism" when it first appeared in England around 1910—had started to gain a measure of acceptance in local circles. Ironically, Lewis's experiences at the front had made him uneasy about the dehumanizing effect of the abstract style he had been perfecting in 1914, and his own work now took an insular turn toward more naturalistic representation. Lewis had once again managed to misplace himself: he became the most English sort of artist—a portrait painter—at the precise moment English audiences were becoming more European in their tolerance for abstraction.

Divided loyalties also contributed to his disastrous views on foreign policy during the thirties. As with the practice of his art, Lewis's political behavior seems to have been rooted in a desire to promote cultural diversity within the domain of Western civilization. While the League of Nations was proving itself ineffectual against the rising tide of nationalism in Europe, and while the English were growing increasingly confirmed in their worst fears about the hostile intentions of their neighbors on the Continent, Lewis wrote in 1936 and 1937 two polemical works that argued that England should follow an essentially internationalist policy, at least insofar as this meant keeping an open door to Germany. Lewis's position seems to have been informed as much by self-interest as by fellow-traveling attraction to authoritarian rule: his career had already been derailed once by a European war, and as an artist, he would have much to lose by the renewal of hostilities; avant-garde movements of the sort Lewis deemed essential cannot flourish apart from the free exchange of people and ideas across borders. Lewis was not alone in wanting to maintain peaceful relations with Hitler, of course; it remained the policy of the British government through the better part of the decade. Hitler's aggression after Munich shocked Lewis as much as it did the politicians, and in two books published in 1939, he disavowed his former ingenuousness about German intentions. Unfortunately, Lewis's earlier books remained in print (one came out in a cheap edition at the time of the German invasion of Czechoslovakia), and one of the two later books only appeared three months after the outbreak of war, by which time nobody needed to be told that Hitler was a villain. But the issue of politics in Lewis's career had now become moot for another reason: in September 1939, Lewis commenced an unhappy period of geographical misplacement back in North America, undertaken in the vain belief that he would find greater opportunity to exercise his talents as a portrait painter.

A number of Lewis's contemporaries had found new homes across the Atlantic by the end of the thirties, and one can imagine that Lewis might have followed suit. His former mentor, Ford Madox Ford, had been teaching at a small college in Michigan for several years before his death in June 1939; both W. H. Auden and Christopher Isherwood had moved to New York in January that year. On several occasions during his six-year residence, Lewis tried to make the arrangement permanent, actively seeking artist-in-residence positions at several American universities (an ambition that he continued to pursue even after his return to England in 1945). But once again his heterogeneous cultural alliances seem to have undermined his chances of finding a comfortable niche in his ancestral homeland. As an Englishman, he found America unbearably commercial; as a European, unbearably provincial (though Canada's French population somewhat alleviated the Anglo-Saxon monotony). Nor did the fact of his having been born in America appreciably help the situation; in some ways, it actually made matters worse. Soon after Lewis arrived in 1939, he went to look up some of his relatives in Buffalo, New York. The results were not encouraging. One cousin thought Lewis "a kind of screwball," and Lewis later referred to his somewhat snobbish relations as "shits."[10] The net effect of the encounter seems only to have reinforced Lewis's sense of not belonging in America. Lewis managed to recover a semblance of his prewar reputation upon returning to England but continued in the ways of cultural misplacement. At a time when the English were turning inward once again, preoccupying themselves with the dismantling of the empire and the creation of the welfare state, Lewis became an outspoken advocate of maintaining cultural ties with America and the Continent and of the eventual establishment of some kind of world government.

A second internal division involved Lewis's equal commitment to two different arts, which to a degree has earned him the suspicion of full-time practitioners (and critics) of one art or the other. With the exceptions of Blake and possibly Rossetti, no other Englishman so fully devoted himself to painting *and* writing. Lewis traced his interest in the two arts back to the activities of his parents: "My mother and father's principal way of spending their time at the period of my birth was the same as mine now: my mother painting pictures of the farm house in which we lived, my father writing books inside it."[11] His own career, he tells us, began at the age of eight as a chronicler of the wars between Redskins and Palefaces: "These lines of lifeless foemen converge, where they meet gesticulation is sometimes indicated. There is much action in the text, but practically none in its visual accompaniment" (*RA* 118). Ironically, when painting became a serious vocation for him as a student at the Slade, he first gained recognition from teachers and upperclassmen as a writer, having composed numerous Petrarchan and Shakespearean sonnets. "To these elders I was known as a 'poet,'" Lewis remarks in his autobiography. "The Fine Arts they imagined were already in good hands, namely their own" (*RA* 123). Lewis's first published works were in prose, however, not poetry. His account of the writing of his first story both illuminates the nature of his creative process and also serves to distinguish him from the few other English artists who worked in both words and paint:

> It was the sun, a Breton instead of a British, that brought forth my first short story—*The Ankou* I believe it was: the Death-god of Plouilliou. I was painting a blind Armorican beggar. The "short story" was the crystallization *of what I had to keep out of my consciousness while painting.* Otherwise the painting would have been a bad painting. That is how I began to write in earnest. A lot of discarded matter collected there, as I was painting or drawing, in the back of my mind—in the back of my consciousness. As I squeezed out *everything* that smacked of literature from my vision of the beggar, it collected at the back of my mind. It imposed itself upon me as a complementary creation. That is what I meant by saying, to start with, that I was so *naturally* a painter that the two arts, with me, have co-existed in peculiar harmony. There has been no mixing of the *genres.* The waste product of every painting, when it is a painter's painting, makes the most highly selective and ideal material for the pure writer. (*WB* 374)

Curiously, Lewis in this passage asserts the priority of painting over writing in his career, while covertly arguing that only the ideal painter can be an ideal writer; he also tells us that the two arts coexist within him in "peculiar harmony," at the same time implying a violent struggle between the two modes of understanding ("As I squeezed out *everything* that smacked of literature"). To some degree, the language in this passage simply reflects Lewis's commitment to the romantic belief that art emerges through conflict: the short story comes into being on account of a struggle between *both* his cultural alliances (Breton versus British) *and* his artistic instincts (painting versus writing). Lewis's insistence upon separation can also be seen as part of a larger movement to establish the unique formal properties of the various arts, a movement that gathered strength at about the time when photography began to challenge the mimetic supremacy of traditional painting. The mechanical accuracy of photographs obliged painters to see that their work involved as much mediation as representation and told them that photographs would always surpass paintings when optical fidelity was the goal. But if painting was a medium, so too was photography, one condemned to a certain kind of "vulgar realism," as its detractors pointed out. Though less visually accurate, painting could *see* where the photograph could only observe. In the late 1870s, James McNeill Whistler urged artists to paint something beyond what was before their eyes and to begin thinking of the natural world not as a "model" but rather as a "key" to the complex experience of perception and understanding.[12] The shift from model to key, readily apparent in the practice of a late-nineteenth-century artist such as Paul Cézanne, anticipates the more radical move toward wholly nonrepresentational art in the early twentieth century. If an artist could not re-create the physical object on canvas, why should he even bother to try? A painting should be nothing more or less than a painting—not a thing or a narrative or a dissertation. As Wassily Kandinsky explained the matter in *The Art of Spiritual Harmony*, "The impossibility and, in art, the purposelessness of copying an object, the desire to make the object express itself, are the beginning of leading the artist away from 'literary' colour to artistic, i.e. pictorial aims."[13] Lewis would have been well acquainted with this way of thinking from his years in Paris and had already executed a number of works in a radically abstract style by the time Kandinsky's influential book appeared in English in 1912.

But while Lewis recognized the opportunities opened up by abstract art, he also must have felt its limitations. In the struggle for possession of the real, art may have gained the high ground from science and technology by shifting from imitation to spiritual harmonies, but at the same time, it lost the texture of the ordinary, which perhaps has only lately been recaptured in the work of the photo-realists. The point of the artistic revolution for Lewis seems to have been less liberation than limits: an awareness that no single style of art [14] and no single art among all the arts could encompass the full register of any experience. Thus, the moral of the story about the beggar is that painting and writing have their inherent limitations. Lewis's subject had an imposing physical presence that could be captured only by a visual medium; but the blind Armorican also belonged to a mythological tradition that could not be conveyed except in words. Efforts to overcome this division by mixing the arts would only result in blunting the formal precision of each medium. Synesthetic projects of artists such as Richard Wagner ignored another important insight of the revolution in the arts: that not only could no single style or art encompass an experience, but no single artist could either. The attempt to do so reveals a desire to see the world with the eyes of God, perhaps a respectable position for a romantic but certainly not for a modern.[15]

Lewis's acute sense of aesthetic boundaries is closely related to his awareness of an estrangement between the human and the divine, which, to the extent that it has influenced his artistic practice, has probably been the most significant factor in his poor critical reputation. T. S. Eliot touched upon this issue in a 1955 review of Lewis's apocalyptic novel *Monstre Gai*, a sequel to *The Childermass* (published over a quarter-century earlier), when he remarked that the latter work showed a marked gain in *"maturity"* over its predecessor:

> The difference in maturity between *The Childermass* and *Monstre Gai* is not merely that the philosophy is riper or more explicit or more coherent: there is, I believe, also a development in humanity. In the first part of *The Childermass* one is too often, and too irritatingly reminded that Pulley and Satters belong to Mr. Lewis's puppet gallery. It is not that their creator *failed* to make them real—it is that he *denied* them more than a measure of reality. Just as one of them seemed about to behave like a human being, instead of like a caricature (though a caricature which only Lewis could have drawn) the author would give a little twitch of the string (and how often, and how tiresomely, we are reminded that Pulley is a "little" man) to put him in his place: "if you are going to try to behave like human beings I'll slap you back into your puppet box."[16]

In short, Lewis refuses to present us with "rounded" characters with whom we can readily identify. Even on those few occasions when Lewis attempted to write popular fiction (because he desperately needed the money), he rejected what Hugh Kenner calls "a cardinal motif of best-sellerdom, empathy: a sequence of small unfakeable indications that a good time is being made available for us all to share, that the writer in some fundamental important way enjoys the world he is presenting."[17] Lewis's unwillingness to play fiction by the rules of the game could have been chiefly a consequence of temperament and disposition. There have always been writers who took a sardonic view of their fellow man and similarly employed an aesthetic of caricature to express their scorn; Lewis himself recognized the affinities between his own art and that of Ben Jonson, whose work he did not otherwise hold in high esteem (*MWA* 91). Personal considerations aside, however, we should be aware that Lewis's practice does reflect some of the changed thinking about man and his place in the scheme of things current in the late nineteenth and early twentieth centuries. What distinguishes Lewis from his contemporaries was his determination to pursue these insights to their unpleasant logical conclusion.

Lewis came to maturity at a time when the ideas of Darwin, Marx, Nietzsche, and, to a lesser extent, Freud had already begun to frame discussions of every subject from politics to paleontology. Underlying this intellectual upheaval at the end of the nineteenth century was the notion that men had not so much *discovered* the world as they had *invented* it. Consider, for example, the traditional postulates about something as fundamental as time and space. The Bible authoritatively placed the origins of the universe at a point some six thousand years ago—a long time, certainly, but not much longer than the span of cultural memory. Darwin's expansion of the time scale from six thousand to several millions of years made the biblical account appear as the prejudiced contrivance of a tragically short-lived creature whose history now seemed less a beginning and an end than a mere episode in some larger evolutionary process. Similarly, our conception of space lost its absolute character. Stephen Kern observes that in the early years of this century not only did scientists assert that people of different cultures have different perceptions of space, but that the various species of animals experience distinct spatial realities. Kern continues: "This reminder that there are complete worlds with distinctive spatial orientations scattered all along the phylogenetic scale challenged the egocentrism of man."[18]

More radical still than the undermining of time and space was the attack upon the idea of truth itself. Two thousand years ago, Plato asserted against the Sophists that an unchanging reality lay somewhere behind the confusing multiplicity of experience. Philosophers since Plato had argued about our degree of access to this reality (which eventually became identified with God), but not until the nineteenth century did anyone seriously doubt its ultimate existence. Then Friedrich Nietzsche announced, in effect, that the Sophists had been right all along: that the metaphysical system of the West was a linguistic artifact, a peculiarly successful piece of rhetoric that served and reflected a variety of human needs:

> What then is truth? A movable host of metaphors, metonymies, and anthro-pomorphisms: in short, a sum of human relations which have been poeti-cally and rhetorically intensified, transferred, and embellished, and which, after long usage, seem to a people to be fixed, canonical, and binding. Truths are illusions which we have forgotten are illusions; they are metaphors that have become worn out and have been drained of sensuous force, coins which have lost their embossing and are now considered as metal and no longer as coins.... [Mankind] forgets that the original perceptual metaphors are metaphors and takes them to be the things themselves.[19]

The arts contributed in their various ways to this assault upon absolutes. Arguably the most influential painting of the early twentieth century, Picasso's 1907 work *Les Demoiselles d'Avignon* (allusions to which may ap-pear in Lewis's own painting as early as 1909[20]) leads the viewer to at least two important recognitions: first, that human beings do not stand apart from their environment but are rather continuous with it, arising from and sinking back into its intersecting planes and angles; and second, that the artist can present his subject from only a small fraction of an apparently infinite number of possible perspectives. In fiction and poetry, James Joyce's and T. S. Eliot's use of the "mythical method" (as the latter described it[21]) instead of a cause-and-effect, temporally sequenced narrative to organize their material implied the reversibility of time and the irrelevance of individual identity: someone wandering the streets of contemporary Dublin or London could be the avatar of a person (or any number of persons) who had participated in the heroic struggles of ancient Greece (or the struggles of some other time and place).

But Lewis came to believe that while this new understanding of the world challenged human egocentrism, it failed to replace it with a modus vivendi appropriate to our changed circumstances. Indeed, one could argue, as the theologian Mark C. Taylor recently has, that since the Renais-sance each displacement of man from his once pivotal place in the cosmic order has left him in an increasingly dominant position vis-à-vis his natural, cultural, and spiritual environments: "[The] inversion of heaven and earth effectively shifts value from the divine to the human subject. Far from suffering the disorientation brought by the loss of center, modern humanism is self-confidently anthropocentric. While denying God, the humanist clings to the sovereignty of the self."[22] In *A Portrait of the Artist as a Young Man*, Stephen Dedalus explains that the "personality of the artist . . . refines itself out of existence," not to diminish the artist but, on the contrary, to bring him to a condition " like the God of the creation."[23] A similar paradox obtains in *Ulysses*, long praised for its celebration of a contingent universe in which character dissolves, narrative voices multiply, and people and things roil around together in an Irish stew of space-time; yet Lewis sensed that these goings on bespoke not the self-consciousness of an ephemeral creature on a speck of interstellar dust but rather an authorial virtuosity, a hubris about one's creative power that surpasses the imaginative daring of eighteenth- and nineteenth-century fiction, just as modern technology surpasses the material power of earlier ages. Lewis almost certainly had Joyce in mind when one of the characters in his satire *The Apes of God* (1930), attacking what today we would call the survival of the subject, observes the simultaneous appearance of "(1) a school of unabashed personal Fiction, and (2) a universal cult of 'impersonality'"; he goes on to complain that this appearance of impersonality *"is a wonderful patent behind which the individual can indulge in a riot of personal egotism, impossible to earlier writers, not provided with such a disguise"* (AG 259, 260). To the extent that a reader identifies with the authorial presence in *Ulysses*, he or she vicariously participates in this celebration of the human as divine.[24]

Biographical accounts of Wyndham Lewis portray him as a self-centered man, thoroughly convinced of his own importance in the world (the legacy perhaps of having been the only child of a woman abandoned by her husband) and openly contemptuous of those who failed to acknowledge his genius. Yet for the better part of his career, Lewis practiced an iconoclastic art founded on the assumption that modern science had indeed knocked man off his cosmological high horse and brought the reign of humanism to an end. His visual art first disassembled the human form, then eliminated it altogether, and finally offered it grudging admission to a chilly world of eternal artifices; his fiction, as noted earlier, turned people into puppets and spun out tragical narratives that, unlike *Oedipus* or *King Lear*, refuse to end with affirmations of human dignity. In a sense, Lewis carried out the project that his contemporary T. E. Hulme envisioned as "A Critique of Satisfaction." At about the time Lewis was experimenting with abstraction in painting and prose, Hulme was trying to formulate a systematic philosophy free from anthropomorphism. He believed that he had identified a common mistake in all modern philosophies and wanted to rectify the problem:

> The philosophers share a view of what would be a *satisfying* destiny for man, which they take over from the Renaissance. They are all satisfied with certain conceptions of the relation of man to the world. These *conclusions* are never questioned in this respect. Their truth may be questioned, but never their *satisfactoriness*. . . . These *canons of satisfaction*, which are the results of an entirely uncritical humanism, should be subject to a *critique*.[25]

Had Hulme survived World War I and gone on to elaborate his critique of satisfaction, he might have encountered two of the problems that eventually led Lewis to withdraw from this position of radical antihumanism. First, no matter how one tries to step outside his particular perspective and imagine the world from the world's point of view, one cannot honestly claim to have seen anything except through human eyes. Hulme himself indirectly acknowledged the problem when he recalled hearing a philosopher whose objective vocabulary and scientific method he admired give a lecture on his religious views, and suddenly realizing that "the overwhelming and elaborate method [of his philosophy] only served to express a perfectly simple and fallible human attitude."[26] Much of Lewis's criticism from the late twenties onward has a curiously postmodern feel to it precisely because he devotes himself to showing the abuses of objectivity and thus revealing the ghost in the machine. Lewis also saw a problem that Hulme never seems to have recognized: that any attempt by a man to step outside the circle of his needs and offer a wholly disinterested account of the world must itself be looked upon as an act of hubris. Man would thus claim for himself a power that medieval theologians denied even to God: the right to will Himself out of existence. The impact of these developments in Lewis's thinking marks the turning points in his artistic practice, as we shall see later.

That one cannot *not* be human, that throughout life one remains a prisoner of nature, culture, and language, for Lewis constituted a tragic awareness. But given the fact that one had to live as a man or woman, what kind of life ought one to pursue? Or to put the question in a more self-interested way, what sort of social and individual behavior would ensure the survival of a world sympathetic to art? Whatever the precise answer, Lewis believed that it would still involve an acute sensitivity to limits. To be human does not require one to abandon the critique of satisfaction and embrace the values of a humanism that sees the world created in our own image. Indeed, Lewis continued to believe that behavior in accord with the humanistic values whose origins Hulme traced back to the close of the Middle Ages was making *any* kind of life on earth increasingly impossible. Although committed to a rhetoric of artistic progress and development early in his career, Lewis later came to realize that the momentum of modernity toward making the world over in our own image (the goal of Western technology, modernity's most characteristic expression) ultimately destroys the context for meaningful human activity.

Anxiety over the effective use of material and intellectual power will always be the luxury of ostensibly successful communities. Serious misgivings about the imposition of human values upon nature (and indeed, the recognition of "nature" as a separate entity with a life of its own) begin to surface in Europe only with the beginnings of the industrial revolution. Jean-Jacques Rousseau, whose ideas about man and nature Lewis critiques in *Tarr*, identified man's fall from grace—his estrangement from himself and others—with the introduction of agriculture and metallurgy,[27] arts that allow men to see the earth not as a power and a spirit worthy of respect, but merely as an instrument for the satisfaction of their own desires. The English romantic poets who followed Rousseau in the last years of the eighteenth century were part of the first generation in history to observe catastrophic social and ecological changes within the span of a single lifetime. By his mid-thirties, Wordsworth had witnessed not only the French Revolution but also the numerous effects of what Lewis would bitterly call the discovery "that England was really a coal mine" (*RA* 121). An excellent summary of the consequences of human success can be found in John Stuart Mill's *Principles of Political Economy*. Mill, an admirer of the romantics, who took solace in Wordsworth's poems during a period of youthful depression, looks ahead to the time when the human species populates every corner of the globe. But he despairs

> in contemplating the world with nothing left to the spontaneous activity of nature; with every rood of land brought into cultivation, which is capable of growing food for human beings; every flowery waste or natural pasture

ploughed up, all quadrupeds or birds which are not domesticated for man's use exterminated as his rivals for food, every hedgerow or superfluous tree rooted out, and scarcely a place left where a wild shrub or flower could grow without being eradicated as a weed in the name of improved agriculture. If the earth must lose the great portion of its pleasantness which it owes to things that the unlimited increase of wealth and population would extirpate from it, for the mere purpose of enabling it to support a larger, but not a better or happier population, I sincerely hope, for the sake of posterity, that they will be content to be stationary, long before necessity compels them to it.[28]

Mill focuses upon the loss of "pleasantness," a practical tonic (which he also found in Wordsworth) for the nerves of men and women cut off by urban life from regular contact with scenes of natural beauty. Other writers of the period, notably Dickens and Arnold, went beyond the utilitarian question and considered the effects of a technologically sophisticated civilization upon man's sense of himself and his place in the cosmos. These responses, which look more to spiritual than pragmatic concerns, have been summarized by J. Hillis Miller in his study of nineteenth-century English literature, *The Disappearance of God:*

The industrialization and urbanization of man means the progressive trans-formation of the world. Everything is changed from its natural state into something useful or meaningful to man. Everywhere the world mirrors back to man his own image, and nowhere can he make vivifying contact with what is not human. Even the fog is not a natural fog, rolling in from the sea, but is half soot and smoke. The city is the literal representation of the progressive humanization of the world. And where is there room for God in the city? Though it is impossible to tell whether man has excluded God by building the great cities, or whether the cities have been built because God has disappeared, in any case the two go together. Life in the city is the way in which many men have experienced most directly what it means to live without God in the world.[29]

As Miller's passage indicates, the apprehension of "what is not human" has traditionally been the province of religion. When Hulme wanted to distinguish his position from that of humanism, he too chose the term "religious," though with a certain amount of reluctance. He wanted his readers to understand that for him religion had no necessary connection with receiving baptism or going to church on Sunday. Hulme observed:

It would perhaps have been better to have avoided the word religious, as that to the "emancipated" man at once suggests something exotic, or mystical, or some sentimental reaction. I am not, however, concerned so much with religion, as with the attitude, the "way of thinking," the categories, from which a religion springs, and which often survive it. While this attitude tends to find expression in myth, it is independent of myth.[30]

A few artists of Lewis's generation, most notably T. S. Eliot, found religious orthodoxy strong enough to shatter the mirror of a humanized nature that condemns man to solipsism. (In *After Strange Gods*, Eliot forcefully presents the argument against human hegemony and praises the Southern Agrarians in his original University of Virginia audience for opposing unlimited industrial development.[31]) Most, however, found the established religious myths and symbols inadequate for their purposes; in an age when science has so undermined the stability of religious myth that theologians have seriously debated the merits of emptying religion of its mythical content,[32] the artist's adoption of an orthodox religious viewpoint can easily be interpreted as a reactionary gesture, as Hulme himself feared.

Lewis belongs in this latter company, which includes not only Hulme but also Joyce, Pound, and, to a lesser extent, W. B. Yeats. All of them share in varying degrees a commitment to modernity: the idea that the forms of artistic and intellectual life must somehow respond to the changing conditions of material life. Accordingly, Lewis refused to bind himself to a traditional worldview, as, for example, Eliot bound himself to Christianity. On the other hand, Lewis and his modernist contemporaries broke from many of their immediate predecessors in doubting that change could be identified with progress and perfectability. Some years before the shock of World War I made pessimism fashionable for a "Lost Generation," Hulme had called for the revival of the doctrine of Original Sin and a general acknowledgment of human limits in an infinitely vast and mysterious universe. In his first volume of memoirs, Lewis reflected upon the value of Hulme's contribution to the philosophical debate about the nature of man:

For people who had definitely become queasy, after listening for a good many years to adulation of the mortal state—of man-in-the-raw—this theology acted as a tonic. The atmosphere had become fuggy with all the greasy incense to Mr. Everyman. And here was somebody who had the bright idea of throwing the window open. There were the stars again! And even if the Star of Bethlehem *was* among them, well what matter! (*BB* 102)

Hulme, a philosopher, insisted that his commitment to the religious attitude was both absolute and impersonal: "It is not . . . that I put up with the dogma for the sake of the sentiment, but that I may possibly swallow the sentiment for the sake of the dogma."[33] Lewis, an artist, does allow a measure of sentiment to influence the forms of his religious expression. As we shall see later, while Lewis holds an essentially Catholic/classical view of man's subordinate place in a graduated cosmic hierarchy, he often presents himself as an inspired poet-prophet closer to the Protestant/romantic tradition of individual witness. Moreover, while Hulme claimed that the religious attitude could find expression independent of myth, Lewis never dispensed with myth entirely (even in his iconoclastic vorticist period) and almost seems to have reinvented Christian myth as an appropriate medium for his mature religious vision.

Although Lewis's career does not exhibit as orderly a progression through various phases as Joyce's, his development does follow a path reminiscent of the one that Kierkegaard outlined for the person who struggles with the temptations and disappointments of modernity.[34] One begins in an "aesthetic" stage characterized by feelings of resentment at the loss of the sacred to human progress and the turning inward to a cultivation of those rare and evanescent sensations (such as love) that seem emissaries from the divine. When the emptiness of this exercise becomes apparent (as Kierkegaard demonstrated in his various analyses of the Don Juan legend), the individual attempts to locate the focus of ultimate concern in the shared life of the community around him. This "ethical" stage often sees the development of intense social and political commitments. And yet, to the extent that the ethical demands the subordination of the particular to the universal (to obey the law is not always to do what one knows is right), it implies a certain flattening out or even evasion of existence. An individual life possesses a value that exceeds that of any ethical imperative to which it must be sacrificed in whole or in part. At this point one passes into the "religious" stage, which Kierkegaard understood as an unmediated encounter with the conditions of one's own existence.

This movement from self to other, accompanied by a paradoxical increase in self-knowledge, can be traced throughout modern literature. We see its outlines in the idealized progress through lyric, epic, and dramatic genres that Stephen Dedalus describes for the artist in *A Portrait*, and that Joyce himself seems to have followed (with a number of detours) in his own career from the poems of *Chamber Music* to the theatrics of *Finnegans Wake*. Lewis, because of his peculiar love/hate relationship with romanticism, would never enunciate a theory of personal growth and development, but this general scheme nonetheless provides a useful approach to his career. His early works (*Mrs. Dukes' Million, The Enemy of the Stars, Tarr*) partake of the brooding aestheticism of a young artist in the last years of Victorian England; his works of middle age (*The Childermass, The Apes of God, Snooty Baronet, Time and Western Man*) consist of harsh social satire and extensive nonfiction analyses of politics and ideology; and in old age, after World War II and the coming of the atomic age, he turns (most notably in *The Human Age*) to serious theological speculation as a way to transcend the increasingly destructive impulses of humankind.

Part of the excitement in reading Wyndham Lewis is suggested by Fredric Jameson's remark that in him we discover "a modernism which is still extant and breathing, an archaic survival, like the antediluvian creatures of Conan Doyle's *Lost World*."[35] But as this also implies, Lewis's work has about it a monstrous and inhuman quality, which, if it has served to keep him alive, has also excluded him from the mainstream of a literary tradition that, despite occasional bows toward the dissolution of subjects, still values the human image above all else. In a way, Lewis's absence from survey courses and anthologies (not to mention publishers' lists) has been as it should be: his skepticism about the ultimate value of man in the cosmos probably runs deeper than that of any modern writer, and readers can perhaps be forgiven for having shied away from him. In the study that follows, therefore, I do not propose to domesticate Lewis according to the tenets of a humanist tradition he consistently rejected, but rather to place him in the context of a religious outlook we can learn to appreciate, if not always love.

2

In Praise of Life

The Aesthetics of Deadness

Wyndham Lewis, Aesthete

Lewis's commitment to modernity entailed a certain impatience with the past, which extended even to his personal history: "How many novels are intolerable that begin with the hero in his cradle?" he asked in the introduction to a volume of memoirs (*BB* 1). His own novelistic practice favored such characters as the hero of *Tarr*, who "impressed you as having inherited himself last week" (*T* 37).

But Lewis did begin somewhere, as he more willingly acknowledged later in life. In an often cited letter of 1941 to his old friend and mentor, T. Sturge Moore, Lewis laments the series of events that has left him stranded in North America and goes on to recall the pleasures of an earlier time:

> How calm those days were before the epoch of wars and social revolution, when you used to sit on one side of your work-table and I on the other, and we would talk—with trees and creepers of the placid Hampstead domesticity beyond the windows, and you used to grunt with a philosophic despondence I greatly enjoyed. It was the last days of the Victorian world of artificial peacefulness—of the R. S. P. C. A. and London Bob-

bies, of "slumming" and Buzzards cakes. As at that time I had never heard
of anything else, it seemed to my young mind in the order of nature. You—
I suppose—knew it was all like the stunt of an illusionist. You taught me
many things. But you never taught me *that*. (L 293)

Lewis came of age in a world that was still peaceful but not wholly
untroubled, as Moore's philosophic despondence and awareness of illusion implies. The Victorians had inherited the spiritual crisis attendant
upon the industrial revolution's progressive humanization of nature and,
with their genius for engineering and public administration, had exacer-
bated the problem, making the spiritual and natural worlds seem increasingly remote. The question of just how to establish vivifying contact with
what is not human thus became a major preoccupation throughout the
latter decades of the nineteenth century.

By the 1890s, a distinctly aesthetic response to the crisis had emerged,
exemplified in the writings of Walter Pater, Oscar Wilde, and others. While
conceding that science had reduced direct experience of the world "to a
swarm of impressions," Pater asserted in the conclusion to his influential
study *The Renaissance* that one could achieve fulfillment by cultivating an
ability to receive and appreciate sensory data: "While all melts under our
feet, we may well catch at any exquisite passion, or any contribution to
knowledge that seems by a lifted horizon to set the spirit free for a
moment."[1] For the aesthete perception alone, as the Greek word implies,
could redeem a world from which one felt increasingly estranged. Alan
Robinson has summarized the aesthetic solutions of the period as "the
replacement of naturalistic objectivity by varieties of anti-materialist transcendentalism."[2]

Moore's early poetry, like that of his close friend W. B. Yeats, reflects a
strong commitment to the aestheticism of the 1890s. Yvor Winters, the only
critic of note to praise Moore's verse, identifies the poet's theme as "his own
relationship to the Romantic tradition, the tradition of rejuvenation
through immersion in sensation."[3] Lewis met Moore as early as 1902,[4] and
although Moore's lasting effect upon his style seems to have been negli-
gible, Lewis certainly recognized a kindred spirit in the older writer. At
least two letters to his mother written during his early years in Paris show
Lewis asking her to forward books by Moore (L 16, 17). Lewis's own verse
of the period, consisting mainly of a group of about forty sonnets[5] that
might well be described as Pre-Raphaelite imitations of Shakespeare, dem-

onstrates his attachment to the concerns of aestheticism: the indifference of the world, the primacy of the self, the redemptive power of art. The concluding sestet of "To the Spirit of Poetry" provides a fairly typical example:

> Our minds are all some buried saviour's tomb,
> But rarely woken from pollution's gloom;
> And nought but a low sound of mourning more
> Assails its depths,—no clamours as of yore:
>   One night shall not the watchers at the door
>   Find a white angel in corruption's room?[6]

Words such as "woken," "gloom," "nought," and "yore" mark the poem as the product of its time; Ezra Pound employed the same kind of diction throughout the first decade of the century until, as he tells the story, Ford Madox Ford rolled on the floor after a reading of Pound's third volume of poetry showed him "trapped, fly-papered, gummed and strapped down in a jejune provincial effort to learn, *mehercule,* the stilted language that then passed for 'good English' in the arthritic milieu that held control of the respected British critical circles."[7] More recently, Donald Davie has described this idiom as "romance language in the sense that it is the language of historical romances written in late-Victorian and Edwardian England; it is not a medium in which anything can be communicated forcefully or crisply."[8]

Moore, a member of respected British critical circles, offered his protégé encouragement in a letter of 1908: "Of all the poetry which I have read by my contemporaries, those who are alive now, it is these sonnets which gave me the most sense of a new possibility, a new creation, and consequently there is no writer alive whom I desire to accompany and communicate with [more than you]."[9] In retrospect, Lewis seems to have had better instincts about his career than Moore, and although never abandoning poetry altogether, he increasingly devoted himself to efforts in prose. By the time of Moore's letter, Lewis had probably written some of the short stories based upon his Breton experiences, which would appear in little magazines over the next couple of years. The prose of these sketches (some of which we will examine more closely in the next chapter) shows none of the pseudoarchaic diction of his poetry; indeed, one is tempted to say, as Pound said of Eliot after reading "Prufrock" for the first time, that Lewis had succeeded in modernizing himself on his own. He also employed this unaffected style in his most ambitious literary work before *Tarr*, a novel written between 1908 and 1910 but not published until twenty years after Lewis's death under the title *Mrs. Dukes' Million*. The work is important to an understanding of Lewis's development because it is at once the fulfillment and exorcism of Lewis's early aestheticism.

In the cover letter accompanying the manuscript to a literary agent, Lewis goes out of his way to distance himself from the work. He describes it as a "miserable pot-boiler" and insists that "it was done to get if possible a little money so that I could complete comme il faut my other novel"—a reference to *Tarr*; he also notes that he selected chapter titles on the basis of what he thought would be most "vulgarly effective" and signals a willingness to remove certain unflattering remarks about the press if the agent saw any possibility of serial publication (*L* 43). Despite these mercenary disclaimers, *Mrs. Dukes' Million* can be read as an ingenious and intellectually sophisticated mystery novel that belies the indifferent attitude of its author.

Mrs. Dukes, an amiable if outspoken old woman, has lived in the junk shop near Oxford Street that her husband left behind when he walked out on her some thirty years before. Unknown to Mrs. Dukes, her husband removed to Liverpool, where he prospered but never remarried. He thus directed in his will that upon passing from this life (an event that immediately precedes the action of the novel), his estranged wife should receive his one-million-pound estate. Though news of Mr. Dukes's demise has not yet found its way to Mrs. Dukes when the story opens, word has reached the mysterious Raza Khan, an Eastern potentate living in London who heads a gang of criminals dedicated to the staging of elaborate impersonations for personal gain. He has decided that the current situation affords him an opportunity to defraud a stupid old woman of her inheritance and conspires to kidnap Mrs. Dukes and replace her with one of his own "Actor-Gang" until the money comes safely into his hands.

When we become better acquainted with the Khan, however, we realize that he is less concerned with money than with art. What matters to him, he explains to a new recruit, is the successful displacement of predictable events by a design that allows the individual the fullest expression of his creative potential: "I wanted to see actors no longer bound by the 'piece' they had to play, but to *act* and *live* at the same time" (*MDM* 66). He goes on to compare what he does to Maeterlinck's staging of *Macbeth* in various rooms of a house, the audience following the actors around and observing them from various perspectives, "as though it were really taking place" (*MDM* 66). If on occasion the Khan's art *does* lead him into criminal activity, so much the better, for most laws exist to protect the timid and frustrate the ambitious (some people would consider Napoléon a criminal, he says angrily at one point).

The Khan always keeps a lookout for exceptional acting talent, and one night he finds it in a young man who has a mere handful of lines in a second-rate theatrical production. Hercules Fane, the actor in question, manages to support himself with occasional minor roles in the theater, but his true ambitions lie elsewhere: "His spirit was a poet's, he was not a verse-writing poet, but a prose-writing poet—even after the slight disappointment of this revelation, which we kept back as long as possible, we shall still continue to refer to him as a poet" (*MDM* 59). After a brief interview with the Khan, the impecunious Fane reluctantly agrees to join his company.

Fane soon learns that his task will be to understudy the role of Mrs. Dukes that is currently being played by another member of the gang, Evan Royal. The narrator tells us little about Royal's history beyond the fact that earlier successes as an actor have turned him into something of an "arrogant young scoundrel" (*MDM* 116). Soon afterward, Royal reflects upon his situation as he gazes out the window early one morning: "'To lie here smoking in this chilly dingy room, supposed to be an old woman, considering my plans for the day, twenty minutes after sunrise, few people awake for a mile around, except the poor dull boring old policemen—the feeling of loneliness and strangeness—there is *stimung* in it, as the Germans say, a certain swagger'" (*MDM* 117). But he goes on to say that after two years in the Khan's service, the thrill of stepping outside the bounds of legal propriety has vanished: "always this same cold, mechanical scheme of robbery—always this blight of sordidness!" (*MDM* 117). Royal decides that he wants out of the whole business and later persuades Fane to join him in a scheme to abscond with the one-million-pound inheritance themselves. After what Lewis must have deemed the requisite number of seriocomic misadventures, Royal, Fane, and the Khan's half-European niece, Lucy (with whom Fane has fallen in love), manage to escape both the police and the Khan's henchmen and to establish themselves under new identities in Paris. Here, we presume, the three of them live happily ever after.

The plot of Lewis's novel rests upon two premises of aestheticism: the corrupt nature of the social and material worlds, and the redemptive power of the individual artist's imagination. In *Mrs. Dukes' Million,* life not only imitates art but is transformed by it, the whole world becoming the stage for a master playwright's productions. "One of the present players in my company," the Khan explains to Fane during their first meeting, "is playing his part six thousand miles away from here, without audience, but none the worse for that" (*MDM* 66). Imagination cannot function in the absence of world, however, and often the brute material that an artist employs will undermine his creation; the artist also depends upon the world to provide him with adequate food, clothing, and shelter. From this tragic awareness grows the occasionally melancholic disposition of the aesthete. In a passage that we know from the letter to his agent alludes directly to Lewis's own predicament, Evan Royal reflects upon the practical dilemma of the Khan:

> " I believe my employer to be a remarkable man, he has somewhat the same feelings as myself. But like many artists he is unfortunately poor, and is compelled always to do only the things that pay, and alas! also, only in the *way* that pays. What we are doing now need not be a pot-boiler, but it is. What a terrible thing poverty is! He needs about a hundred thousand a year to carry on his company, to keep it up properly, and go on with his fantastic projects. The result is that he has to be thinking constantly of money, money. This preoccupation enters into all our schemes, and spoils them." (*MDM* 117–18)

The plot and theme of *Mrs. Dukes' Million* show Lewis's debt to aestheticism, but other aspects of the novel indicate a more critical attitude toward the program as understood by his older contemporaries. Consider, for example, the curious doubling of protagonists. After a fifty-page exposition leading up to the replacement of Mrs. Dukes with a member of the Actor-Gang who had been living in her house as a lodger, Lewis introduces us to Hercules Fane. Fane is an attractive character who would be a suitable hero in almost any work of popular fiction. Although he eventually becomes involved in an underhanded scheme, he promises himself to withdraw if and when he is asked to do something illegal, and he makes it very clear that he would never have joined the gang in the first place had he not been so desperately poor. Fane does, however, possess one characteristic that sets him apart from more conventional heroes: his artistic temperament. Here he begins to fall in love with the heroine: "Being of a very romantic disposition—so much so, indeed, that we have been compelled often to refer to him as a poet, as the only means of conveying an idea of the excess of these romantic tendencies in him—he was extremely alive to the exotic charms of his colleague, the beautiful Lucy (*MDM* 199)." While Lewis often pokes fun at the conventions of the "pot-boiler," on this occasion, his mockery focuses squarely upon the overheated sensibility of his artist-hero, who can hardly retain his composure in the presence of feminine beauty. The satiric perspective on Fane had actually been adopted as far back as his introduction in a chapter entitled "An Inflammable Young Poet." There the narrator informs us that "Hercules Fane, despite his Christian name . . . was short, not even of medium height," and lacks the splendid presence that sometimes allows an extra to eclipse a star (*MDM* 57). His unusual surname further modifies our impression of him. Fane means "sanctuary" or "temple" and has a possible provenance in Keats's rather cloying hymn to the goddess of self-consciousness, "Ode to Psyche" ("Yes, I will be thy priest, and build a fane / In some untrodden region of my mind"); the word also evokes the world of late-Victorian historical romance mentioned earlier. Taken together, his names signify a man too precious and otherworldly to realize his grand ambitions. He is more acted upon than acting and, in the last analysis, is unable to resolve the conflicts of the narrative on his own.

Fane contrasts sharply with Evan Royal, who increasingly becomes the center of attention as the novel progresses. Royal subscribes to a more hard-boiled kind of aestheticism, which surfaces when he convinces Fane to join him in double-crossing the Khan:

> "I don't do this for money, as I have told you already, but for fun—not innocent fun, because I am not a particularly honest man, anyway, but fun all the same; a funny sort of fun of my own. . . . I was born for adventure. The only way of getting a sufficient amount of adventure, and always on tap, for my very big appetite in this country is being a criminal. I don't particularly mind being a criminal, but it naturally hampers one, and cuts one off from all decent people. But in certain parts of the world I could secure as much adventure as was necessary for my health . . . without going out of my way. I should get it as an ordinary citizen. I should not have to become a sharper and outcast to get it." (*MDM* 280)

Despite the selfish and amoral attitude he adopts here and elsewhere in the novel, in one respect Royal shows greater consideration for others than the ostensibly more thoughtful Fane. Royal's desire to have adventure as an ordinary citizen without having to become "a sharper and outcast" tacitly acknowledges the social context of aesthetic experience. Unlike the Khan, who undermines the life of the community, or Fane, who withdraws from it into the world of his own passions, Royal wants to be both an artist and a citizen (though "ordinary citizen" seems a rhetorical excess: a few lines later he announces, " 'I shouldn't at all mind being president of a South American republic, for instance' " [*MDM* 280]).

Mrs. Dukes' Million moves toward something that is absent from all other Lewis novels until the final (and not fully complete) version of *The Human Age:* a happy ending. Both heroes find satisfying lives abroad, though here again the differences between them tell us something about Lewis's progress from the other side of Sturge Moore's worktable to leadership of the English avant-garde. We last see Fane standing in the Museum Galleries of the Luxembourg Gardens in his new identity as one Mr. Edgar Pope: "Fane was still a poet, only now instead of being a poet in prose, he was a poet in paint." We also learn that on account of his "charming talents" as a painter, which earn him "considerable sums of money," he has anonymously returned his portion of the loot to the rightful owner (*MDM* 365). As we might expect, Evan Royal (now known as Richard Neal) has felt no such compunction; but on the other hand, "the more heroical, filibustering Royal" has had more ambitious plans and has achieved greater fame than his companion, whose new name (an apparent cross between Alexander Pope and Edgar Allan Poe) still implies something vaguely neurasthenic. Royal, who began the novel masquerading as a portrait painter, has now become an artist in the medium of the machine:

> This young Englishman who had lately astonished Europe with the accounts of his amazingly daring aeroplane flights, published by all the papers, was proposing to astonish them still more. It was he who had flitted around the topmost peaks of the Alps in his wonderful biplane, and who had done all the most romantic and most perilous things that the new sport yet had to boast of. He had lived amongst the clouds and snows of mountains like an eagle; he had passed a night at sea, in the Mediterranean, with his machine, especially adapted for alighting on the water. He was, the papers pointed out, like a seamew—this flying man. (*MDM* 363–64)

This talk of eagles and seamews and flying men recalls Stephen Dedalus's vision of "a hawklike man flying sunward above the sea" in Joyce's *Portrait of the Artist as a Young Man*,[10] a novel roughly contemporary with *Mrs. Dukes'* (but unknown to Lewis until its publication in 1916). Like Stephen

Dedalus, Royal dreams of forging the uncreated conscience of his race, though he chooses to employ mechanical rather than mythological means: "it was now an open secret among inventors that he had already prepared a machine which would at last solve all, or nearly all, the problems of aviation, so that at last aviation would no longer be a perilous sport for a few courageous men, but would come within the reach of any man who had money enough to buy a machine" (*MDM* 364). It is tempting to read forward from Royal's desire to bring aviation to the masses toward Lewis's later attempts in novels and essays to secure a respected place for the arts in society. In *Mrs. Dukes' Million*, however, the focus remains on the integrity of the artist's vision, not on its social utility; indeed, the narrator makes a point of remarking that Royal has not approached the building of airplanes with altruistic motives, but "entirely as business speculation" that promises to yield an immense personal fortune (*MDM* 364).

The movement from Hercules Fane to Evan Royal marks a transition from a detached to an engaged aestheticism, from the modesty of Yeats's suggestion at the end of the 1890s that the arts should be pursued "for ourselves and our good friends,"[11] to Lewis's announcement in *BLAST* that the vorticists "will convert the king if possible" (*B1* 8). Lewis's meditations on aestheticism continue in *Tarr*, the novel that his "miserable pot-boiler" had been intended to subsidize. This work provides both an exhibit of, and an argument for, a radically new kind of art.

Lewis wrote *Tarr* over a period of several years, during which he also executed a large number of paintings and drawings in an increasingly nonrepresentational style. Although the novel did not appear until 1916, Lewis's apparent preference for the daring aviator over the charming painter in *Mrs. Dukes'* indicates that he had already committed himself to an avant-garde program by 1910. (A small drawing entitled *The Theatre Manager*, which arguably registers the earliest influence of cubism in Lewis's visual art, also dates from this time.[12]) Pronouncements in *Tarr* thus reflect a pattern of thinking that predates the emergence of his revolutionary vorticist persona in 1914.

Tarr shares with Joyce's *Portrait* an interest not only in developing a new medium of expression, as Ezra Pound had noted in his early essay on Lewis, but also in discovering the origins of the artist who would employ it. Although Frederick Tarr, a young English painter living in Paris, gives the impression of having "inherited himself last week," the narrator's passing allusion to his childhood early in the novel belies his self-possession and reveals a continuing pattern of inner conflict:

> A rude and hard infancy, according to Balzac, is best for development of character. A child learns duplicity and hardens in defence. = An enervating childhood of molly-coddling, on the other hand, such as Tarr's, has its advantages.—He was an only child of a selfish, vigorous mother. The long foundation of delicate trustfulness and childishness makes for a store of illusion to prolong youth and health beyond the usual term. Tarr, with the Balzac upbringing, would have had a little too much character, like a rather too muscular man. As it was he was a shade too nervous. But his confidence in the backing of character was unparalleled. You would have thought he had an iron-field behind him. (*T* 38)

In short, Tarr wants to be an Evan Royal flitting among the topmost Alpine peaks of the spirit but instead often finds himself, like Hercules Fane, weighted down by the desires of the flesh and the pangs of conscience. The novel opens with Tarr's resolution to break off a longtime love affair with an attractive but rather unintellectual German woman, Bertha Lunken, whose ambitions for marriage and family present a serious threat to his artistic career. Tarr cannot bring himself to make a clean break with her, however, and decides upon a policy of gradual withdrawal, a plan greatly facilitated by the appearance of a boorish, untalented, and aging art student named Otto Kreisler. Tarr encourages an affair between Kreisler and Bertha that allows him the emotional breathing space to achieve the desired state of indifference toward his former mistress. But Kreisler, whose story eventually consumes five of *Tarr*'s seven sections, does more than relieve Tarr of an emotional burden; his life of noisy desperation, culminating in acts of rape, manslaughter, and suicide, also serves Tarr as an important lesson in the failure to master one's instinctual life.

An indication of Tarr's apparent progress toward self-mastery is his liaison with Anastasya Vasek, who becomes the focus of his attention in the concluding section of the novel. Though on one level Anastasya simply replaces Bertha as an outlet for Tarr's sexual energies, she comes closer to being an expression of his artistic ideals, impressing Tarr one evening as a statuesque "apparition in solid white" (*T* 306), as against the "German pastry" offered by Bertha Lunken (*T* 305). Tarr's conversations with Anastasya provide the author an occasion to comment upon the fate of Otto Kreisler and to present a discursive explanation of the proper relationship between art and life. (As Pound observed, "when Tarr gets things off his chest, we suspect that the author also is getting them off his own chest."[13]) During one of these exchanges (which roughly parallels the discussion of aesthetics in the last chapter of *A Portrait*), their attention turns to the nature of art itself:

> "There is bad art and bad life. We will only consider the good. = A statue, then, is a dead thing; a lump of wood or stone. Its lines and masses are its soul. Anything living, quick and changing, is bad art, always; naked men and women are the worst art of all, because there are fewer semi-dead things about them. The shell of the tortoise, the plumage of a bird, makes these animals approach nearer to art. Soft, quivering and quick flesh is as far from art as an object can be."
>
> "Art is merely *the dead*, then?"
>
> "No, but *deadness* is the first condition of art. A hippopotamus' armoured hide, a turtle's shell, feathers or machinery on the one hand; *that* opposed to naked pulsing and moving of the soft inside of life, along with infinite elasticity and consciousness of movement, on the other.—Deadness, then," Tarr went on, "in the limited sense in which we use that word, is the first condition of art. The second is absence of *soul*, in the sentimental human sense. The lines and masses of the statue are its soul. No restless, quick flame-like ego is imagined for the *inside* of it. It has no inside. This is another condition of art; *to have no inside*, nothing you cannot *see*. Instead, then, of being something impelled like an independent machine by a little egoistic fire inside, it lives soullessly and deadly by its frontal lines and masses."
> (*T* 299–300)

This impromptu manifesto still has the power to shock readers after more than half a century. Critical taste in fiction has not changed appreciably over the years in the sense that most works continue to be held to an implicit standard of vitality: how lifelike do the characters appear? do they engage the reader's sympathy? can we imagine ourselves in their places? Rarely, if ever, do critics praise a book for its deadness. Lewis's position seems doubly perplexing in light of his commitment to an aggressive aestheticism that proposed a large-scale transformation in consciousness through the medium of art; deadness hardly seems an adequate catalyst for such a revolution.

Lewis's preference for lines and masses at the expense of soul has its origins in a philosophical split within the aesthetic movement of the 1890s.

The late Victorians responded to increasingly popular mechanistic theories of human behavior (evident in the literary practice of the naturalist school) with an "anti-materialist transcendentalism" that attempted to restore the sense of mystery that urban and industrial progress had crowded out of modern life. Yeats and Moore asserted the absolute supremacy of mind over matter and endeavored "to supplant the contemporary world with a more congenial and autonomous world of the imagination."[14] Their pre-occupation with folktale and mythology implies a belief in the power of the mind to utterly transcend the physical limitations of time and space. Other artists, including Arthur Symons and many New English Art Club painters, all distinguished by a receptivity to "the dispassionate, scentific detachment of French Impressionist painting," believed that the transcendent experience would come only of a "sympathetic interaction" between mind and world.[15] Both positions emphasize the importance of individual consciousness in compensating for the loss of something once available from revealed religion and a life close to nature, but while Yeats could dispense with the material world from the outset, Symons accepted the world as a necessary instrument of consciousness. The two positions also reveal distinct ideological biases: the former inclines toward oligarchy with its concentration of spiritual power in the minds (and only the minds) of the few; the latter is more democratic in allowing for the dispersal of spirit throughout the sensible world and in maintaining that spirit exists only through an interaction of mind and matter.

Mrs. Dukes' Million would seem to have been written from the oligarchic perspective outlined above: Evan Royal, more at home among the Alpine summits than in the petite bourgeoisie precincts of London, can lay claim to a spiritual-heroic pedigree going back to Byron's Manfred. Two features of the book complicate this picture, however, and indicate Lewis's uneasiness with the idea of an autonomous and omnipotent imagination. First, none of the characters, with the possible exception of Mrs. Dukes's idiot son, Cole, have stable identities. In fact, Lewis encourages the reader to accept the consummate artistry of the Actor-Gang's miming skills. When Evan Royal puts on makeup and adopts the verbal mannerisms of Mrs. Dukes, he *is* Mrs. Dukes for all intents and purposes. (Even her son, who seems to intuit the change, quickly accepts Royal as his mother.) The same holds true for other members of the gang. Watching his beloved Lucy in the guise of a homely charwoman, Fane is possessed by a "melancholy fancy": " What if she were *really* like this, and if the charming girl she appeared to him, when her make-up was discarded, was the untrue and unreal aspect of her?" (*MDM* 154). Later on, when Royal decides to leave the Khan, a series of changes in identity facilitates his escape; he becomes, in turn, a member of a German band, a "dapper young man of fashion" in London, a tourist in Paris, a student in Munich, and, eventually, the aviator Richard Neal. The Khan himself remains a cipher. Not only does he come from the mysterious East, but his name is not even a name; as Royal observes, " he's a Median prince, a Parsee. . . . He has one peculiarity, I believe, and that is that he has no name. All his names, and he has about a dozen, are titles" (*MDM* 184). Thus, although Lewis's hero may lean toward a philosophical idealism, his creator premised a novel upon a radical nominalism where appearances count as reality and signs signify no Platonic ideal of selfhood.

A second problem involves Evan Royal's ambitions at the end of the novel. Royal wants to build a safe and reasonably inexpensive airplane that would allow "all the people who had hung back from participating in the new sport because of its dangers" to share the excitement of aviation. The implication is that the artist differs from the common man not in kind but in degree, and that the artist may have a responsibility to share his vision with a world that can appreciate and understand it. This broad conception of the place of art in society stands far removed from Yeats's sometime notion of the artist creating things only for himself and a few select friends.

These inconsistencies in characterization tell us that while Lewis's contempt for the workaday routines of modern life drew him to the figure of the artist who can transform the world through the power of imagination, his exposure to insights of the physical and behavioral sciences, showing the complex relation of the self to forces beyond its conscious control, made impossible an unquestioned faith in that imaginative power. Evan Royal has the power to effect radical change in the world, but at the same time, he takes shape before us as a collage made out of bits and pieces of that same world.

The aesthetic principles elucidated in *Tarr* affirm and extend the principle of opposition between mind and world. "Art is identical with the idea of permanence," Tarr tells Anastasya. "It is a continuity and not an individual spasm" (*T* 299). The artist infuses his raw material with a quality that lends immortality to the final product. *He* performs the magic; the material *does* nothing. Tarr's insistence upon deadness as a condition of art continues to assert the artist's supremacy over his creation. But we might go on to ask why Tarr illustrates his aesthetic theories with reference to sculpture. Lewis himself wrote and painted but never worked in stone. This intractable medium offers greater resistance to imagination than words or paint, requiring the brute force of a strong arm and a chisel. A sufficiently gifted poet could compose an epic in the privacy of his own mind, but the sculptor cannot come as close to realizing his vision without turning to the world outside imagination. Thus, while Tarr's first condition of art celebrates the genius of the artist, it also serves to remind writers and painters of the limitations imposed upon them by an environment that can no more be denied by imagination than death can be denied. The deadness underlying the fully realized artifact implies its indifference to and separation from the living artist's original vision.

Aesthetic Theory: Hulme, Worringer, Shklovsky

The outlines of Lewis's aesthetics of deadness can be seen with greater clarity in the work of two contemporaries who undertook a more systematic approach to the philosophy of modern art. T. E. Hulme based his theories partly on his reading of Continental aestheticians and partly on the practice of English artists including Jacob Epstein, David Bomberg, and Lewis himself; his ideas in turn exerted some influence on the course of art and literature in England. The writings of the Russian formalist critic Victor Shklovsky were unknown to Lewis and his associates, though Shklovsky's theories emerge from an intellectual milieu that closely parallels that in England at the time, and his ideas about how art radically estranges familiar objects unknowingly provided one of the best commentaries on Lewis's narrative technique in *Tarr*.

Although Hulme believed in the value of a religious attitude that would acknowledge the nonhuman context of human actions, he usually preferred to address particular aesthetic problems in his essays rather than broader theological issues; and the problem that most often engaged his critical attention during his short career was the development of a nonrepresentational approach to poetry, painting, and sculpture. Hulme strongly approved of this trend and advanced an argument that both demonstrated its intellectual sophistication and gave it the appearance of historical necessity. In his most succinct formulation, the argument has three main points:

> 1. There are two kinds of art, geometrical or abstract, and vital and realistic art, which differ absolutely in kind from the other. . . .

2. Each of these arts springs from, and corresponds to, a certain attitude towards the world. . . .

3. The re-emergence of geometrical art at the present day may be the precursor of the re-emergence of the corresponding general attitude towards the world, and so of the final break-up of the Renaissance.[16]

A few paragraphs later, Hulme admits that these developments became clear to him only after he had read the work of the German art historian Wilhelm Worringer and had had the opportunity to discuss his ideas with him at a conference in Berlin. Briefly, Worringer argued that so-called archaic or primitive art had as valid a claim to our attention as the naturalistic art of Greece and the Renaissance. In his doctoral dissertation, translated into English as *Abstraction and Empathy*, he goes on to make two essential points. First, he claims that the history of art is less a matter of ability than of volition.[17] If an African mask looks primitive or unnatural to us, this has less to do with what the artist could accomplish, given the limitations of his skill and his material, than with what he wanted to accomplish. His second point follows naturally enough from the first: that different but equally worthy volitions are behind different kinds of art. An "urge to empathy" has motivated European art since the Renaissance, whereby the artist, wishing to express man's apparent mastery over his physical and social environments, almost casually projects himself into the things he tries to represent.[18] Empathetic art makes no fundamental distinction between self and other; the aesthetic pleasure derived from a work of empathetic art is a form of "objectified self-enjoyment."[19]

Worringer contrasts empathy with an "urge to abstraction," such as motivated the Byzantines, which leads an artist to represent the object of interest as radically estranged from man.[20] He has two possible reasons for doing so: he feels an immense spiritual dread of space and the disconnected phenomena that it contains, and he seeks to take the individual object (or person) out of this unending flux by approximating it to abstract, eternal forms; and/or he has an instinctive respect for the "thing in itself" (as Worringer puts it), understanding that he does not have proprietary rights over everything and everyone, and that, perhaps ironically, his destiny may be better served by not attempting to gain complete mastery of the universe. If the urge to abstraction was once again reasserting itself in the arts, Worringer reasoned, this was because modern man had discovered by "rationalistic cognition" what his primitive ancestor knew by instinct: that there are limits to human knowledge that engender a certain humility in us when we face the riddle of a world that contains us but that we can never quite contain.[21]

Hulme had been as disturbed as Lewis by mechanistic theories of natural processes and human behavior, but also, like Lewis, he had been sufficiently impressed by scientific analysis to reject any notion that the contradictions of modern life could be resolved through the power of imagination alone. For a time, Hulme found an adequate response to mechanism in the writings of the French philosopher Henri Bergson, who proposed, in effect, the existence of two worlds and two methods of apprehending them. Hulme summarized "the general idea behind Bergson's work" as follows:

> It is an endeavor to prove that we seem inevitably to arrive at the mechanistic theory simply because the intellect, in dealing with a certain aspect of reality, distorts it in that direction. It can deal with matter but it is absolutely incapable of understanding life. In explaining vital phenomena it only distorts them, in exhibiting them as very complex mechanical phenomena. To obtain a complete picture of reality it is necessary to employ another faculty of the mind, which, after defining it, Bergson calls intuition. It is useless then to dream of one science of nature, for there must be two—one dealing with matter which will be built up by the intellect, and the other dealing with certain aspects of life which will employ intuition.[22]

We experience the interaction of these two worlds through the two media of intellect and intuition. Crudely speaking, Hulme seems to have understood Bergson's philosophy as a dualism of form and content, the latter in the service of the former. As he observes later in this same essay, "It may be, then, that the function of matter in regard to consciousness is this: It is destined to bring to precision, in the form of distinct personalities, tendencies or potentialities which at first were mingled."[23]

Hulme published his last essay on Bergson in 1913, and while never renouncing his former master, he became increasingly uneasy with such aspects of Bergsonian philosophy as the *élan vital*, a stream of consciousness that suffuses every atom of the universe and makes possible the fit between mind and world. The ideological implications of this philosophy certainly contributed to Hulme's disenchantment. Bergson's emphasis on intuition and flux argues against the preservation of traditional social and political institutions. Hulme, a conservative by temperament and upbringing, opposed during the immediate prewar years such liberalizing trends in

English politics as the reduction of the House of Lords prerogative and supported the broad objectives of the Neo-Royalist *Action française* in France. (After discussions in 1911 with Pierre Lasserre, a leading French conservative, Hulme moved to a position that limited the significance of Bergson's *élan vital*, holding that the experience of the world as animated and ever-changing might somehow be true for the individual but not for the race.[24]) Hulme's commitment to a view of man as a limited creature also conflicts with Bergson's belief in the dispersion of consciousness throughout the material universe. Although Bergson sought to demonstrate the value of mind and its relationship to matter, one can discern in his work an argument that the world is in fact a thinly disguised objectification of human consciousness. Hulme wanted a world more solid than the one Bergson offered him (and perhaps more solid than anything words could provide: at about this time, he forsook literature for plastic art), and Worringer's theories gave him a world that would resist the encroachments of consciousness.

Indeed, Worringer had been wrestling with many of the same conflicts as his English contemporary. He opposed the strictly materialistic approach to art history with a concept of artistic volition that could be modified by, but never subjected to, the accidents of time and space. But while Worringer's contemporaries had proceeded from here on the assumption that the artist would naturally re-create himself in the world around him, aesthetic enjoyment being nothing less than "objectified self-enjoyment," Worringer claimed that the exact opposite could occur and had occurred in the art of the Egyptians, the Byzantines, and various non-Western cultures. "Whereas the precondition for the urge to empathy is a happy pantheistic relationship of confidence between man and the phenomena of the external world," he explained, "the urge to abstraction is the outcome of a great inner unrest inspired in man by the phenomena of the outside world."[25]

For Hulme, Worringer's theory of abstraction preserved the individual self against a reductive materialism, while simultaneously demonstrating the self's ability to move beyond solipsism (Bergsonism, the left wing of English aestheticism in the 1890s, and empathetic art in general merely shifted the venue of selfhood from the body to its immediate surroundings). Because abstract art leads us away from the human form, it can aptly be described as an art of deadness; but death functions here as a master trope for the otherness of "the outside world," which, as Hulme recognized, not only contributes to the making of the modern self but also defines the field and the limits of its activity.

The idea that art should contradict rather than affirm life also figured prominently in the work of the Russian formalist critic Victor Shklovsky. Shklovsky occupied a place in prewar Russian art circles roughly analogous to that of Hulme's in England. He was well acquainted with leading artists in the avant-garde movement and, despite his formal education at Petersburg University, "felt more at home amidst the noise of literary cafés than in the calm atmosphere of university classrooms."[26] Also like Hulme, Shklovsky wanted to confer legitimacy upon the work of the avant-garde by giving it a sound theoretical foundation.

His essay "Art as Technique," an exemplum of early formalist method, begins with a rejection of the doctrine that "art is thinking in images," which Shklovsky identifies with the nineteenth-century philologist Alexander Potebnya and his followers.[27] While Potebnya had recognized the unique qualities of poetic as opposed to ordinary language, he revealed his commitment to a materialist view of art by suggesting that "the purpose of imagery is to help channel various objects and activities into groups and to clarify the unknown by means of the known."[28] In effect, this endorsed "the law of the economy of creative effort," which turned the mind into a machine of limited physical capacity. Shklovsky cites Herbert Spencer's formulation of the matter in *The Philosophy of Style*: "carrying out the metaphor that language is the vehicle of thought, there seems reason to think that in all cases the friction and inertia of the vehicle deduct from its efficiency; and that in composition, the chief, if not the sole thing to be done, is to reduce this friction and inertia to the smallest possible amount."[29] Oddly enough, Potebnya's ideas had also been absorbed by the chief opponents of materialism in Russia, the symbolists, whose agenda closely paralleled that of W. B. Yeats and his associates in England at about the same time. As Victor Erlich describes the meetings of Petersburg's literary and intellectual elite,

> the conversation, combining French "esprit" and German "inwardness", probed with equal zest into Oscar Wilde and Nietzsche, into Eleusinian mysteries and Neo-Kantian philosophy. . . . In these unique gatherings there was some room, to be sure, for snobbish precosity, for blasé estheticism seeking new trills in pseudo-mystical flirtations with the "Absolute". But it can hardly be doubted that the main participants of the Symbolist symposia

brought to them a genuine, indeed a desperately earnest, search for the meaning of life, for a satisfying set of values, however "private" or esoteric.[30]

The symbolists, too, saw the artistic image as a means to an end, not the simplified rational cognition of materialists, but rather an encounter with a hidden spiritual reality: "As the sensitive reader strained himself beyond the 'microcosm' of the poetic image toward its 'deeper' meaning, the perception of the visible symbol ushered in the intuition of the invisible 'substance.'"[31] Although symbolism strives after a transcendent absolute, in practice it turns attention back toward consciousness, where the transformation from the phenomenal to the noumenal occurs. At its most extreme, symbolism reduces all images (drawn from things in the world) to signs in the private aesthetic language of an individual artist; less radically, it functions as an empathetic art, blending things with signs in a way that allows the mind to see its diversity of moods expressed in the world around it.

In "Art as Technique," Shklovsky seeks a *tertium quid* that neither reduces conscious life to a series of physical events nor makes the physical world an event within consciousness. He first of all rejects the notion that art could function in a materialist economy of creative effort by noting that poetic language is frequently more difficult to read and understand than prose. In Japanese, for example, "the poetic language tolerated the admission of hard-to-pronounce conglomerations of similar sounds" not found in the conversational idiom.[32] Art therefore does nothing to support the materialist view that the world can be adequately comprehended as a collection of atoms governed by the laws of physics.

On the other hand, the difficulties that individual works present to the viewer also suggest that art does not recognize an exact parallel between world and mind (much less a sense that world *is* mind). Indeed, a perfect fit between the two would mean a kind of death-in-life. Shklovsky asks us to consider our relation to the objects and events with which we feel most intimate, the things that constitute our daily routine. We rise in the morning, get dressed, eat breakfast, bid our spouses and children good-bye, and go off to work. We meet no resistance and feel little anxiety as we perform these tasks because we have learned to ignore whatever might be strange or uncanny about them (including our reasons for being involved with them in the first place) and have effectively made them as much a part of ourselves as our own limbs. But this narrowing of perception soon begins to work its peculiar magic: life itself gradually disappears. Shklovsky quotes a passage from Tolstoy's *Diary* that illustrates the process:

> I was cleaning a room and, meandering about, approached the divan and couldn't remember whether or not I had dusted it. Since these movements are habitual and unconscious, I could not remember and felt that it was impossible to remember—so that if I had dusted it and forgot—that is, had acted unconsciously, then it was the same as if I had not. If some conscious person had been watching, then the fact could be established. If, however, no one was looking, or looking on unconsciously, if the whole complex lives of people go on unconsciously, then such lives are as if they had never been.[33]

Having successfully assimilated the environment to the rhythms and demands of daily existence, existence loses the solidity that gave it value in the first place. "And so life is reckoned as nothing," continues Shklovsky. "Habitualization devours works, clothes, furniture, one's wife, the fear of war."[34]

The aesthete in Shklovsky recognized art as an act of will, a special event somewhat removed from the domain of ordinary verbal and visual expression; the scholar and scientist in Shklovsky, however, needed to acknowledge the solidity of a world that resisted the efforts of the mind to possess it. His assertion that art "de-familiarizes" objects through such devices as metaphor and metonymy resolves this dilemma, much as Worringer's theory of abstraction resolved a similar problem for Hulme, by continuing to see art as an expression of will, but a will to acknowledge the peculiar forms of things rather than to assimilate other things to the form of the self. Like his futurist contemporaries, Shklovsky sought an art oriented "towards a reality which was in some sense immediate, concrete, actual," one that aimed at "the 'thing,' and not at an idea or an ideal."[35]

Critics since Shklovsky's time have noted with varying degrees of enthusiasm the difficulty of understanding modernist texts, a difficulty that Shklovsky himself seemed to prescribe; Richard Poirier, for example, has used the phrase "grim reading" to characterize the difference between twentieth-century literature and what came before.[36] But for Shklovsky, there was nothing grim about defamiliarization at all; rather, it signaled a reawakening of the senses such as William Blake might have appreciated. "Art exists that one may recover the sensation of life; it exists to make one feel things, to make the stone *stony*. The purpose of art is to impart the sensation of things as they are perceived and not as they are known."[37] By "known," Shklovsky means the way we see (or more likely fail to see) something within the framework of our selfish interests and routines; by "perceived," he had in mind an ex-static perspective from which we see the object in its ontological purity—seeing the stone as *stony* and not as the raw material for fences or axheads.

Aesthetic Practice: *Tarr*

Defamiliarization, abstraction, and the "condition of deadness" can all be seen as attempts to develop an aesthetic that preserves the imaginative powers granted to the artist by romantic theory, while acknowledging a complex network of relations discovered by the physical and social sciences that cannot be fully comprehended within an individual consciousness. To some extent, aesthetic theory followed upon changes in artistic practice during the first decade of the century; Hulme, for example, developed his arguments from careful observation of contemporary literature and, more especially, painting and sculpture. But the often programmatic quality of much early twentieth-century art also indicates that artists responded to prescriptive assertions about their craft. Marjorie Perloff notes that the masterpieces of Italian futurism were painted only after the appearance of manifestos by the futurist impresario F. T. Marinetti, describing the appropriate form and content of those pictures.[38] In Wyndham Lewis, we have an artist who wanted to serve as his own theorist, and who, with the discussion of art placed near the end of *Tarr*, offered a theory for the novel that contains it. Near the end of his life, Lewis remarked that "in writing *Tarr* I wanted at the time for it to be a novel, and to do a piece of writing worthy of the hand of the abstractist innovator" (*L* 552). Turning now to *Tarr*, we can observe several ways in which the general principles of abstraction and defamiliarization inform basic aspects of its design.

To begin, Lewis went out of his way to estrange the plot of his novel from the naturalistic expectations of his readers. That Lewis could put together a novel in a perfectly straightforward manner we know from *Mrs. Dukes' Million* (and few genres test a writer's skill in plot construction as thoroughly as the detective story); but in *Tarr*, he simply did not want to write that way. Some years later, he recalled his thinking on the subject in *Blasting and Bombardiering*:

> *Tarr* was not "constructed," as the commercial pundit calls it. It did not conform to the traditional wavelength of the English novel. There was not a lot of soft padding everywhere, in other words, to enable the eggs to get safely to market, to Boots and to Mudies. Indeed, they were *not* eggs. They were more like bullets. As Mr. H. G. Wells once remarked to me: I did not write novels as he'd been brought up to think of them. But *Tarr* was only the first: and there have been many since then—of my own, for that matter. Today *Tarr* would be accepted as a pretty straightforward narrative. Then it looked queer. (*BB* 88–89)

In the sort of novel H. G. Wells had been brought up on, the principle of continuity reigned supreme. As an author, you were allowed to surprise the reader occasionally, but you could not leave holes in your text through which the unsuspecting reader might fall, even if such textual holes had equivalents out there in the real world. Middle-class Victorian readers wanted the legitimacy of their position in the world affirmed, not brought into question. Liberal democracy, free enterprise, and modern technology promised the greatest good for the greatest number, and authors were expected to join in the march of progress by telling stories in which a logical sequence of events led to a resolution of conflict and uncertainty. Fictional characters, for example, were obliged to have come from some place; they needed a mother and a father (whose identities, if obscure at the outset, would be triumphantly revealed at the end) and an upbringing that would account somewhat for their behavior as adults. But as we have already seen, Lewis wanted to present the hero of *Tarr* as new and unfinished, almost as though he had just risen from the worktable of a latter-day Dr. Frankenstein: "[Tarr] impressed you as having inherited himself last week, and as under a great press of business to grasp the details and resources of the concern"(*T* 37).

The English novel tuned to the "traditional wavelengths" also had to move toward a climax, which provided a definitive measure of the characters and which began the part of the narrative that handbooks call the resolution. *Tarr* does have a climax, which involves a duel between Otto Kreisler and a certain Polish exile who has been guilty of a minor offense to Kreisler's honor. But Lewis seems to have gone out of his way to botch the drama of the moment and deprive it of conventional narrative significance. Kreisler kills the offending Pole, but he does so quite unintentionally when he is knocked off-balance by the Pole's second and involuntarily pulls the trigger of a gun pointed in the direction of his adversary. The confrontation with death, which might otherwise provide a real test of the characters' mettle, turns into a farce, as the narrator acknowledges: "[The] bolt was shot. Kreisler had been unsatisfactory. All had ended in a silly accident. It was hardly a real corpse at all" (*T* 276).

Even more curious is the absence of the novel's protagonist throughout this sequence. In a café the evening before, Tarr had been an observer of the negotiations that lead up to the duel, but he "left when the talking was over" (*T* 265) and does not resurface for another couple of chapters, following Kreisler's halfhearted flight from the law and his suicide in a provincial jail. Nor does Tarr ever have the opportunity to show his *virtu* in anything so dramatic and convincing as individual combat; rather more like Paris, he chooses to dabble in the wars of Venus.

The complications arising from Tarr's romantic entanglements bring us to the problem of the novel's conclusion. The sort of novel that Wells remembered does not have to end with everyone living happily ever after, but it does have to *end*. The reader expects answers to his unanswered questions, an assurance that the forces of chaos released at the beginning of the narrative have been brought back under control, and the satisfaction of knowing that heroes and villains, after their moment in the sun, will return to the same ordinary anonymity inhabited by the reader. Again, *Tarr* does have a denouement of sorts. The hero, having been exorcised of his sentimental and self-destructive impulses by the death of Kreisler, marries his estranged fiancée out of an ironical sense of duty and immediately goes off to live with his splendid Russian mistress. Things seem to be winding down nicely:

> Two years after the birth of the child, Mrs. Tarr divorced him. She then married an eye-doctor, and lived with a brooding severity in his company and that of her only child.
> Tarr and Anastasya did not marry. = They had no children. (*T* 320)

Then Lewis adds a concluding paragraph, which instead of bringing the novel to a point, effectively reopens all of its original conflicts:

> Tarr, however, had three children by a lady of the name of Rose Fawcett, who consoled him eventually for the splendours of his "perfect woman." = But yet beyond the dim though solid figure of Rose Fawcett, another rises. This one represents the swing back of the pendulum once more to the swagger side. The cheerless and stodgy absurdity of Rose Fawcett required the painted, fine and inquiring face of Prism Dirkes. (*T* 320)

From the standpoint of the nineteenth-century novel, these lines destroy any sense of narrative closure and leave Lewis open to the same charge a publisher's reader made against Joyce's *Portrait*, that "at the end of the book there is a complete falling to bits."[39] Who is this woman, Rose Fawcett, with whom Tarr had a sufficiently long and intimate relationship to father a small brood? Lewis introduces this woman just to keep us in the dark about her, as though defying his audience's wish for a final denouement. The same holds true of Prism Dirkes, who rises spectrally at the very end: probably no other English novel introduces a character in its last two words. Of course, a moment's reflection will reveal these two figures as later versions of Bertha Lunken and Anastasya Vasek, between whom Tarr had oscillated throughout the novel. But this awareness does not serve to restore a satisfactory sense of ending. It does, in fact, suggest that nothing has been resolved. Technically, *Tarr* is a tragicomedy: a comedy (the story of Tarr's engagement and marriage to Bertha) that contains a significant tragic element (the death of Kreisler). But the marriage is entirely perfunctory, evaporating in divorce within two years' time, and we cannot be sure that Kreisler's tragedy has had the appropriate cathartic effect upon the hero or has brought him self-knowledge. Reading the last paragraph of *Tarr* anticipates somewhat the experience of sitting through the opening moments of act two of Samuel Beckett's play *Play* and realizing that act two will be an exact repetition of act one; we begin to squirm in our seats and wonder how many times the cycle will repeat during the evening. The printed text of a novel cannot maintain theater's level of suspense—the reader can always flip over the last page of the novel and find the next sheet mercifully blank— but the conclusion, such as it is, gives the reader pause to think that *Tarr* was never meant as a logical and satisfying progress toward equilibrium, but rather as a demonstration of the recursive movement into chaos of a society that, during the years of *Tarr*'s composition, was proving itself at once the most civilized and most brutal in history.

Readers who were thrown off-balance by Lewis's unconventional plot would also have been intimidated by his prose style. Consider, for example, *Tarr*'s opening sentences: " Paris hints of sacrifice. = But here we deal with that large dusty facet known to indulgent and congruous kind. It is in its capacity of delicious inn and majestic Baedeker where western Venuses twang its responsive streets, and hush to soft growl before its statues, that it is seen" (*T* 21). Ezra Pound once remarked of Ford Madox Ford's novels that the prose " lay so natural on the page that one didn't notice it;"[40] Pound said many laudatory things about Lewis (as did Ford, who first published him), but praise for natural-sounding prose was not among them (indeed, he found the "actual writing" of the novel "faulty"[41]). Lewis's prose through the first half of his career brings to mind such adjectives as jagged, discontinuous, abstract. In *Enemy of the Stars,* a closet drama published in *BLAST 1* and composed during the last year of his work on *Tarr,* he experimented with this new style, generating such alien sequences as "The Earth has burst, a granite flower, and disclosed the scene," and "A leaden gob, slipped at zenith, first drop of violent night, spreads cataclysmically in harsh water of evening" (*CPP* 98). A distinguishing feature of these sentences and of many others in the play is paratactic structure, which makes the reader work a little harder figuring out how one thing relates to another. A reluctance to use articles, evident in the second sentence above, also contributes to the vague and unsettling sense of indeterminacy. (The English instructor would correct it to something like, "A leaden gob [!], which slipped at the zenith like the first drop of a violent night, spread cataclysmically in the harsh water of evening.") That Lewis intended to carry these tactics over into the composition of a full-fledged narrative we know from his remark years later that when writing *Tarr,* he wanted to eliminate all the "small fry," grammatical aids such as prepositions, pronouns, and articles, that normally grease the rails of comprehension (*L* 553). *Tarr* could not do without these items, he realized, but as we read the novel, we still have the feeling that something has been left out, and that sentences and paragraphs create as many problems as they resolve.

Returning to the opening lines of *Tarr,* we would probably like some clarification of the relationship between the "sacrifice" of which Paris "hints" and the "large dusty facet" known to persons of "congruous kind." But instead of a helpful transitional phrase, we find the suspiciously mathematical "=" sign. Lewis also achieved an abstract effect in prose by weakening the specificity of nouns and jarring slightly the placement of adjectives. Who exactly are the "kind" that know the "dusty facet"? And if "congruous," what are they congruous with (Paris? one of its facets?)? The remarkable third sentence, balanced upon the almost colloquial "twang," but otherwise reading like a translation from a newly invented German dialect, presents problems of reference due to the repetition of "it" or "its." Rereading the sentence, we can see that "its" must refer to Paris. But what about the final "it"? What is seen ("sacrifice"? "Paris"? or that "dusty facet" again?)?

Stylistically, Lewis's career was almost the reverse of James Joyce's or Henry James's. As he passed beyond middle age, he gave up the verbal pyrotechnics and wrote in a conventionally straightforward way. A number of reasons for the change can be cited. By the late 1920s, the highly mannered style that had once served à épater le bourgeois had itself become a bourgeois cliché in the hands of the dadaists and some of Joyce's lesser followers. Lewis also realized that while abstract prose could be used to good polemical effect in such a squib as *Enemy of the Stars*, it could not handle the various demands of an extended fictional narrative. Indeed, Lewis later insisted that the irregularities of *Tarr* had mostly to do with its hasty composition during the first year of World War I (*T2* 7), and when he had the chance to revise the novel for a second edition, he smoothed out all the rough edges, as these specimens from the opening of the second chapter will illustrate:

> Butcher was a bloody wastrel enamoured of gold and liberty. = He was a romantic, educating his schoolboyish sense of adventure up to the pitch of drama. (*T* 36)
> Butcher was the sweetest old kitten, the sham *tough guy* in excelsis. He might have been described as a romantic educating his english schoolboyish sense of adventure up to the pitch of drama. (*T2* 28)

The descriptive energy of the original has been thoroughly domesticated in the later version: out went the mysterious "=" sign, in came such "small fry" as the adjective "english" and the subjunctive modal "might"; longer sentences also counteract the staccato movement of the 1918 text.

But if Lewis had finally wrung abstraction out of his prose style, he adhered to the radical theory about fictional character that he first worked out in *Tarr*. Early critics noted that despite its title, the commanding presence in the novel belonged to Otto Kreisler, not Frederick Tarr (Lewis admitted in his second autobiography that "the book should have been called 'Otto Kreisler'" [*RA* 165]). Yet Kreisler is also the most mechanical figure in *Tarr*, a self-destructing contraption wired together out of clichés from a decadent romanticism that Lewis principally identified with the philosophy of Friedrich Nietzsche.[42] Everything about Kreisler suggests an absence of the vitality that informs the well-rounded character in more traditional novels. Lewis seems to have been obedient to another standard when creating him: indeed, the first condition of Kreisler is deadness:

Kreisler's room looked like some funeral vault. Shallow, ill-lighted and extensive, it was placarded with nude and archaic images, painted on strips of canvas fixed to the wall with drawing pins. Imagining yourself in some Asiatic dwelling of the dead, with the portraits of the deceased covering the holes in which they had respectively been thrust, you would, following your fancy, have turned to Kreisler seeking to see in him some devout recluse who had taken up his quarters there. (*T* 77)

Kreisler is the first of Lewis's major characters whose power lies not in a capacity to possess life but to oppose it. (Later on, Lewis would further detract from the physical vitality of his antiheroes by equipping them with artificial limbs.) This decision to break with naturalistic canons reflects a view, common to many of Lewis's contemporaries, that the human image in a work of art, no matter how convincingly executed, can never be more than a counterfeit made out of words, paint, or stone. Recognizing this, many artists in the early twentieth-century avant-garde asserted that the value of their work lay in the artifact itself rather than in the subject that the work was "about." (Abstract art, of course, supposedly had no subject.) As the Russian artist Kasimir Malevich exclaimed in a manifesto: "A face painted in a picture gives a pitiful parody of life, and this allusion is merely a reminder of the living. But a surface lives; it has been born."[43] Lewis, however, moved in almost the opposite direction. Although not indifferent to the textures of his media, his mature work shows him to be neither a "painterly" painter nor a "writerly" writer. Rather, his art seeks to preserve a fragile vitality that exists not within the work but beyond its margins. Art does have a relationship to the world (it is not in any sense self-contained, as Malevich suggests), but this relationship is more instrumental or rhetorical than mimetic. Thus, a fictional creation's effect upon its environment is more important than either its adherence to a canon of verisimilitude or its fidelity to inherent formal principles.

The world Lewis created in *Tarr* provides a microcosm of art's instrumental relationship to its surroundings. Otto Kreisler, for example, seems hardly more plausible as an actual person than Coleridge's Ancient Mariner; but like the Ancient Mariner, a specter provisionally returned from the world of the dead, Kreisler by his negative example recalls others to the lives they have almost surrendered to routine and cliché. This prophetic office lends Kreisler's "moody wastefulness and futility . . . a raison d'être and meaning, almost," (*T* 93) and functions on a number of levels in the novel itself. One beneficiary of this futility is Ernst Volker, a minor figure who for some years had been Kreisler's preferred source of credit: "It was Kreisler's deadness, his absolute lack of any reason to be confident and yet perfect aplomb, that mastered his companion. . . . The inertia and phlegm, outward sign of depressing everyday Kreisler, had found someone for whom they were a charm and something to be envied" (*T* 93). Kreisler plays a similar role, though in much tighter counterpoint, with Tarr. He serves as a constant reminder to Tarr of what he will become if he fails to master the forces arrayed against his ambition of becoming an artist: inertia, self-doubt, sentimentality, sex. Near the end of the novel, reflecting upon Kreisler's demise, Tarr comments: "He was an art-student without any talent, and was leading a dull, slovenly existence like thousands of others in the same case. He was very hard up. Things were grim that way, too" (*T* 302). But to all appearances, Tarr had been leading much the same existence during his time in Paris. As he strolls through the Luxembourg Gardens one afternoon, Tarr entertains these gloomy thoughts:

> This place represented the richness of four wasted years. Four incredibly gushing, thick years; what had happened to this delightful muck? All this profusion had accomplished for him was to dye the avenues of a Park with a personal colour for the rest of his existence.
> *No one,* he was quite convinced, had squandered so much stuff in the neighborhood of these terraces, ponds, and lawns. (*T* 232)

Kreisler is both warning and scapegoat to Tarr, an unbeloved companion who in the economy of the novel assimilates the protagonist's liabilities (including the emotional demands of his banal and bourgeois fiancée) and goes tumbling into the abyss otherwise reserved for Tarr.

Of course, if this instrumental theory about Lewis's art is correct, then the fate of the characters in *Tarr* matters far less than that of the living persons around its margins; and the most prominent among these would be the author. Indeed, as if to signal the real purpose of painting pictures and writing novels, Tarr remarks that the first creation of the artistic impulse should be "*the Artist* himself, a new sort of person" (*T* 29). Although the characters in *Tarr* cannot be wholly identified with their author, it would not be wrong to say that Tarr and all the others exist for the sake of their author. Their deadness—an abstract, unfamiliar, two-dimensional quality that to some degree informs all characters in fiction—provided Lewis with a kind of ontological background against which he could attempt to achieve the self-definition that ultimately eludes even the progatonist of his novel (we last see Tarr swinging on a pendulum between "the cheerless and stodgy absurdity of Rose Fawcett" and "the painted, fine and inquiring face of Prism Dirkes" (*T* 320).

Although Lewis rejected the otherworldly aestheticism of his early mentors, preferring instead to engage a reality as tough and independent as the mind he brought to bear against it, he remained an aesthete in the sense that reality still existed to serve the artist's imagination. This partly explains why the revolutionary fervor we see exhibited in *BLAST* and in all of Lewis's pronouncements on art during the immediate prewar years never carried over into the development of an equally revolutionary political program. At its worst, Lewis's call for abstraction, defamiliarization, and simple deadness masks the self-serving polemic of a disenfranchised modern artist who longed for the time, before democracy made all things possible for everyone, when artists were recognized as members of an elite caste, a priesthood whose activities provoked the masses to silent awe. Like the romantic poet Percy Shelley, Lewis and most of his associates in the avant-garde clung to a belief that the artist would remain the legislator of the world, even if unacknowledged. The dialectic of vitality and inertia— the idea that the living need the dead, if only to establish their identity as the living—tells a tale of the artist's dependence upon a somewhat attentive but, above all, docile audience who will provide him with the raw material of his art and a market for his finished products; thus the urge to abstraction can also be accounted the urge to subjugate and exploit. In another conversation with Anastasya, Tarr asserts that an artist's work is actually safer in the hands of an ignorant public, like the English, who though philistine at heart are at least "inquisitive about and tickled by it," than with an " 'artistic' vulgarly alive public" such as you had in France, where "thirty-five million little Besnards" were sufficiently acquainted with the clichés of art to be scandalized by any truly original work (*T* 234–35). The average man in fact wanted nothing more than a life filled with action: commerce, sex, war. "The moment they *think* or *dream*," says Tarr, "you get an immense weight of cheap stagnating passion that becomes a menace to the health of the world. . . . Mute inglorious Miltons are not mute for God-in-Heaven" (*T* 302).

Lewis never abandoned his elitist convictions, but his experience in World War I convinced him that art could not simply change the world by fiat. Looking back upon the period of *BLAST* and *Tarr* from the eve of another war, Lewis wrote:

> I was, I protest again, completely innocent of all political motives. I saw that if London was to be pulled down (and this I advocated, and still advocate) that vested interests would be involved. That much was evident, but even of that I was not over-conscious. While I was full of the problem of "Ancient Lights," the mind of the politician, in the nature of things, was busy with the question of the Royal Prerogative, the Mutiny Act, a Second Chamber . . . I was turning over in my mind the duel of Otto Kreisler, in my novel *Tarr:* but the politician had a whole nation of Teutons on his hands or knew he soon would. (*BB* 51–52)

After the war, Lewis would shift his focus from aesthetic to ethical concerns, as he tried to come to grips with the "vested interests" and other powers that were part of the solid world the youthful artist thought he had desired.

3

From Morality to Metaphysics

Lewisian Satire

Lashing the Public

Wyndham Lewis was not completely oblivious to the social and political environment of art before the war. In *Mrs. Dukes' Million*, the emergence of Evan Royal as the novel's hero tells us that Lewis subscribed to Shelley's view of the artist as legislator: the daring young aviator who flits among the topmost peaks of the Alps wants the attention of an audience; the entrepreneur who develops an inexpensive airplane hopes to transform the lives of the people in that audience. Lewis's early work also shows us an author who believed that the task of changing lives might be a simple matter of dazzling the world with one's genius. In an outburst reported by the variously reliable Ford Madox Ford, Lewis exclaimed: "Verisimilitude—that's what you want to get with all your wheezy efforts.... But that isn't what people want. They don't want vicarious experience; they don't want to be educated. They want to be amused. ... By brilliant fellows like me. Letting off brilliant fireworks. Performing like dogs on tight ropes. Something to give them the idea they're at a performance."[1] Brilliant, perhaps; but the sudden eclipse of vorticism by the outbreak of war in the summer of 1914 provides a sad commentary on the avant-garde's understanding of just what kind of fireworks people wanted. Lewis never quite recovered from this disillusionment.

The seeds of the bitterness that would characterize Lewis's postwar relationship with his audience can actually be found in a number of early short stories, including, most dramatically, "Les Saltimbanques," published in the August 1909 issue of Ford's magazine, *The English Review*. Although he began this story as a holiday diversion from painting, this and his other Breton tales represent Lewis's first serious efforts in fiction. All the stories from this period share an attitude of detachment and disinterest that reveals an origin in fin de siècle aestheticism. As Lewis admitted some years later, he went to France after abandoning art school in London to escape "the drab effects of Victorian mediocrity" (*WB* 377), and in Brittany, he found "a wild and simple country," inhabited by a "people to whom the fundamentals of life [were] still accessible" (*WB* 373).

In one respect, the Celts of Finistere afforded Lewis imaginative liberties that he could not have taken with a more familiar people. Yet the distinctive folkways of the Bretons also threw into relief certain basic principles of human behavior. Indeed, the detachment that characterizes the narrative technique of these stories probably has as much to do with science as romance. While Lewis lived in France, he attended Henri Bergson's lectures at the College de France and probably became acquainted there with new ideas in sociology and anthropology through the work of Émile Durkheim and Lucien Lévy-Bruhl (*WB* 236). Lewis's wish not only to describe personalities but also to identify the rules and mechanisms governing the behavior of people in these traditional communities distinguishes "Les Saltimbanques" from the anonymous potboiling of *Mrs. Dukes' Million*.

In "Les Saltimbanques," Lewis presents a narrator's reflections upon a family of itinerant acrobats not unlike the ones that Lewis himself had met in August 1908.[2] When introduced to us, the husband and wife are overheard talking about the people of the town they have just left behind; both are scowling. The narrator comments that it was their lot to "knock each other about and tie their bodies up in knots before an astounded congregation of country people" (*WB* 237). Because their audiences have no conception of the hardships their life entails, however, the amusement they provide others has become only a source of irritation to them. The narrator's opening meditation eventually distills itself into a certain "nightmare image": "It was as though they were lost in a land peopled by mastodon and rhinoceri. Whenever they met one of these monsters—

which was on an average twice a day—their only means of escape was by charming it with their pipes, which never failed to render it harmless and satisfied. They then would hurry on, until they met another, when they would again play to it and flee away" (*WB* 237–38).

From here the story turns to an account of a performance the narrator attends sometime later in the town of Quimperlé. Everything, he notes, centers around the ongoing repartee between the master of ceremonies (also called the proprietor or head showman) and the clown. Although the narrator recognizes the clown, with his impertinent wit, as "the people's favourite," it is the proprietor whom he "always look[s] out for . . . with special interest" (*WB* 239, 241). At first he seems a cheerless individual, whose repeated calls cannot persuade the audience to take their seats; yet the people have an "inspired presentiment," gazing on him "with the same chuckling exultation that sportsmen do on an athlete whose worth they know, and whose debile or gauche appearance is a constant source of delight to them" (*WB* 239). Their expectations are fulfilled upon the clown's arrival, which brings about a change in the proprietor's nature that the narrator finds "truly astonishing." He engages the clown in a sort of comic boxing match, nimbly springing back and forth as he rains "delighted blows" upon his adversary, while grinning appreciatively at his insolent wit, almost in spite of himself (*WB* 239).

The scene inspires the narrator to detailed analysis. "In the tradition of the circus it is a very distinct figure, the part having a psychology of its own—that of the man who invents posers for the clown, wrangles with him, and against whom the laugh is always turned" (*WB* 240). This psychology includes the projection of a superior air intended to cover the embarrassment of being the constant object of the clown's ridicule. In matters of fashion, he has, like the Germans, a predilection for formal attire. Rarely does he smile, and when he does, it is only to prove that he is not without a sense of humor. He recognizes what passes for being witty, while not actually lowering himself enough to participate in such nonsense.

Here the narrator realizes that what he sees enacted in this exchange between the clown and the proprietor is but another version of the artist's "long pilgrimage through this world inhabited by the public" (*WB* 237), which had earlier suggested to him the image of the mastodon and rhinoceri. The figure of the proprietor, he sees,

> originally stood for the public. Out of compliment to the public, of course, they would provide him with evening dress. It would also be tacitly under-

stood by the courteous management, that although many of those present were in billycocks, that their native attire was evening clothes, or at least "smokking," as it is called abroad.

Also the distinguished public would doubtless appreciate the delicacy of touch of endowing its representative with a high bred inability to understand the jokes of his inferiors, or be a match for them in wit. In the better sort of circus he speaks in an obviously gentlemanlike voice—throaty, unctuous and rounding his periods. (*WB* 240)

What Nietzsche found in his study of Western civilization, Wyndham Lewis discovered in a Breton circus: the triumph of a slave ethic that seeks to right the injustices of nature by allowing the weak to dominate the strong through sheer force of numbers. Although the proprietor cannot match the clown in agility or wit, and his oily deportment reflects the hollow pretensions of his constituency, he (and the public he represents) runs the show.

Knowing no other means of gaining a livelihood, the performers resign themselves to their unhappy fate and, like the hunger artist in Franz Kafka's fable, may even become connoisseurs of their own humiliation. At one point during the show, the proprietor steps forward and announces that since the local authorities will not allow his daughter to appear on stage, he will have to perform the next set of acrobatic feats himself. Despite "a creaking and cracking of his joints of a most alarming nature," he executes a series of somersaults and contortions that leaves the narrator applauding wildly. He suddenly realizes, though, that his enthusiasm has drawn the attention of the acrobat, who now seems to look over at him "with a mixture of dislike and reproof." But the hostility is directed against everyone in the audience and brings along with it a certain compensatory satisfaction: "he treated all of us rather coldly, bowed stiffly and walked back to the cart with the air of a man who has just received a bullet wound in a duel, and refusing the assistance of his friends, walks to his carriage" (*WB* 243).

But not all members of the troupe find an outlet for resentment in the cultivation of pathos. About midway through the performance, the proprietor's wife, whose restless figure the narrator has observed lurking in the background, advances toward the stage and starts haranguing the audience:

" Here are hundreds of people standing round, and there are hardly a dozen sous on the carpet. We give you entertainment, but it is not for nothing. We do not work for nothing! We have our living to make as well as other people.

This is the third performance we have given to-day. We are tired and have come a long way to appear before you this evening. You want to enjoy yourselves but don't want to pay. If you want to see any more loosen your purse-strings a little." (*WB* 244)

As the narrator goes on to explain, her indignation stemmed not from her high opinion of the troupe's performance, but rather from the belief that the money thrown at their feet came as reparation for the trouble, inconvenience, and fatigue of their existence. The price of admission was a punishment in the form of a fine, and what made this punishment all the more satisfying from the standpoint of the performers was their awareness that the audience in fact received nothing for their money:

> The reflection that all these people parted with their sous for so little would be the only bright spot in the gloomy Adrien Brower of their minds. They felt that they were getting the better of them in some way. That the public was paying for an idea, for something that it gave itself, did not occur to them, but that it was paying for the performance as seen and appreciated by them, the performers. (*WB* 238)

The traditional Breton artist, it turns out, shares with his twentieth-century European counterpart an acute sense of estrangement from his audience.[3] Because art concerns itself as much with the supernatural as with nature (the acrobat, after all, challenges the laws of physics), people accustomed to measuring experience by a standard of simple common sense do not comprehend it. This inevitably leads to suspicion that the artist is out to hoodwink the public by creating works that fail to affirm a stable relationship between appearance and reality (or, as with Andy Warhol's Brillo boxes, to affirm it so crudely as to expose the banality of the public's idea of transcendence). And yet, precisely because a work of art breaks the rules of common sense, it becomes an object of unending fascination. Ultimately, the power of the thing must be contained. For those with adequate resources, this means an act of appropriation: the actual purchase of the object, or in the case of a performance art, the purchase of rights of access and enjoyment. But what has the new owner really bought for his money? From the artist's viewpoint, the owner has a piece of canvas smeared with paint, or an aesthetic experience of a few minutes duration. Neither does full justice to the process of artistic creation because, in a sense, the complete work ("the performance as seen and appreciated by them, the performers") never leaves its creator's mind. What distinguishes modern art from that of earlier periods is the degree to which artists have focused attention on the limits of the artifact (or text or performance) itself: the nonrepresentational art of the last hundred years forces the public to an awareness of the interpretive element ("something that it gave itself") in art appreciation. Thus, the modern artist not only hoodwinks the public but also rubs its collective nose in the fact.

Oddly enough, the proprietress's sally receives an "amiable" response, as her demand for money reassures the audience about the quality of the performance. This leads the narrator to surmise that the public not only deserves punishment but actually *wants* to be punished. The administering of pain in measured doses relieves the fear of unexpected suffering and argues for the possibility that a rational principle (though a grim one) governs experience:

> The people (or the people that I chiefly know, these Bretons) are spiritu-
> ally herded to their amusements as prisoners are served out their daily soup,
> and weekly square inch of tobacco. The spending of their wages is as much
> a routine as the earning of them. Also in their pleasures—and when buying
> them with their own money—they support the same brow-beating and
> discipline as in their work. The circus proprietor and his wife represented
> for the moment the principle of authority, and they received the reproof as to
> their slackness in spending their money, as they would a master's just abuse
> if they showed a slackness in earning it. (*WB* 245)

By the time the proprietor's wife steps forth to "lash the public" again, we sense that Lewis has at least partially restored the artist to his position of natural superiority. But three paragraphs from the end, things take an unexpected turn. A small boy in the audience begins jeering at the proprietor. Neither he nor the clown can make him stop, and the story ends on a distinctly apocalyptic note:

> [The boy] would no doubt have met death with the exultation of a martyr,
> rather than renounce this transfigured image of an old and despondent
> mountebank—like some stubborn prophet that would not forego the
> splendour of his vision—always of the gloom of famine, of cracked and
> empty palaces, and the elements taking new and extremely destructive
> forms for the rapid extermination of man. (*WB* 247)

Since the narrator at one point calls the boy a "poet" and notes how his outburst "in some very profound and strange way tickled" the showman's vanity, we might see him as an ally of the performers (*WB* 247). The "comedy of existence" that suddenly bursts in upon him is the recognition of how absurd it is that talented people should have to tie themselves up in knots and generally make fools of themselves before an unappreciative crowd. (A final paragraph added to the proofs of a 1927 revision of the story bears out this interpretation: the boy's action effectively dissolves the assembly and causes the saltimbanques to look back upon the performance as "a good show" [*WB* 104].) On the other hand, the boy's behavior toward the "old and despondent mountebank" may simply express the public's indifference to the fate of the artist. He remains for them (again like Kafka's hero) just a minor diversion who loses what little respect he does command when the novelty of his act wears thin. However we approach the ending, "Les Saltimbanques" leaves us with an impression of Lewis as a writer who will retaliate against any audience that denies him the recognition he thinks he deserves.

Through the Vortex

Although "Les Saltimbanques" anticipates Lewis's mature understanding of the relationship between art and society, the actual path of his career in the immediate prewar years would lead us to believe that he planned his early stories more as exorcism than prophecy: around his Breton heroes— an old mountebank, a blind beggar, a suspicious innkeeper—he constructed scenarios of paralysis and despair that, having been played out in words, did not have to be enacted in life. (The stories thus fulfill the same psychological and aesthetic needs as his novel *Tarr*.) When Lewis concluded his protracted adolescence on the Continent in 1909, he returned to England with the all but announced intention of becoming a major figure in contemporary arts and letters. An apocryphal story attributed to Ford describes how Lewis, "wearing a long black coat buttoned up to his chin," and generally affecting the manner of a Russian anarchist, walked into Ford's lodgings while the latter was taking a bath, and announcing "in the most matter-of-fact way that he was a man of genius," proceeded to read the manuscript of a story that he wanted Ford to publish in *The English Re-*

view. Although Lewis later claimed that he had merely left a packet of manuscript for Ford to consider (probably on the advice of their mutual friend, the poet Sturge Moore), the anecdote gives us a good idea of the impact that Lewis wanted to make—and was making—in established literary circles.[4]

Lewis's association with another important little magazine of the time sheds further light on the character of his prewar ambitions. In 1910 and 1911, he published, successively, an essay and a short story in A. R. Orage's *The New Age,* a journal dedicated to the coverage of all aspects of English cultural life—politics, philosophy, economics, and the arts.[5] Although *The New Age* began as an "independent socialist weekly" with ties to Fabianism, its contributors often shared little more than a dissatisfaction with the materialistic values of bourgeois democracy and, beyond this, a vague longing for a more organically constituted society. This accounts for the otherwise anomalous appearance in its pages of writers such as G. K. Chesterton and T. E. Hulme, who believed in Original Sin and called for the establishment of authoritarian social and political institutions. Orage himself favored guild socialism, a variation on the medieval system of craft unions, which governed both the material and spiritual aspects of a worker's life. In its more radical formulations, guild socialism resembled the revolutionary syndicalist movements on the Continent; Orage, however, was uncomfortable with the notion of class struggle and dreamed instead of a revolution in consciousness that would, in effect, return Europe to the Middle Ages and a time when all men were supposedly united by a common understanding of transcendental values. Orage's solution to the crisis of liberalism has been described by Miriam Hansen as "an idealistic short-cut," a phrase that again recalls the strong aesthetic undercurrent in political debate before the war.[6]

Although Lewis's involvement with *The New Age* seems to have been limited to two contributions, neither of which follows the magazine's philosophy in any programmatic way, his 1910 essay entitled "Our Wild Body" does share with Orage an idealistic approach to cultural crisis. The essay takes up the broad philosophical question of the mind's relationship to the body, an issue that would not have seemed abstruse to readers accustomed to the ongoing debate in the early part of this century between vitalism and mechanism. After opening with the observation that the English never really talk about their bodies *as* bodies, Lewis launches his argument in a metaphysical direction, remarking that "it is not . . . the body that is ailing, but our idea of the body" (*WB* 251). He then compares the Anglo-Saxon idea of the body to that held by the French and Germans. The English, he says, fear their bodies. Their dedication to personal hygiene and pursuit of robust health through indulgence in sports is simply a way of "daunting and taming" the body (*WB* 254). The typical Englishman goes through life either never touching his fellow man or knowing physical contact only in the form of schoolboy roughhousing; the finer discriminations that would come from acknowledging the actual virtues and vices of the body remain unknown to him. His Continental neighbors, however, take a more equanimous view of their persons. "The Frenchman regards our bodies as children," explains Lewis, "and when the minds, like two fathers, have become friendly, it seems natural to him that the bodies also should become better acquainted and have their little sport" (*WB* 252). For the more serious-minded German, the body is "the vessel of his life, the receptacle of his life vowed to honour, and the symbol of his recklessness" (*WB* 256).

While the general movement of Lewis's argument is against the prudery and inhibitions of the preceding generation, and in this sense shares a mission with the writings of D. H. Lawrence, we should note that Lewis, while enfranchising the body as a working partner with the mind, also confirms its subordinate status: thus the Frenchman sees it as a mischievous but well-meaning child; the German, as the necessary instrument for the assertion of his will. Like Orage's antiquated guild socialism, Lewis's metaphysics of the body reflect a desire for an organic community in which the head exercises appropriate control over the heart, reason over the emotions, the one over the many. Indeed, if we approach the mind/body dualism as a political metaphor, we see that the essay once again reveals the obsessive preoccupation of Lewis's early work: the relationship between genius (the artist) and the world that supplies genius with both inspiration and material support (the audience).

The unconscious political agenda of "Our Wild Body" provides another testament to Lewis's naïveté before the war. While most of his prewar writings were fictional narratives with a foreign setting (usually France), here he addresses a distinctly English question in a work of nonfiction; but by choosing to employ a broadly philosophical discourse, he transforms a political conflict (the struggle between artist and audience) into a personal dilemma. Now instead of having to unravel a complex web of historical, social, and economic forces, he can talk about the need for simple changes in individual attitudes. The external forces that do remain in Lewis's thinking have been reduced to a residue of national stereotypes ("the Continental gentleman," "the sanguine son of democratic France") that can be moved about as easily as pieces on a checkerboard.

The last of Lewis's Breton stories appeared in print in early 1911. Although he probably began work on his novel *Tarr* later that year, most of his energies from then until the spring of 1914 were directed toward painting and drawing. In these endeavors, as in his writing, Lewis showed a predilection for the "idealistic short-cut": the notion that a change in consciousness initiated by artists and intellectuals could revolutionize everyday life in the modern world. Besides the gallery exhibitions that brought him a measure of recognition as a painter, Lewis also accepted commissions that promised to liberate art from the stuffiness of its usual venues. In 1912, Lewis and three fellow artists decorated the Cave of the Golden Calf, "London's first ultra-modern, arty nightclub," which had been opened by Frida Strindberg, the wealthy wife of the Swedish play-wright.[7] A year or so later, he became involved with Roger Fry's Omega Workshop project. Fry, an influential art critic and impresario who had taken it upon himself to explain modern art to an uncomprehending British public, established the Omega as a place that would produce various arts and crafts after the manner of William Morris. Artists would receive a salary for their anonymous production of textile and wallpaper designs, furniture, murals, screens, and various other domestic bric-a-brac; their income from the Omega would help support them in their more experimental activities. During his brief three-month tenure at the Omega, Lewis painted only a few screens and candle shades and generally resented working for a man whose artistic taste he considered philistine.

He eventually broke with Fry over the latter's handling of a commission that the Omega had received for a "modernist room" at the Ideal Home exhibition sponsored by the *Daily Mail*. (Lewis believed that Fry had cheated him out of an assignment for decorations that the newspaper had specifically intended for him.) In March of 1913, Lewis and several other artists who had become disaffected from the Omega opened the Rebel Art Centre. Education was to be a primary objective of this new enterprise. The prospectus spoke of the centre as a place that would, "by public discussion, lectures and gatherings of people, familiarize those who are interested with the ideas of the great modern revolution." A resident art school would provide students with "something like the natural teaching of the artists' studios during the best periods of European art."[8] The Rebel Art Centre also produced a variety of domestic furnishings in direct competition with the Omega, though this end of the operation seems to have engaged Lewis less than its various propaganda functions. Nonetheless, a display of fans, scarves, boxes, and a table at a public exhibition moved the young sculptor Henri Gaudier-Brzeska to write that "the new painting [was also] capable of great strength and manliness in decoration."[9]

Although the centre closed its doors four months after opening due to personal and philosophical differences among its members, it gave Lewis a platform from which to launch his most ambitious project of the prewar years, the avant-garde journal *BLAST*. In *BLAST*, the curious mixture of aesthetic and utopian strains in Lewis's thought found its purest expression. As editor of *BLAST* and chief impresario of vorticism, the movement that served to give the magazine a focus, Lewis presided over the announcement of a definitive break with the past, which together with similar movements in France, Italy, and Russia constituted what Marjorie Perloff (following Renato Poggioli) has characterized as the "Futurist moment": "the brief utopian phase of early Modernism when artists felt themselves to be on the verge of a new age that would be more exciting, more promising, more inspiring than any preceding one."[10] In the spring of 1914, Lewis could at least entertain the possibility that the revolution in the arts would be answered by a parallel movement in society. The brief manifesto that opens the journal announces: "Blast will be popular, essentially. It will not appeal to any particular class, but to the fundamental and popular instincts in every class and description of people, TO THE INDIVIDUAL" (*B1* 7). A few lines below this, the possibility of converting the king to vorticism is announced. Talk of a vorticist king can be dismissed as mere drollery, but there is no doubt that Lewis and his associates had a sincere (if selfish) interest in promoting social change. Consider alone the format of *BLAST* : its telegraphic diction and gargantuan typography, key elements also in the rhetoric of popular journalism and commercial advertisement, represent a serious effort to find a language that could motivate the urban mass audience to action.

But no revolution was forthcoming, and it is unlikely that one acceptable to Lewis would have occurred in England even had war not broken out just a few weeks after the appearance of *BLAST*. Part of the reason for this failure to turn an avant-garde movement into a popular one lay in the tendency to think in aesthetic rather than political terms—to believe that a change in the collective consciousness could be imposed from above through the agency of a few brilliant minds. In a sense, Lewis never fully acknowledged the reality of his audience. At times it seems that an audience was no more alive to him than the canvas that he painted on. We see evidence of this attitude even on the occasions in *BLAST* when Lewis makes a direct address to his readers. For example, while the proclamatory tone of the "Blasts" and "Blesses" and the "Manifesto" that compose the opening pages of Lewis's journal evoke the spirit of a popular political movement, the rhetorical devices he employs presuppose a passive audience that has no choice other than to accept the *ex cathedra* pronouncements of its superiors. A further sign of Lewis's indifference to public response is apparent in the text of the "Manifesto" itself, which begins with the assertion "Beyond Action and Reaction we would establish ourselves" and proceeds to characterize artists as mercenaries who fight for "NO-MAN'S" cause other than to "Stir up Civil War among peaceful apes" (*B1* 30–31). The attraction to military metaphors here and elsewhere in *BLAST* also implies a faith in the efficacy of simple and unilateral solutions to the world's problems (a view evidently shared by the prospective combatants on the eve of the First World War). Near the end of *BLAST,* Lewis does offer support for one recognizable political cause, the suffragette movement, though again his motivation seems to have been aesthetic rather than moral or political. " WE ADMIRE YOUR ENERGY. YOU AND ARTISTS ARE THE ONLY THINGS . . . LEFT IN ENGLAND WITH A LITTLE LIFE IN THEM," he announces, but then he goes on to warn them against the inadvertent destruction of artwork: " IF YOU DESTROY A GREAT WORK OF ART you are destroying a greater soul than if you annihilated a whole district of London. LEAVE ART ALONE, BRAVE COMRADES!" (*B1* 151–52). At this point in his career, the notion that works of art might possess ideological content and thus have a role in political debate does not seem to have occurred to him.

The war obliged Lewis to reconsider his views on this issue and a variety of others. As early as his contributions to the second issue of *BLAST,* which appeared in July 1915, he began to talk about art not as something that exists in pristine isolation from its surroundings (as his advice to the suffragettes implies), but as one important cultural phenomenon among many. The "Editorial" that opens the second issue begins: "*BLAST* finds itself surrounded by a multitude of other Blasts of all sizes and descriptions" (*B2* 5). In the " War Notes" that follow, Lewis speculates on the causes of the war (commercial jealousies, the German romantic spirit) and considers some of its possible effects (the death of imperialism). He also recognizes that art can function as a purveyor of ideology, explaining in his first note that the reason why the kaiser had suppressed cubism and expressionism was that he feared the puritanical spirit behind abstract painting would discourage consumption and thus cause German trade to suffer (*B2* 9). This new awareness of the artist's environment was accompanied by a discursive style that implicitly, if grudgingly, acknowledged the reader as a participant in an intellectual exchange. Whereas his prose in *BLAST* No. 1 aspired to the condition of Nietzschean epigram, in No. 2 Lewis wrote paragraphs and took the trouble to construct logical arguments (though he did not abandon the vatic style altogether).

But it was his experience in the trenches that really transformed the aesthete of the fin de siècle into the social critic and satiric novelist of the twenties and thirties. Looking back from a distance of twenty years, Lewis observed that more than anything else his service in France and Flanders had provided him with a *"political* education": "I, along with millions of others, was standing up to be killed. Very well: but *who* in fact was it, who was proposing to kill or maim me? I developed a certain inquisitiveness upon that point. I saw clearly that it was not my German opposite number. He, like myself, was an instrument. That we were all on a fool's errand had become plain to many of us" (*BB* 187). Lewis's new understanding of the relationship between politics and art is evident in *The Caliph's Design: Architects! Where Is Your Vortex?* (1919), which he described to his patron, the American art collector John Quinn, as "an appeal to the better type of artist to take more interest in and more part in the general life of the world, if only in the interest of his own shop, and to attempt to change the form-content of civilized life" (*L* 110).

While the appearance of the word "Vortex" in the subtitle implies a continuity with the aesthetic project outlined in *BLAST*, the address to "Architects" demonstrates the change in focus of Lewis's concerns. The essay opens with a brief parable of Lewis's invention about the caliph of Baghdad. Dissatisfied with the appearance of his capital, the caliph executes a vorticist design for a new city and directs his chief engineer and chief architect to draw working blueprints by ten o'clock the next morning on penalty of death. After recovering from the shock of their master's command, the architect and engineer work through the night to devise a set of plans faithful to the caliph's vision, which they present to him the next morning. The parable concludes: "And within a month a strange street transfigured the heart of that cultivated city" (*CD* 20).

Up until now, Lewis had paid scant attention to architecture, despite the fact that many of his abstract paintings have the rectilinear look of a modern urban skyline. But to draw buildings is one thing, to draw with the expectation of seeing one's design realized in brick and mortar is something quite different. As Lewis observes in *The Caliph's Design:* "Architecture is the weakest of the arts, in so far as it is the most dependent on the collective sensibility of its period" (*CD* 43). The painter and, to a lesser degree, the sculptor can work in virtual isolation given the modest material requirements of their art. But the architect must necessarily work for someone else, and the most ambitious architectural projects demand the resources of entire communities. Defective public taste would not stop an artist from painting a picture, but it could effectively forestall the construction of an important architectural monument.

Why then should a painter be concerned about the plight of the architect? Indeed, the painter's imagination is such that it can inhabit a vacuum. "I do not need to have a house built with significant forms, lines, masses, and details or ornament, and planted squarely before my eyes, to know that such significance exists, or to have my belief in its reality stimulated" (*CD* 37). He goes on to observe that, in theory, an artist can do quite well without the possibility of materially realizing his vision. But theory does not always translate into practice. In practice, "the society of which [the artist] forms a part, can, by its backwardness, indolence, or obtuseness, cause him a series of inconveniences; and above all, can, at certain times and under certain conditions, affect his pocket adversely and cause him to waste an absurd amount of time" (*CD* 39). Without an enlightened audience, in other words, the artist cannot make a living doing what he does best but must either dedicate himself (as Lewis was doing in *The Caliph's Design*) to the education of the public or surrender himself to the production of the bric-a-brac that satisfies vulgar tastes. Lewis also acknowledged that while environmental limitations mean nothing to the Rembrandts and Van Goghs of the world, material conditions do affect the many artists who, though lacking genius, may still be capable of respectable work: "Set a rather poor artist down in a roadway, ask him to draw a street of houses in front of him. If the houses were of good and significant build, he would be more likely to do a good and significant painting than if they were such clumsy, and stupid, lineless, massless, things as we invariably find ourselves in the midst of today" (*CD* 35–36).

Lewis's formulation of the relationship between artist and society in *The Caliph's Design* strongly influenced the direction of his career during the next two decades. A utopianism that survived from his leadership of the London avant-garde combined with his introduction to political realities on the Western Front confirmed his belief that the artist had a role to play in the development of mass culture—though whether the leading role seemed more doubtful now. In a short chapter entitled "The Public Chosen," he announces that in *The Caliph's Design* he seeks "a socially wider and not necessarily specialist public" (*CD* 41). But while Lewis expresses an interest in reaching a wider public, and on several occasions notes the "inconveniences" for artists that can result from an unfavorable environment, he continues to insist upon the artist's principled indifference to his audience. This indifference lies behind the curious assertion Lewis would make in the twenties and thirties that though his work addressed such public issues as war, revolution, and economic reform, he had little personal interest in politics. Rather, he expected us to see his polemical writings as advice on how to avoid embroilment in political debate.

While the politician in Lewis sought a "socially wider public," the tone of his writing often conveys the impression of an artist who resents having to explain the obvious to an audience he knows he does not really need. This resentment undermines the artist's studied indifference and, by a turn critical to an appreciation of Lewis's fiction, leaves the reader less a passive observer than a villain and a victim.

Evidence of this latent hostility can be found in the author's preface that precedes the parable about the caliph of Baghdad. Here Lewis offers a brief account of the situation of painting in postwar Europe:

> The spirit that pervades a large block—cube, if you like—of the art of painting to-day is an almost purely Art-for-Art's sake dilettantism. Yet you find vigour and conviction; its exponents, Picasso, Matisse, Derain, Balla, for example, are very considerable artists, very sure of themselves and of the claim of their business. So you get this contradiction of what is really a very great vitality in the visual arts, and at the same time a very serious scepticism and discouragement in the use of that vitality. (*CD* 9)

The passage reflects the widely held view that European artists and intellectuals had been demoralized by the war and were now living in the ruins of a heroic age that began a few years after the turn of the century and ended abruptly in the summer of 1914. Cubism and the various other avant-garde movements once promised to expand the reach of human consciousness but had lately retreated into what Lewis called "the Nature-morte school," which squandered its genius on monotonous still lifes of apples and mandolins. Of course, by calling Picasso a "Nature-mortist," Lewis was carrying on a polemic of *BLAST* that sought to distinguish vorticism from Continental movements by criticizing the relatively static quality of cubism. But in this preface, Lewis does not immediately pursue the attack against his fellow painters. Rather, he proceeds with a description of the contemporary art world as a corrida: here art is a "little bull" toyed with by "crowds of degenerate and dogmatic Toreros" who drop down at random from the audience into the arena (*CD* 10). Must the professional artist accept the blame for this ridiculous state of affairs? Not at all, according to Lewis:

> It is evident that the Public is at fault. Why does it not insist on a better type of Bull in the first place, a more substantial type of art, that would be capable of driving all but the best performers from the Arena? If the public cannot think of a new type of Bull at the moment, and is not willing to take a new brand of beast that we are rearing on trust, let it at least put into the Circus some fine animal from Nineveh or rake the Nile valley for a compelling and petulant shape. (*CD* 10)

In sum, though Lewis emerged from the First World War a more socially conscious artist, acknowledging the role of the audience in the production of art, he also believed that an intellectually lazy public—not the artist himself—was responsible for the poor quality of contemporary art. The war had fulfilled the prophecy that Lewis had intimated (and probably hoped to exorcise) in "Les Saltimbanques": that the world would make a mockery of art despite the heroic efforts of genius. But if "Les Saltimbanques" predicts the artist's betrayal by his audience, it also shows that he could do more about it than simply maintain his deportment, like a man who has received a bullet wound in a duel and walks back to his carriage unassisted. For almost the next twenty years, taking his cue from the wife of the circus proprietor, Lewis would step forward to the middle of the circle and lash his public.

After the War

Lewis's creative work in the immediate postwar years also shows greater sensitivity to the context of art. We see the change as early as 1917 in some pen and ink sketches that Lewis drew while recovering from trench fever in France. As Walter Michel observes of these casual depictions of townspeople and hospital staff, "for the first time since the 1909 *Theatre Manager,* the civilized world is represented: humans, clothed or uniformed, with hints, even, of bourgeois settings."[11] Later that year, Lewis turned to the problem of representing the *un*civilized world of men and arms when he received an appointment as an artist with the Canadian War Memorials project. Although the relatively naturalistic style of the pictures he painted to fulfill this commission merely reflects Lewis's attempt, in Augustus John's words, "to reduce his 'Vorticism' to the level of Canadian intelligibility,"[12] other drawings from the period carefully attend to bodily contours and suggest that his war experience had taught him to respect the limits that nature imposes upon mind, even the mind of genius. Unlike other avant-garde artists of the prewar years (most notably the Italian futurists Balla and Severini),[13] Lewis did not (and would not) abandon the abstract style but now seems to have decided that abstract forms had a genetic relationship to forms in nature. Writing many years later in *Rude Assignment* about his changing style, Lewis commented: "War, and especially those miles of hideous desert known as 'the Line' in Flanders and France, presented me with a subject-matter so consonant with the austerity of that 'abstract' vision I had developed, that it was an easy transition" (*RA* 138).

The war showed Lewis that the world had a place *in* his art; it also made him more attentive to the relationship *between* the world and art. Up through the publication of *BLAST,* Lewis operated on the rather idealistic assumption that the public would be transformed by the appearance of artistic genius in its midst. Like all revolutionaries, the artist might have to propagandize for his convictions—he might even have to set off an explosion or two, figuratively speaking—but the essential justice of his cause and the progressive spirit within history itself would eventually carry the day. After the war, Lewis approached the public less as a block of inert matter than as a dynamic force that one had to reckon with, for better or worse. Near the opening of a 1919 letter to his American patron, John Quinn, Lewis echoes Oscar Wilde's aphorism about romanticism and the rage of Caliban, observing: "As you know, in England one is up against the least imaginative and the most self-satisfied public in the world. They suppose that an artist is entirely occupied with *them.* They are accustomed to get *exactly* what they want. They have not the haziest conception of a man as an artist, with different, in most cases opposite, standards to their own" (*L* 103). He concedes, however, that although smug and unsophisticated, the English public has a certain fairness about things absent in the French. (Because Continental audiences *think* they know all about art, they are more likely to try to tell the artist his business.) Lewis then goes on to suggest that in his current one-man exhibition entitled *Guns* (which included pictures completed during his tenure as a war artist), he hoped to enter into a sort of dialogue with his public. Despite his complaint a couple months earlier to the art critic Herbert Read that *A Canadian Gun Pit* was "one of the dullest good pictures on earth" (*L* 102), on this occasion, he explains that the naturalistic style of the work will help persuade viewers of his credentials as an artist and validate his prewar forays into abstraction; he even chides himself for not having adopted this more conciliatory procedure at the outset:

> It will be more difficult henceforth in the set politics of London for certain gentlemen to assert that myself or my companions are "spoofers" & so on. I feel that I should have rendered all concerned a service had I done this earlier. For the public's eye first struck a canvas of mine when I was already experimenting beyond the zone of that eye's comprehension or special knowledge of the subject. (*L* 104)

Admittedly, the moderate rhetoric of this letter shows Lewis on his best behavior. He was not about to denounce the public in front of one of its wealthier representatives, who, mainly as the result of Ezra Pound's assiduous cultivation, had become the premier customer for his paintings and drawings. Lewis probably had no more affection for the English public in 1919 than he had had five years earlier. But this letter demonstrates that Lewis was now giving serious thought to the ethical questions connected with the production of art: how does the world find a place in what I do? how will my art affect the lives of those in my intended audience? who *is* my audience? what effect will the audience have upon the future course of my work?

Some tentative answers to these questions can be discerned in Lewis's most visually arresting work of the immediate postwar years, a series of drawings first shown at his 1921 exhibition, *Tyros and Portraits*. In his Tyro drawings, Lewis created a set of fashionably attired grotesques chiefly identified by the toothy grins they flash at the viewer. Although Lewis defined a Tyro in the foreword to the exhibition catalog as "an elementary person; an elemental, in short" (*WB* 353), these figures seem less universal than the anonymous officers and men that populated his war paintings of a few years before. The style of clothing and accessories indicates a setting among the comfortable bourgeois of the early twenties, and the presence of one work entitled *Mr. Wyndham Lewis as a Tyro* suggests that persons known to the artist lurk somewhere behind these caricatures. We might say that Lewis's use of abstraction is more focused and deliberate here than it had been in his prewar pictures. The steely angularities of the *Timon of Athens* illustrations present a criticism of everything fleshly and mortal in human existence; the Tyros, on the other hand, provide a negative commentary on a particular way of life, without implying that the artist stands outside life itself in a heaven of aesthetic ideals. In his foreword to the catalog, Lewis acknowledges the more limited scope of his Tyros, proudly noting his debt to the English caricaturist William Hogarth, an artist not known for the transcendent qualities of his work. He also explains that he created this new race to help "frighten away" English dilettantes (meaning Roger Fry and the Bloomsbury circle) who, clinging to a few scraps of Continental theory, saw modern art as a convenient escape from the complexities of social and political life (*WB* 353, 354).

The Tyros were a rather short-lived phenomenon in the development of Lewis's visual art, lasting only about a year. Bernard Lafourcade writes that the impulse behind the Tyros was more literary and philosophical than pictorial, an assertion supported by Lewis's remark in the catalog that "these partly religious explosions of laughing Elementals are at once satires, pictures and stories" (*WB* 354). Perhaps Lewis decided that the two-dimensional surface did not lend itself to the telling of the kind of stories that needed to be told if one was going to understand the origins of war and revolution, events that profoundly affected the situation of the artist. (Lewis later admitted that "from 1924 onwards writing became so much a major interest" that he worked at painting and drawing only in intermittent bursts.[14]) Still, the Tyros serve to announce the confrontational style that would characterize Lewis's writing of the next ten years, most notably in *The Apes of God* and *Snooty Baronet*.

Before passing on to these longer works, let us briefly mark the stylistic transition in Lewis's fiction by looking at "Sigismund," a short story published in the Winter 1920 issue of *Arts and Letters*, about the time he must have commenced work on the Tyros. In many respects, "Sigismund" is a domesticated version of one of Lewis's Breton tales, and it is precisely this domestication that makes the story a minor landmark in his career. Since Lewis's Brittany naturally existed at one remove from the English reader, the peculiar excesses of a character's behavior could always be ascribed to inherent differences of national temperament. But no distancing of this sort would be possible with "Sigismund," whose ambience is thoroughly Anglo-Saxon. In a gesture calculated to set the farcical tone of the story, the narrator first introduces us to Pym, Sigismund's bulldog—that most English of beasts—whom Sigismund proudly escorts around London. Though Pym is "the ugliest, wickedest, most objectionable bulldog that ever trod the soil of Britain," because he is a *bulldog*, whose forebears had done romantic things, Sigismund has implicit faith in the nobility of his pedigree (*WB* 163). Their partnership continues for several years until the day when Sigismund discovers his passion for a buxom lady of equally noble pedigree, Deborah Libyon-Bosselwood. After a slapstick courtship (which at one point sees a jealous Pym affixing his teeth in Deborah's "eighteenth-century bottom"), the couple weds.

It soon becomes apparent, however, that Sigismund's passion for his bride is less amorous than cultic. Immediately upon their return from the church, Sigismund attempts to read the secrets of his bride's palm: "The Mount of Venus, for him, was to be sought on the base of the thumb, and nowhere else" (*WB* 166). He studies the creases of her hand in search of further confirmation of Libyon-Bosselwood antiquity but is dismayed to discover few lines of any sort: "The Palmer Arch, it is true, had its accompanying furrow, rather yellow (from which he could trace the action of Deborah's bile) but clear. The Mars line reinforced it. Great health: pints of blood: larders full of ox-like resistance to disease. It was the health sheet of a bullock, not the flamboyant history of a lady descended from armoured pirates" (*WB* 166). Undeterred by these ill omens, Sigismund escorts Deborah around London much as he had done with Pym, showing off the authentic Roman curve of her nose and the subtle hint of Viking in her blue eyes.

His audience on these occasions is an interchangeable lot of ex–public school types, who, like Sigismund, acquire an identity only through the adoption of various fetishes and tics. Typical of the group is Reddie Gribble-Smith, whom Sigismund calls an "awful nice feller," but whose existence the narrator dismisses with the remark: "This particular cliché propelled itself through life by means of a sort of Army-laugh" (*WB* 170). Although Lewis adopts a satirical attitude toward his material in "Sigismund," the world he describes here is much the same world as that whose spiritual malaise Eliot would diagnose in *The Waste Land*. For both

men, Europeans had suffered a debilitating loss of will in the aftermath of
the war and could no longer think critically about the past or create new
ideas appropriate to the future. Indeed, Sigismund's interest in astrology
and palm reading, like Madame Sosostris's faith in her "wicked pack of
cards," reveals a deep-seated fear of change. Lewis further satirizes this
attitude when he shows us his protagonist's fascination with a book on the
upper classes that he happens upon in the Bosselwood Chase library.
Deeply impressed with what he finds, Sigismund reads several passages
aloud to Deborah:

> These luckily-born people have a delicious curve of the neck, not found in
> other kinds of men, produced by their habit of always gazing *back* to the spot
> from which they started. Indeed, they are trained to fix their eyes on the
> Past. . . .
> The thoroughfares of life are sprinkled with these backward gazing
> heads, and bodies like twisted tendrils. It is the curve of grace, and chal-
> lenges nobly the uncouth uprightness of efficiency.
> That class of men that in recent years coined the word "Futurist" to
> describe their kind, tried to look forward, instead. This is absurd. Firstly, it is
> not practical: and, secondly, it is not beautiful. This heresy met with bitter
> opposition, curiously enough, from those possessing the tendril-sweep.
> Unnecessary bitterness! For there are so many more people looking *back*,
> than there are looking forward, and in any case there is something so vulgar
> in looking in front of you, the way your head grows, that of course they never
> had much success. (*WB* 171–72)

The ideal romance with the past would find satisfaction only in death, and
accordingly, the selection concludes with praise for the dead, who "have
learnt not to expect too much of existence, and have a lot of nice habits that
only demise makes possible" (*WB* 172).

This ironical preference for death over life (like *The Waste Land*'s assertion
of winter's warmth) reflects not only the author's objective view of a
cultural crisis, but also his personal frustration in having tried to do
something about it. As a former leader of the English "Futurists," Lewis
believed that his efforts to make people confront the consequences of
modernity in their lives had been repudiated by masses of men who
stubbornly looked backward instead of forward. These included not only
members of the ruling aristocracy, whose obstructionism could almost be
excused, but also the educated middle classes, who ought to have known

better. By characterizing the victorious majority as a deformed race of beings with bodies like twisted tendrils, Lewis was taking upon himself the role of the proprietor's wife in the Breton circus he had seen years earlier. In "Les Saltimbanques," the hostility between artist and audience had been displaced into fable: Lewis was not an acrobat and his readers were not Breton peasants. But "Sigismund" pulls no punches. Lewis *was* a futurist (a detail that would not have been lost upon readers of the journal *Arts and Letters*, where the story first appeared), and his audience on this occasion would have been people who moved in roughly the same circles as Sigismund and his cronies. The aesthete's nightmare that genius would be accorded the reception of a clown had been realized, and Lewis responded by punishing his audience as the Bretons had finally punished theirs.

One day while putting the finishing touches on his private collection of English historical art ("Mary Queen of Scots over and over again: Fotheringay: many perfect deaths: the Duke of Cumberland holding the candle for the surgeon amputating his leg" [*WB* 174]), Sigismund is drawn to the main part of the house by a loud commotion. Arriving at the entrance, he discovers that in a fit of rage his wife has thrown one of the maids to her death from the top of the stairs. Sigismund is secretly enraptured with this robust expression of Bosselwood nobility. He does not realize, however, that before his obsession with the past had finally driven her mad, Deborah had conspired with her brother to have Sigismund committed. The men in the white coats come for Sigismund just a few minutes before the police remove Deborah to jail, and the story ends with both husband and wife permanently ensconced in an asylum. In "Sigismund," satire works as an instrument of revenge: the futurist condemns the ruling class and their bourgeois lackeys to a place that confirms the insanity of their rejecting the avant-garde in 1914 and instead leading the world into war. Lewis's next major satire would be an effort to deliver the coup de grace to the collectors and connoisseurs who still dominated English arts and letters.

Beyond Classical Satire: *The Apes of God*

Described in a 1981 afterword by Paul Edwards as one of the "pessimistic masterpieces of modernism" (*AG* 630), *The Apes of God* was intended by Lewis as a major pronouncement upon European civilization that would invite comparison with *The Waste Land* and *Ulysses*. He began the novel in 1923, and it is reasonable to think that the feverish pace of his activity during the next few years was partially motivated by a desire to show that the promise of *Tarr* would be fulfilled in a monumental work, just as the promise of "Prufrock" and *A Portrait* had been fulfilled. As early as 1920, Lewis explained to John Quinn that he had not done so already only because he had lost four years in war service (one of the few important modernists to be so affected), and he urged Quinn "to have another look" in five years, by which time he would have accomplished his first "*complete*" work (*L* 120).

When *The Apes of God* finally appeared in 1930, it produced an effect opposite from what the author had intended. Instead of establishing his reputation as an important literary figure, it relegated him to the status of an unreadable eccentric. Few readers had patience for the baroque style that Lewis invented as the appropriate medium to describe the hothouse environment of bourgeois-bohemian England. Those who did have patience read the book chiefly as a roman à clef by an author who was using literature to get back at his enemies. While *The Apes of God was* a roman à clef and Lewis *did* use it to settle scores with a number of people who had offended him, he wanted his portraits from life to be recognized as the totems of a sick and dying culture. As Ezra Pound remarked in 1931, eighty years hence "no one will care a kuss" who was who in the novel, but "the colossal masks will remain with the fixed grins of colossi" (*AG* 634). These apologies for the book's importance aside, Lewis's failure with *The Apes* to write a successful novel of manners and mores points to an important metaphysical strain in the development of his satiric art.

The Apes of God begins and ends in the household of Sir James Follett, a hoary old baronet, and his wife, Lady Fredigonde Follett, who, though well into her nineties, still entertains the dreams of a young socialite. Their utter senility and decrepitude reflect Lewis's view of the state to which the traditional ruling class in England had fallen—a descent confirmed by the General Strike of 1926, against whose backdrop the novel reaches its denouement. The next generation of Folletts holds small promise for the future, avoiding even the appearance of responsible behavior. In the novel's first chapter, we meet the androgynous Horace Zagreus, a middle-aged Follett nephew, who makes a career of staging elaborate practical jokes for his rich friends and seeking out physically attractive young men whom he advertises to the world as so many budding young geniuses. The action of Lewis's episodic work begins when Zagreus arrives at the Follett estate to introduce his most recent protégé, a nineteen-year-old Irishman improbably named Dan Boleyn, to his aunt and uncle (Zagreus is keeping a watchful eye on the ultimate disposition of the family fortune). From here we follow Dan's "apprenticeship" in how to succeed as an artist by ingratiating himself with the wealthy dilettantes, or "apes," who oversee bohemia. Under Zagreus's direction, Dan makes a number of forays into this world, including visits to a Follett cousin who prides himself on his whip collection, a neurotic vanity publisher and bookseller who writes bad novels, and a lesbian painter who forces the painfully modest Dan to pose in the nude. In the second half of *The Apes,* Dan accompanies his mentor to the country estate of Lord Osmund Finnian-Shaw (a thinly disguised caricature of Osbert Sitwell), where Zagreus assures him that he will have the opportunity of observing "the lively spectacle of how Apehood may affect an entire family"(*AG* 322). Zagreus has been commissioned by Lord Osmund to perform a pantomime at a lavish Lenten Freak Party he is giving. Dan's bungling of his simple part in the pantomime weakens Zagreus's faith in his nonexistent genius and paves the way for the inevitable transfer of his attentions to yet another youthful protégé.

Lewis called *The Apes of God* a satire, and in many respects, the work accords with the conventional assumptions about the genre. Michael Seidel, analyzing the motivations behind satire, observes that "satirists generate their own insecurities and then elaborate a fable in which they attempt to displace themselves from what they have generated."[15] Although Lewis would have bristled at the notion that he generated his own insecurities, he undoubtedly felt threatened by a number of social and economic trends during the twenties; in *The Apes of God,* he sought to distill these movements into the grotesque stereotypes that people his narrative.

The predominance of these stereotypes signaled the final decay of heroic values in modern Europe. Lewis believed that at one time the elite had aspired to positions of visible wealth and power without embarrassment. But the situation changed with the transition from a producer to a consumer economy and the concomitant growth of bourgeois democracy. Henceforth the position of the elite depended more and more upon the participation of the middle and lower classes—as civil servants, engineers, teachers, industrial workers, and, above all, as consumers. It was now in their interest to mask their superior status lest the appearance of privilege alienate the masses, upon whom their continued well-being depended. And so, just as English royalty exchanged their crowns and stoles for business suits, the monied classes began to adopt the folkways of the proletariat. Indeed, they often went the lower classes one better by cultivating a taste for the primitive and the perverse. Consider, for example, the case of the amateur painter and whip collector Dick Whittingdon, whom Zagreus briefly characterizes in a set of marching orders he issues to Dan one morning:

> he was not only too old as he regretfully decided but far too clumsy and not very clever (as well as bald and rheumatic) to become an Oxford-voiced *fairy-prince*. So Dick Whittingdon cast around for some recognized vice that might compensate for this social handicap. The pornographic literature of the camp and barracks (and for Dick the horizon of Letters was more or less that) suggested a solution. So he is a noted amateur *flagellant*. Whip in hand, Dick Whittingdon faces the world. It is the birch-rod of the decrepit gallant, in the old love-books, that gives the poor man a face, and enables him to hold up his head in a universe of dogmatic perversion. (*AG* 138)

Another more common manifestation of this will to weakness was the public's increasing fascination with youth, which Lewis called "the cult of the child." Of course, since not everyone could be young, older persons were obliged to convey the impression of youth through close association with the young—and the more pubescent the companion the better. In this regard, Zagreus is unsurpassed. When he introduces the nineteen-year-old Dan to Sir James as "too young to have done much [yet]," despite his having written "one most lovely poem," the old man naturally supposes that Dan works in free verse:

> A look of momentary indignation appeared in the face of Horace Zagreus.
> "Not at all—it is in a quite traditional metre. Absolutely the *youngest* generation, sir, do not write in free verse—they have gone back to *quite* traditional forms."
> "Have they? That is very interesting."
> "Yes quite the youngest generation! It is only, you will find, the thirties and the forties that believe in violent experiment—the *very youngest generation*" Mr. Zagreus thundered, his eyes flashing "are super-victorian now, if you like—are classical *to a man!*"(*AG* 40)

In *The Art of Being Ruled* Lewis offered this analysis of the popularity of the child cult in postwar Europe:

To grow up, to do what Peter Pan so wisely refrained from doing, is to think and struggle; and all thinking is evil, and struggle is useless. Give up your will; cease to think for yourself; regard your employer as your good, kind father or uncle: leave everything in his hands.

Barrie's play, *Peter Pan,* is to our time what *Uncle Tom's Cabin* was to the Civil War period in America. It gave expression to a deep emotional current, of political origin. The *refusal to grow up* of Peter Pan was the specific found by the *narquois* mind of the Zeitgeist for the increasing difficulties connected *with* growing up. (*ABR* 185)

As we noted earlier, Lewis identified the source of this refusal to enter into adult life in the subconscious reaction to the horrors of the war. Culturally shell-shocked by the most destructive outburst in the history of "civilization," people sought refuge from their anxieties in various ideologies—sadism, infantilism, anarchism—that one way or another promised to free the individual from the struggle for complete self-realization. Oddly enough, these same motivations contributed to a phenomenon that constituted the primary objective of Lewis's satire in *The Apes of God:* the increased attraction of the educated middle classes to the profession of artist. Lewis believed that the democratization of culture since the French Revolution had simultaneously lowered critical standards and encouraged anyone with a modicum of skill and sensitivity to think that he or she could become an artist. Since the image of the artist in popular culture derived from the romantic "man of feeling"—a somewhat neurasthenic figure who rejected the will to power behind modern civilization—being an artist in postwar England signaled one's temperamental distance from the holocaust on the Western Front and all that had led up to it.

Lewis had romantic sympathies also, but more in line with Blake and Shelley, who saw the artist as a warrior-prophet leading a revolution in consciousness, if not in social reconstruction. For Lewis, monied amateurs such as Whittingdon and Zagreus lacked the artistic talent and moral courage to fulfill the true artist's mission. Because a real change in the status quo would endanger the sources of their material well-being, what little work the "apes" did produce invariably had a sentimental or *passeiste* quality. A typical example would be the work in progress by a rival of Zagreus named Melanie (possibly the Bloomsbury painter Vanessa Bell), described as "a bright picture, full of the Warm South, with a bright volcanic blush, parched stucco farm-shacks, plages and so on" (*AG* 125).

Lewis was convinced that the presence of wealthy amateurs in the art world undermined the ability of professionals to earn a decent living. Despite an abiding faith in the power of his art, Lewis, like other avant-garde artists of his generation, had "not yet wholly resigned himself (at least secretly) to having forever lost the advantages inherent in cultural situations dominated by taste rather than by genius."[16] Although he berated others for wanting to live in the past and devoted himself in his nonfiction to exploring the links between modernity and modern art, his continued disappointment over his lack of popular recognition probably indicates, to cite Renato Poggioli again, "an unconfessed grief for more secure and happy times—when the creator could count on a public, not large but faithful, attentive, compact, and integral, to which he was bound by the sharing of identical presuppositions, by the same system of social, aesthetic, and ethical values."[17] In *The Apes of God*, Lewis holds Bloomsbury and the Sitwells responsible for the breakdown in shared aesthetic principles that genius still finds useful, if not absolutely necessary. When not damaging the cause of art in practical ways by occupying all the available studios in London and Paris (*AG* 120), the amateur debases the general level of taste by producing work that merely expresses the maker's narcissism: it "does not challenge their conceit, and it fraternizes with the fundamental vulgarity with which they have not parted." But since these persons possess money and influence, *"they are identified, in the mind of the public, with art and intelligence"* (*AG* 121). Their visibility in the gossip columns of the press and their saturation of the market with second-rate books and paintings makes it almost impossible for the genuine artist to gain acceptance for, and thus a living from, work that by its very nature must run against the grain of received opinion.

In a short newspaper interview published at the time of his Tyro exhibition in April 1921, Lewis asserted, "Satire is dead to-day. There has been no great satirist since Swift" (*WB* 359). He went on to say that because the present age had so little capacity for moral discrimination, most people would be unable to recognize written satire if they saw it; therefore, he had decided "to get at them" with his visually potent Tyros.

But Lewis had evidently changed his mind about the appropriate vehicle for satire by the time he began writing *The Apes of God*. He decided that a mixture of verbal burlesque and grotesque, combined with sheer volubility, could force people to sit up and take notice. To ensure this effect,

Lewis orchestrated the book's reception by publishing soon after its appearance a sixty-page pamphlet that laid out his theory of satire. Once again Lewis acknowledges the tutelary presence of Jonathan Swift, as in this passage where he explains the nature of satiric humor:

> In Swift, in Dryden, in Pope, it is not the "natural," "bubbling" laughter of Shakespearean comedy that you should expect to find, any more than you would look for a jovial heartiness in a surgeon at work, or, if you like (to take a romantic illustration), in an executioner. It would decidedly be out of place. *Laughter* is the medium employed, certainly, but there is laughter and laughter, and that of true satire is as it were a *tragic* laughter. It is not a genial guffaw nor the tittivations provoked by a harmless entertainer. (*SF* 45)

The spirit of the premier satirist in English prose oversees *The Apes of God:* its presence is felt when Mr. Zagreus announces that each and every person is "objectively unbearable" (*AG* 257) and on those many occasions when the narrator ridicules a character for his physical appearance, if not, indeed, his physicality. But Lewis adopted more from Swift than his posture of savage indignation. Beneath the undeniable verbosity of *The Apes* lies a book with a plan as simple as *Gulliver's Travels:* an ingenuous hero, his mind somewhat dulled by exposure to the conventional wisdom of his day, undertakes a journey among peoples whose monstrosities mirror the folly of those much closer to home. Lewis's Gulliver is Dan Boleyn, a barely literate young Irishman with pretensions to literary genius; his Lilliputians, a community of upper-middle-class bohemians who conspire to destroy the talented persons whom they cannot exploit for their own petty ends; and his Houyhnhnms, or rather Houyhnhnm, the invisible Pierpoint, a painter cum philosopher who is known to the reader only through the text of an unpublished "encyclical" on apery and his "broadcasts" on related topics through the mouths of his various disciples.

But *The Apes of God* shares more with *Gulliver's Travels* than the broad outlines of a picaresque plot. The marked style of Lewis's narrative also owes something to Swift's prose, or at least to the philosophical assumptions behind it.

In *The Apes of God,* Lewis committed himself to the methods of a "personal-appearance writer"(*MWA* 101), choosing to describe only what could be perceived with the naked eye. This insistence upon exact physical description was meant to counter the "romantic" tendencies in Joyce,

Virginia Woolf, and other writers, which had caused them, Lewis believed, to become lost in the labyrinths of their own minds and to overlook the infinitely grander vistas of the world outside the self. Lewis carried his methods to such an extreme, however, that the commonsense reality of his fictional universe often disappeared beneath an encrustation of detail, rendering the narrative of *The Apes of God* more difficult to follow than the extended "stream of consciousness" episodes in *Ulysses* that he himself had denounced for their darkness and obscurity (*TWM* 91–92).

While Lewis criticized the aims of psychological novelists throughout the twenties and thirties, he directed his most violent attacks against those who were in a sense at the *opposite* pole from such writers as Joyce and Woolf. These were the philistines of science, men and women who interpreted the insights of Darwin, Einstein, and others as proof that there was no ghost in the machine after all, but who then, blind to the implications of this supposed truth for themselves, proceeded to look down upon their fellow humans as only so much psychochemical hardware. In *Time and Western Man*, Lewis cited as a particularly crude proponent of this philosophy the American R. M. Yerkes, who developed "intelligence tests" for the Army during the First World War. In fact, what the tests measured, Lewis argued, was a person's ability to conform to a certain model of behavior, and a rather imbecilic one at that. Silly as the intelligence tester might appear, the mere existence of his profession indicated a significant intellectual trend in the modern world. With evident horror, Lewis quoted (and italicized) this sentence from the writings of Yerkes: *"Great will be our good fortune if the lesson in human engineering which the War has taught us is carried over, directly and effectively, into our civil institutions and activities"* (*TWM* 330). Thus we can observe that when Lewis denounced his "romantic" contemporaries (and the partisan is often harder on wayward allies than on obvious adversaries), it was either because they had failed to recognize the dehumanizing elements in their own belief systems (the noble savage, for example, can be seen as a mechanism of instinct), or because their leaps into the abyss of the self implied, at best, little hope for altering the conditions of everyday life or, at worst, an all-consuming egoism.

Here we can begin to see how Lewis's intentions paralleled Swift's, and how the book's apparent obsession with external detail, though officially directed against his "romantic" contemporaries, finds its true satiric object in the mechanist worldview of the twentieth century. Not that the twentieth century invented mechanism: much of the humor in *Gulliver's Travels* arises from the hero's insistence upon reasoning his way to the obvious, as though only with the aid of Newton and Locke could he see that the Lilliputian emperor's decision to blind him instead of killing him outright showed something less than royal magnanimity. Swift wanted to defend man against what now seems to have been inevitable: his reduction to a set of quantifiable needs that could be conveniently (and profitably) satisfied by an industrial system founded upon materialistic principles. Two centuries later, Lewis tried to fight the same battle. *His* adversaries included Karl Marx and Maria Montessori, the educator, on his left, and the behavioral psychologist James B. Watson on his right—a seemingly motley group, but bound together, in Lewis's mind, by their application of discoveries in natural science to various projects in "human engineering," with a consequent diminution in the mystery of man's "human divinity" (a Blakean expression Lewis uses in *The Childermass*) and a weakening of the bonds between persons.

In *The Apes of God*, Lewis registers the effect of these developments in the comic, ultraempirical style that denotes a whole society of Gullivers who have surrendered themselves to mechanical metaphors for thought and action. Simple communication becomes arduous, too, when a universe of shared experience (however riddled with myth and superstition) is rationalized for efficiency's sake. People in *The Apes* talk profusely, and sometimes with great rhetorical skill, but it is equally apparent that hardly anyone listens to anyone else, a fact that accounts for the exasperating repetitiousness of much of the dialogue.[18] Even the absent protagonist of the novel, the painter-philosopher Pierpoint, has a problem in this area: he is not a man speaking to men, but a disembodied voice that makes "broadcasts" through his disciples—broadcasts that, like the radio programs the term alludes to, can easily be tuned out by his listeners.

Lewis's method does represent a departure from classical satire in one important respect. While satirists usually wrote in a language that reflected universally acknowledged, if rarely attended to, standards—Pope's orderly rhymes and Swift's lucid prose, for example, appeal to the eighteenth-century reader's faith in reason—Lewis's style remains highly idiosyncratic, making it hard to see how he intended to align himself with anything universally acknowledged. Evidence elsewhere in *The Apes of God* suggests that Lewis did not see himself laughing *with* his readers at his satiric creations, but rather, continuing a pattern first noted in "Les Saltimbanques" and affirmed with "Sigismund" and the Tyros, laughing *at* his creations *and* his readers. In Pierpoint's "Encyclical" to Mr. Zagreus, we find this criticism of "bohemians," which now included only those who could afford to become one:

> Paris where there are incomparably more people living on familiar (and naturally contemptuous) terms with Art than anywhere else, is in reality a very large club for the well-to-do. The well-off find the studio-café society the only one in which they are free to live as they choose. It is unnecessary to say that these large groups of people, numbering many thousands, are not for the most part occupied in any pursuit more exacting than that of paying calls, and acting as clients to the Paris night resorts. A floating population of very young students lends the necessary air of "bohemian" illusion and juvenility to the large idle cosmopolitan settlements. They provide constant human currents and freshets in which the hardened old sinners can fish. (*AG* 119)

Lewis had spent most of his twenties in Paris, frequenting cafés, paying calls, painting less than he should have—the bohemian life, in other words. Paris was his Golgonooza, his city of art, but Paris could just as well have been any large metropolis with a reasonably sophisticated population and a university campus or two. Yet these were the only places where people could be expected to take much of an interest in *The Apes;* certainly he had not written it for the working class.[19] Thus, the overwhelming majority of prospective readers would necessarily have been apes themselves, persons with whom Lewis believed he had nothing in common.

This brings us to the paradox of Lewisian satire, a problem that Lewis himself acknowledged and one that explains why, despite his intense interest in social issues, Lewis is more accurately characterized as a philosophical and religious writer. In *Satire and Fiction,* Lewis noted that the classical satirist was essentially a moralist, attacking his enemies from a position that his readers could recognize as normative. Robert C. Elliott, an astute modern commentator on the art of satire, supports this view: "Usually (but not always—there are significant exceptions) [the satirist] operates within the established framework of society, accepting its norms, appealing to reason (or to what his society accepts as rational) as the standard against which to judge the folly he sees. He is the preserver of tradition, the true tradition from which there has been grievous falling away."[20] Among the significant exceptions, Elliott notes in passing, was Wyndham Lewis.

Lewis saw two problems with a satire based upon accepted moral standards. First, moral satire had a certain publicity value that actually flattered the ego of the victim: "For all those satirised by Juvenal, or smarting beneath the scourges of most other satirists, have been able at a pinch to snigger and remark that 'Yes, they *knew* they were very *wicked!*'" (*SF* 43). Secondly, the satirist who subordinated his art to an external system automatically limited his freedom of expression. Lewis claimed that the greatest satire would be nonmoralistic because "no mind of the first order has ever itself been taken in, nor consented to take in others, by the crude injunctions of any purely moral code" (*SF* 43).

A nonmoralistic satire such as *The Apes of God* dealt with man, not manners, and examined "a *chronic* ailment (manifesting itself, it is true, in a variety of ways) not an *epidemic* state, depending upon 'period,' or upon the 'wicked ways' of the particular smart-set of the time" (*SF* 50). Nonmoralistic satire was "doubly deadly" because it did not secretly envy its victim for bucking social convention and thus did not give back with one hand what it had taken away with another. For the same reason, however, the nonmoralistic satirist would always find himself the enemy of society, which would feel insulted at his indifference to its cherished principles of normative behavior. In *The Apes of God*, Lewis seems to have gone out of his way to alienate any possible "society" that might find an ally in him. The plain man would find the style obtuse and the subject matter irrelevant; the bohemian who might be able to appreciate both would find himself the target of scathing attacks, and would not appreciate the novel's immense bulk—the original edition weighed around five pounds—which Lewis intended to ensure that his apes would feel physically as well as mentally uncomfortable. This leaves us with the impression that the only adequate reader would be someone possessing genius equal to the author (though it would seem that there will always be too few of these around to provide artists with the decent living they deserve).

But even this hypothesis is flawed since eventually genius itself becomes an object of satire. Dan Boleyn, the young poet and apprentice ape-hunter, is reputed to have genius, yet he cannot navigate from one part of London to another without constant reference to his street guide and directions from policemen of whom he barely has the courage to make inquiries. Sustained thought or conversation severely taxes his intellectual resources (reading two or three pages of text exhausts him). Every now and then someone sees through the pretense. The hostess at a tea party Dan attends wonders aloud if he's some kind of automaton, asking him point-blank, " 'Is it true, Mr. Boleyn, that somebody has *made you*—that you have been manufactured like the—Hoffman doll?' " (*AG* 205).

Dan *has* been made by Horace Zagreus, his mentor in a bizarre apostolic succession that leads back to Pierpoint. In a note to Dan prefacing an extract from Pierpoint's "Encyclical," Zagreus had written: *"I believe absolutely in your genius.* You are a child of the Moon, when I first set eyes on you I knew it, you possess the *virtus vegetandi.* I solicit the privilege of being your gardener at this crisis, oh delicate moonflower. Have I your permission?" (*AG* 117). But if Dan is really as stupid as he appears (and he is), what can we be expected to think about Zagreus? He must either be an ape himself, pretending to have talents he does not possess, or a cynical genius whose adoption of ape values is yet another sign of the age's decadence. Whatever the case, he remains an unlikely prophet of an order that would restore the proper boundaries between artists and audiences, and that would return to art the legislative function it lost at just about the time Shelley felt the need to proclaim it. Among the few details about Zagreus that do emerge, we learn that before the war he was a "notorious practical joker," who once took virtual possession of the palace "for about ten minutes," by dressing up as a Guards Officer and disarming the sentries at the gate (*AG* 214). The name Zagreus is itself something of a practical joke, being a title of Dionysus, god of the irrational forces threatening to undermine the civilized order that Lewis sought to defend in *The Apes of God* and his other books of the twenties. On another occasion, when someone misapprehends the correct pronounciation of his name, Zagreus acquires the Dickensian tag-name "Thug Rust," which reinforces our impression of him as a charlatan.

As Dan implicates Zagreus in the practice of apery, so does Zagreus implicate the mysterious Pierpoint, whose wisdom Zagreus often "broadcasts," but who in the course of 625 pages never honors the reader with a personal appearance. With Pierpoint, we run into a real problem, because we know from reading Lewis's nonfiction that Pierpoint's opinions come with an authorial *nihil obstat;* the "Encyclical," for example, which analyzes the relationship between art and society in postwar England, reads like a condensed version of *The Art of Being Ruled.* Having pursued the fictional chain of being back to Pierpoint, we must now take the next logical step back to *his* maker and consider whether Pierpoint's poor judgment should cause us to doubt the assumption of genius in the author himself.

The Apes of God thus presents us with a dialectical argument that turns the book into an example of what Stanley Fish describes as a "self-consuming artifact":[21] a work whose basic premise (that the rational mind can distinguish truth from falsehood in art) is dissolved through a series of narrative events (each demonstrating the limits of intelligence), which lead the reader to the intuition of a truth that lies beyond reason (that art is an expression of the supernatural). In fairness to Lewis's announced intentions, we might describe the book as intensely "self-critical" rather than "self-consuming": the substance of Pierpoint's analyses in the "Encyclical" and the various "broadcasts" so closely parallels the content of Lewis's essays and letters that it would be presumptuous to claim that *The Apes of God* reaches the *aporia* modern criticism demands of its canonical texts. But though we never reach the point where the narrative completely unravels itself, we feel a momentum pulling us in that direction. This is especially so in the second half of the book, which follows the movements of the principal characters during the Finnian-Shaw Lenten party. After nearly 250 pages of dialogue and broadcast designed to show the Finnian-Shaw commitment to the ideals of a decadent romanticism, the narrative reaches an apparent climax with Zagreus's attempt to perform a "Vanish" or disappearing act. The absurdity of Pierpoint's chief disciple practicing the art of illusion can hardly be lost upon the reader; neither is it lost upon another disciple named Starr-Smith, who claims to be Pierpoint's political secretary. Soon after the "Vanish," Starr-Smith leaps up onto the stage and calls Zagreus to account:

> "You are playing the same game Zagreus as the people whom he [Pierpoint] denounces—whom *you* denounce!"
> "I denounce all that he denounces!"
> In solemn tones Horace assented.
> "That is it! But you are as bad as the rest!" (*AG* 594)

Since Starr-Smith has come to the party dressed in a black shirt and is alternately referred to as "Blackshirt" and "the Fascist," we might assume that he embodies the emotional astringency that Lewis cautiously admired in fascism as he understood it in the 1920s. Starr-Smith would thus become a fixed reference point in a universe otherwise dissolving into illusion. Yet even he seems to have been infected with the slippery metaphysics of the novel, telling Dan earlier in the evening: " 'Why do you suppose I am here with two more, who are volunteers, as 'fascists' of all things, to-night? Nothing to do with *Fascismo*—the last thing—can you guess? It's because I picked up three khaki shirts for a few pence and dyed them black—the whole outfit for the three of us did not cost fifteen bob! That is the reason'" (*AG* 509). Starr-Smith's final report to Pierpoint only confirms his unreliability, for in it he claims to have been severely beaten by the effeminate Dan, when in fact Dan never laid a hand on him. When the novel ends with the relative status of everyone almost unchanged from the beginning—the Folletts holding sway behind the walls of their estate, the apes occupying all the available studios, and Horace Zagreus promoting a newly discovered young "genius"—the reader will feel that he, too, has been the victim of an elaborate literary confidence game.

Religious Satire: *Snooty Baronet*

In numerous essays of the twenties and thirties, Lewis conducted a vigorous polemic against Freud, Bergson, and others who asserted the primacy of the unconscious in human behavior. He claimed to prefer a classical anthropology that identified the essential man with his powers of reason. As with many of the positions he held at this time, his commitment to reason derived largely from his experience in the war. For Lewis, the violence and unpredictability of modern warfare fulfilled the romantic vision of a world in which men no longer restrained the promptings of desire. Without the order that the conscious mind imposes upon experience, men quickly descended to the level of animals and machines. (The political implications of this philosophy were obvious: in *The Art of Being Ruled*, Lewis observes that "the western democratic principle has always been too anarchic to be sensible" [*ABR* 69] and calls for the establishment of a strong central government under such a figure as Lenin or Mussolini). But given Lewis's public affirmations of rational principles, the question remains: how did he come to write such a profoundly anarchic book as *The Apes of God*, one that undermines the willfulness and self-possession even of its autobiographical hero, the painter-philosopher Pierpoint?

To answer this, let us briefly review the evolution of Lewis's attitude toward reason during the first part of his career. In his early stories and paintings, Lewis celebrated the lawless spirit of Breton peasants who inhabited the margins of European civilization. Their impulsive and often violent manner of self-expression contrasted favorably with the tightly controlled passions of the English middle classes. In a 1910 essay, Lewis coined the term "the wild body" to describe this raw, physical side of human existence, which served as the primary reservoir of creative energy (*WB* 251).

Strangely enough, almost as soon as Lewis articulated the doctrine of the wild body, he began to retreat from the vitalist position and adopt an increasingly analytic approach to nature (including human nature). The critical factor here seems to have been the influence of cubism, an aesthetic movement whose preoccupation with media and perspective implicitly acknowledges the mind's intervention in our image of the world and of ourselves. The cubist painter, like the scientist, transcends the chaos of everyday experience and presents for the viewer's inspection the principles that enable us to understand what we see: lines, angles, vertices, polygons, and so forth. Evidence of this analytic approach is obvious in Lewis's visual art from *The Theatre Manager* onward and can also be seen in his fiction as early as *Mrs. Dukes' Million,* with its artist-hero who consciously tinkers with identity and later achieves mastery in the most glamorous high-technology field of his day, aviation.

The appearance of a flying machine in his 1910 novel indicates another factor pulling Lewis away from aestheticism and toward a more positivist outlook: his belief that an artist's work should be rooted in the experience of the present. If modernism can be defined as a conscious effort by artists to acknowledge the triumphs and tragedies of the industrial revolution, then Lewis deserves to be called the arch-modernist of the twentieth century. And since the processes of social, political, and economic modernization derive in large part from the applications of science, it seems only natural that science should have become one of Lewis's foremost concerns. This commitment to modernity influenced not only his choice of subject and setting, but also his method of composition. For years, Lewis tried to give the impression that he approached the writing of a novel the way an engineer undertakes the design of a high performance aircraft, keeping abreast of the very latest developments in materials science and fabrication techniques.

At all events, by the time of his second important essay, "Inferior Religions" (1917), Lewis had redefined "the wild body." He saw it less as an affirmation of the ineffable life force that aestheticism wanted to defend against the encroachments of science than as further proof of the mechanistic principles that inform all activity in the natural world. He now described his Bretons as "puppets" and "men-machines" and offered the general observation that most lives present "a spectacle as complete as a problem of Euclid" (*WB* 315). Lewis had not exactly abandoned the idea of transcendence but rather had come to doubt that the highest values would necessarily be human values. Indeed, like Hulme, he recognized a certain theological element in science: the indifference of the rational mind promised a means for recovering the ontological purity of a world that had been buried under three or four thousand years of self-interested myth.

By the mid-1920s, however, Lewis was no longer fighting the battles of either the scientists or the aesthetes. Both positions, he realized, exaggerated the uniqueness and the impact of scientific thinking. The war had forced Lewis to take a more pragmatic view of art and ideas, and in *The Art of Being Ruled*, he argued that science was just another cognitive instrument that, like all such instruments, reflected the immediate and often petty interests of its users:

> But here we arrive at one of the most significant delusions of the present time, to which in passing we must devote some attention. The popular notion that science is "impersonal" is one of the first errors we are called upon to dispel. The *non-impersonality* of science should at all cost be substituted for the idea of its personality.
>
> Science itself, to start with, when it first began its revolution, was a force of nature pure enough: a thing and not a person. But this impersonal thing men have now got hold of and harnessed, to a great extent. So pure science is one thing: its application another; and its vulgarization a third. (*ABR* 34)

When the ideal of scientific objectivity had entered into modern fiction ("principally from Flaubert," according to Zagreus, who broadcasts Pierpoint [*AG* 259]), the pernicious effects of its vulgarization were plain to see. On the one hand, there had arisen "a universal cult of 'impersonality'" (*AG* 259), evident, for example, in the work of James Joyce, a writer obsessed with the accuracy of his facts (using a watch and map to calculate the movements of his characters, corresponding with Aunt Josephine in Dublin about the basement entryway to 7 Eccles Street), and committed to the pose of a God-like detachment from worldly events. But Joyce could also be seen as representative of an equally influential "school of unabashed personal Fiction" (*AG* 259), since few writers were as autobiographical as he or, indeed, provoked such intense interest in their personal lives. Zagreus explains the paradox in a conversation with one of the "apes":

> "You see, Li, *a mask of impersonality merely removes the obligation to be a little truly detached*. The writer like Jane Austen (her personality according to the methods of the time in full view) had that imposed upon her. When the personality is in full view, the person has, in all decency, to be a little impersonal or non-personal. *The 'impersonality' of science and 'objective' observation is a wonderful patent behind which the individual can indulge in a riot of personal egotism impossible to earlier writers, not provided with such a disguise.*" (*AG* 259–60)

Zagreus goes on to assert that the more a person believes himself to possess "superhuman *impartiality*," the more he can be expected to behave in a manner both human and partial (*AG* 260). A man is a man, not a god or a machine, and if that man happens to be a writer, he must impose upon himself the conditions that Austen could take for granted, lest he become a hypocrite or, in Lewis's terms, an "ape of God." This obligation to acknowledge the limitations of authorship accounts for the "self-consuming" movement of the argument in *The Apes of God* and encourages us to see Lewis as a writer who set out to create a deliberately imperfect fiction.

Signs of this methodical imperfection abound in *Snooty Baronet*, Lewis's first work of fiction after *The Apes of God*, and a book that builds upon the insights of its predecessor while leaving it far behind. *Snooty Baronet* is the product of Lewis's periodic desire to write a popular novel that would ensure him a measure of financial security, though it is obvious from the third paragraph, in which the narrator apologizes for opening his story in the style of a "gunman bestseller," that Lewis doesn't take the genre seriously enough to actually write one. The action centers around the figure of Sir Michael Kell-Imrie, a peg-legged war veteran who has made a career writing books that illustrate the behavioristic foundations of human psychology. (Not surprisingly, he takes a rather sardonic view of his fellow man; thus his nickname, Snooty.) In an effort to keep him in the public eye, his literary agent comes up with a bizarre scheme to have Snooty travel to Persia, where, while doing research for a book on the ancient cult of Mithras, he will be "captured" by a group of bandits and held for a ransom. Though Snooty feels nothing but contempt for his agent (and the public he represents), he goes along with the idea, always considering ways to exact revenge.

Until recently, Lewis's critics have dismissed *Snooty Baronet* as a minor work, calling it "pointless" and "wayward. "[22] The novel seems to lack the polish of revision, and, in fact, Lewis wrote it under contract in a period of about three months. In the mid-1970s, however, Timothy Materer proposed that readers should carefully distinguish between the narrator (Snooty) and the author and should approach the book with the same appreciation for irony that allows Nabokov's *Lolita* to be read as an affirmation of the human values Humbert Humbert almost destroys.[23] Materer suggests that Snooty's callousness simply exposes the underlying brutality of a civilization that sent young men off to lose legs and lives in the trenches of France.[24] Another attempt to redeem the novel comes from Bernard Lafourcade, the editor of the recent Black Sparrow Press edition of *Snooty Baronet*, who sees the book as a precursor to postmodern fiction, with all its attendant anxieties about the disappearance of the subject. For Lafourcade, the novel is an "existential farce" in the tradition of *Tristram Shandy*, which allows the author to "test the ambiguities of his own [empiricist] vision" (*SB* 264, 263).

In *Snooty Baronet*, Lewis finds several ways to remind the reader that the power of disinterested observation does not properly belong to the human subject. He begins by employing a first-person narrator, a technical device that the master of psychological realism, Henry James, once called the most "barbarous" means of telling a story. Next we notice that he has abandoned the verbose "external" style of *The Apes of God*, whose long, groping sentences confronted the reader with "a principle of immense mechanical energy"[25] that seemed calculated, despite Pierpoint's warnings, to achieve the illusion of impersonality. He replaced it with something chatty and impulsive, a style that is unembarrassed by the casual syntax that records the play of stimulus and response under the cranium of the novel's behaviorist hero. Snooty's preface to a discussion of Mithraism is typical: "I suppose now I have to boil down for you what I read. I offer it in tabloid. It's difficult to compress all the facts. Never mind.—Read this of course if you like, if you don't do the other thing, you are not obliged to. It is of no great importance that you should know it. It was one of the stepping-stones in my translation to Persia" (*SB* 87).

Lewis also intrudes upon the fictional world he creates in *Snooty Baronet* with a determination equalled only by Joyce's efforts to *exclude* himself from *Ulysses*. On more than one occasion, he puts in a cameo appearance under such a flimsy disguise that even the reader who knows nothing about the author beyond his name will realize that Lewis is having his little joke.

The most amusing of these comes in the fifth chapter, when Snooty, during one of his many excursions into self-justification, compares himself to the eighteenth-century politician and disciple of Burke, William Windham. Quoting liberally from the Earl of Rosebery's introduction to *The Windham Papers* (*SB* 279), Snooty compares himself to a Windham renowned for his independence, extremism, and powerful resentments—characteristics that would also be part of a candid assessment of the other Wyndham whose name appeared on the title page.

Admittedly, the cameo can have an ambiguous significance. On the one hand, it usually remains the prerogative of the master craftsman. The journeyman dare not tease the audience with his presence lest he imply that his work does not have a life of its own and needs someone there to coax it along. (This partly explains the absence of the author's photograph on the dust jackets of most first novels.) But when Alfred Hitchcock appeared for ten seconds in a movie starring James Stewart or Cary Grant, it was clearly a matter of Cardinal Richelieu winking at us from behind the throne of Louis XIII, reminding us who was making this whole universe go round. The very brevity of Hitchcock's appearances further contributed to the effect, telling us that he did not *have* to assert his presence, which extended to every detail of the production.

Yet the cameo is undeniably a rip in what might otherwise have been a seamless garment. It shatters the satisfying illusion of *ex nihilo* creation and forces us to see that there is, after all, a ghost in the machine. And the smallness of the cameo role might just as well be taken as a self-conscious belittling of authorial authority, a gesture done in the spirit of the Feast of Fools, where the king played slave for a day and acknowledged certain unhappy truths about his exalted station.

This brings us to Lewis's most compelling argument against the notion that man, or whatever man creates (no matter how technically accomplished), could be the measure of all things: Snooty himself. Snooty's typically obnoxious behavior toward others can be traced back to a period of convalescence at the end of the war when he read Herman Melville's *Moby Dick*. Snooty was first drawn to Melville's novel because of Ahab, "the patron-saint, in our English Letters, of the One-legged" (*SB* 62). At about this time, too, he had decided upon a career as a sort of amateur marine biologist and had even gone on to write a successful book about deep-sea fishing.

But the more that Snooty thought about *Moby Dick* (which had become almost an obsession for him), the more he realized that his sympathies lay not with Ahab but with the whale: "I saw Captain A. as the spear-head of the Herd. He stood for Numbers. It was *he*, in fact, who was the giant!" (*SB* 63). The bloodthirsty Ahab, harpoon in hand, represented a civilization so committed to a Nietzschean slave-ethic that all its energies were directed to the destruction of "the great solitary floating colossus that was the private soul" (*SB* 63). Now having discovered that he was "*another* Ahab, but of opposite sign" (*SB* 63), Snooty sets out to develop a plan of attack against the real Leviathan, mankind. He decides, in effect, to hang them by their own rope, one by one. Since man was "compacting with the insects" to sweep away all noble values, Snooty undertakes the study of man "upon exactly the same footing as ape or insect" and, indeed, in his first behaviorist work dissects the lives of a pair of former army comrades "as if they were lice" (*SB* 64).

It should be apparent by now that Snooty's philosophy of the one and the many closely resembles Pierpoint's ideas about genius and apehood, and thus leaves Snooty open to similar charges of hypocrisy. But Snooty is more conscious of his existential limitations, admitting that what he does to others he might just as well do to himself: "I do not hide behind the waving arms and nodding heads of my marionettes. Anything but—why, I will dance a *pas de quatre* with the worst of them, and I will pick myself to pieces for the benefit of the Public as soon as look at it! As readily as I would pick a member of the Public to pieces I will pick my own self, bit by bit" (*SB* 102). Still, Snooty is not a perfect behaviorist because he shows in his actions a certain air of superiority with regard to other members of his species. All this changes one day when Snooty is walking down a London street and is attracted by the spectacle of an automaton "behaving" in the display window of a hatter. While he stands there with several other passersby watching the performance, he first amuses himself by noting the likenesses between this mechanical mannequin and his boorish literary agent. He goes on to consider that at the moment the mannequin is actually *more* real than his agent because in the absence of measurable behavior, the behaviorist has no choice but to conclude that a person has simply blinked out of existence. But as he continues to observe the thing's behavior, it gradually dawns upon him that there is also no absolute, empirically demonstrable distinction between the puppet and *himself*:

As the man at my side observed me putting on my hat, I was for the first time placed in the position *of the dummy!* I saw all round Behavior as it were—for the first time. I knew that *I* was not always existing, either: in fact that I was a fitful appearance. That I was apt to *go out* at any moment, and turn up again, in some other place—like a light turned on by accident, or a figure upon a cinematographic screen.—And must I confess it? I was very slightly alarmed. I saw that I had to *compete* with these other creatures bursting up all over the imaginary landscape, and struggling against me to be *real*—like a passionate battle for necessary air, in a confined place. (*SB* 138)

Since the text of Snooty's narrative is identical to that of Lewis's novel (on the next to last page, Snooty tells us that the *"Book of the Month Club* have taken up these papers, entitling them . . .'SNOOTY BARONET' " [*SB* 251]), the preceding passage can be read as a seriocomic expression of the author's own existential doubts. In a Lewisian universe, no man has an automatic *right* to existence, not even Wyndham Lewis. Hugh Kenner has remarked that Lewis's fiction "concerns itself with the unreal, with gradations of unreality,"[26] that is to say, with the rhetoric we employ to excuse the trouble of our coming into the world and to give it the appearance of meaning. Writing fiction—writing satiric fiction on the order of *Snooty Baronet,* in which people knock one another about in a "passionate battle" for the necessary air of reality—was just such a self-serving rhetoric, to be perfectly honest about it, and so it is only natural that the author should follow his characters up the scaffold.

The self-consuming ironies of *Snooty Baronet* remind us once again that Lewis had less interest in developing a coherent social critique than in articulating a theory of human nature. At the root of that theory was an understanding of man as a creature whose natural limits obliged him to act in his own self-interest. People customarily want to believe only good things about themselves, however, and so over the centuries men have tried to paper over the violent and inhospitable acts they have committed against others to further their own ends. Every now and then, someone comes along who does see through the mystifications: Lewis, for example, devotes several chapters of *The Lion and the Fox* (an extended meditation on Shakespeare's politics) to Niccolò Machiavelli's *The Prince,* which he praises as a critique of satisfaction "that forces civilization to face about and confront the grinning shadow of its Past, and acknowledge the terrible nature of its true destiny" (*LF* 76).

Lewis's skeptical approach to human institutions can be compared to that of the contemporary French critic René Girard, who sees the laws and rituals of civilized life as the encoding of forgotten acts of violence that underlie the social order: patricide, theft, war, repression, and so on.[27] Building on Girard's insight, Michael Seidel asserts that satire "blows history's cover" by decoding these now legitimized acts of violence and thus revealing the actual bases of civilization: "In satire the necessary displacements of history—the cover-up rituals—are represented by more overt forms of the violations they are supposed to replace. Girard holds that what was once unthinkable becomes, after a fashion, legal. The satirist maintains that what is represented as legal is really unthinkable."[28] When Jonathan Swift confronted England with the terrible nature of its relations with Ireland, he proposed cannibalism as only a slight exaggeration of the legal status quo. In *Snooty Baronet*, Lewis wanted to expose the loss of the divine in man by a culture whose dedication to the control of all human and natural energies meant the rationalization of every unchecked impulse. He faced a more difficult task than Swift, however, because the liberal institutions that had developed since the eighteenth century prided themselves on their humane and sympathetic approach to individual needs. Throughout *The Art of Being Ruled*, for example, Lewis tried to show the absurdity of believing that the consumption of mass-marketed goods and services could be a means of self-realization, or that the violence required to maintain the international system upon which the wealth of the bourgeois nations depended actually served the interests of the "savage" races. Not surprisingly, Snooty himself would have preferred life in a more openly violent society and on one occasion falls into a reverie about the possibility of a Mithraic Europe:

SOL INVICTUS at Stonehenge, instead of the Archbishop of Canterbury at Canterbury. Delightful! The Magi officiating in a semi-mazdean temple where Westminster Abbey now stands (a big bull-ring between it and the Tate). And our Government next door (assembled in a very fine building of Persepolitan pattern) not forced as at present to apologize to the ridiculous Bengalee for having thought of the machine-gun first or having invented electric light and airplanes! The King-Emperor would visit Delhi in great pomp every year or two, and a few thousand heads of traitors would be brought in bags from all parts of India and heaped up in a pyramid outside his residence, as if our George were Ashurbanipal! What a transformation don't you agree! (*SB* 90)

But since Europeans practiced (or did not practice) a religion whose "humanitarian sentimentalism" (*SB* 90) could mystify even the most heinous crimes, the rottenness in Denmark can be revealed only by stratagem. And so, in *Snooty Baronet*, Lewis gives us a character whose brutally mechanistic assumptions about his fellow man differ in degree but not in kind from the assumptions embodied in our commercial, educational, political, and, of course, military institutions.

Lewis attains the most eloquent expression of his rage near the end of *Snooty Baronet* in a veritable aria of misanthropy. His outburst is occasioned by the death of his friend Rob McPhail (modeled upon the South African poet Roy Campbell), who has succumbed to wounds received during an impromptu bullfight in the south of France. Although McPhail had been taunting the bull, Snooty, who had been visiting his friend en route to Persia, concludes that he had done so only to show up the professional toreadors, and that in fact, McPhail, like Snooty, was thoroughly "antiman" (*SB* 193). Still, despite his obvious attachment to McPhail, Snooty does not abandon his behaviorist principles in the midst of tragedy and reports that upon hearing the bad news he experienced no emotion beyond a certain annoyance. He further considers that he no longer likes McPhail as much now that he is dead: "There is nothing more to like! After all I could not *marry* a dead person! So how could I *like* one, really?" (*SB* 193). Perhaps aware that his readers might still be shocked at his behavior Snooty offers this apologia:

> I am not perhaps a good friend. It may be I am not a good companion. The Shan Van Vocht, the snooty sibyl of the Gael—I can hear her grinding out her ceaseless imprecations, against all that goes upright—it has come now to be that! Within the twilight of my race's days, the hostile silhouette (once that of tradition, of the hated next-door neighbour) grows vaster beneath our eyes—but also far more impersonal. No people are exempt. Not *someone,* but *everyone,* has blundered! The Shan Van Vocht squats there calling Chaos about her—as *Chaos comes!* It is the soul of a defeated race, that nothing can reconcile to its unhappy lot—but at last it sees that not its next-door neighbour merely (a nation *telle ou telle*) but that ultimately all mankind is responsible for its misfortunes.—And that blood of the cantankerous is in my veins, I am very much afraid. Expect nothing out of my mouth, therefore, that has a pleasant sound. Look for nothing but descriptions out of a vision of a person who has given up hoping for Man, but who is scrupulous and just, if only out of contempt for those who are so much the contrary. (*SB* 232–33)

The appearance here of the Shan Van Vocht ("the poor old woman," a personification of Ireland and also the title of a famous revolutionary anthem) can be ascribed to Snooty's Gaelic ancestry and his general dislike of authority. But it might be worth noting that Celtic literature had a tradition of poetic invective in which Snooty would have been right at home. The angry words of these ancient bards were understood to have supernatural powers, and indeed, the Irish language itself insisted upon the identification of satire and magical spells.[29]

Snooty will not be satisfied with mere imprecation, however, and eventually acts upon his dark vision, murdering his agent in cold blood just as the bandits who have been hired to kidnap him arrive on the scene. Naturally, Snooty feels no guilt, since he had known all along that his agent was just a mechanical puppet; indeed, his pleasure in remembering the second rifle shot inspires him to end a chapter by quoting the first line of Keats's *Endymion*, "A thing of beauty is a joy forever!" (*SB* 240). But to his surprise and even mild irritation, the world simply refuses to acknowledge his antisocial behavior when the events of his Persian expedition become known. The one European witness to the shooting denies Snooty's culpability, and the king himself believes that after "suitable treatment" Snooty would return to his senses (*SB* 252).

Snooty's freedom at the end of the novel tends to confirm Lewis's claim that he wrote a "metaphysical" satire, whose mission was more properly religious than moral. Seidel observes that the satirist is tolerated "because he has in him something that is sacred and prophetic,"[30] and Elliott identifies him specifically as the *pharmakos*, or scapegoat, whose vestigial forms can still be identified in most religions. Although he will be denounced by society and runs the risk of punishment, "he is quite unrealistically privileged in legend and literature because he represents our own (and presumably the author's) suppressed aggressive impulses."[31] In *Snooty Baronet*, Lewis thus carries out a priestly function, exposing and perhaps exorcising modern man's frustration at having created a world that is gradually denying him divinity.

4

Religious Sensibilities

Inferior and Superior Religions

Lewis began his literary career writing sonnets, moved on to novels about art and artists, eventually became a satirist and social critic, and ended with an unfinished trilogy about life after death. This movement through a variety of forms and subject matters recalls the Virgilian paradigm, which conducted the aspiring writer up the scale from pastoral to didactic to epic poetry. Virgil's model allowed a poet to exercise his talents in the relative security of Arcadia before moving on to the real world of men and arms.[1] Later, the progression from pastoral to epic signaled the maturing artist's willingness to forgo the private pleasures of the imagination and place his gifts at the disposal of the community.

In the mid-nineteenth century, Kierkegaard, though not writing with Virgil specifically in mind, modified this scheme to reflect more accurately the condition of the modern artist. The progress Kierkegaard charts from the aesthetic to the ethical to the *religious* sphere, where an *individual* (like Abraham on Moriah) encounters the Absolute, implies the artist's estrangement from the shared cultural experience assumed by the writer of classical epic. Though the desire to tell (in Pound's words) the "tale of the tribe" would persist well into the twentieth century, the idiosyncratic form of many modern epics hints at an equally strong wish to transcend culture once and for all.

Of course, literary careers do not follow the ideal trajectories that critics plot, nor should we expect them to, since each stage in a dialectic incorporates something of what comes before and after. Although *The Human Age* arguably fulfills Lewis's ambitions as a religious writer (or would have if he'd lived to complete it), we find him there wrestling with many of the same aesthetic problems that preoccupied him in *Tarr*. On the other hand, *Tarr*'s "aesthetics of deadness" represent Lewis's disenchantment with humanism and his desire for an art like that of the Egyptians that acknowledged man's cosmic insignificance—his desire, in short, for a religious art.

The word *religion* comes from the Latin *religare*, which means "to bind back." In simplest terms, then, religion concerns itself with man's awareness of limits and his dependence upon things outside the self. Although Lewis came to maturity at a time when religious scepticism was already well established among artists and intellectuals, he always seems to have been sensitive to the existential constraints upon human freedom. We find a seriocomic treatment of this issue in the 1917 essay "Inferior Religions," which had originally been composed as an introduction to a collection of his Breton stories. Looking back upon these studies in the "wild body" that he had completed several years earlier, Lewis was now able to identify their unifying principle:

> These intricately moving bobbins are all subject to a set of objects or one in particular. Brobdingnag is fascinated by one object for instance; one at once another vitality. He bangs up against it wildly at regular intervals, blackens it, contemplates it, moves around it and dreams. All such fascination is religious. Moran's damp napkins are the altar cloths of his rough illusion, Julie's bruises are the markings of an idol. . . .
>
> All religion has the mechanism of the celestial bodies, has a dance. When we wish to renew our idols, or break up the rhythm of our naivety, the effort postulates a respect which is the summit of devoutness. (*WB* 315)

In his famous essay on the comic, Henri Bergson wrote that we laugh at the man who behaves with "a certain *mechanical inelasticity*, just where one would expect to find the wideawake adaptability and the living pliableness of a human being."[2] We laugh, in other words, when someone acts like a machine instead of the semidivine creature described by poets and philosophers. Lewis's idea of the "wild body" (distilled from his observations of ordinary Breton folk) turns Bergson upside down and asserts that in fact most human behavior *is* machinelike and that we ought to laugh, or at least be taken with surprise, when someone acts in a thoughtful or creative manner.

Lewis's theory goes beyond mere drollery, however, by insisting that mechanical movement, far from proving a defect in man's design, shows how much he belongs in a universe where even the motion of the stars has been choreographed in advance. Indeed, a man's domestic routine provides in microcosm the same refuge and security that he feels in the "big religions" (*WB* 316). For example, in the story entitled "Brobdingnag," a fisherman and part-time innkeeper beats his wife, Julie, at more or less regular intervals to purge his violent impulses and maintain the equilibrium of his normally placid existence. The beatings also help to strengthen the marriage by letting Brobdingnag show his affection for his wife as he nurses her back to health. One day Brobdingnag returns to his village from a fishing trip to discover Julie with her arm in a sling. It seems that the baker's cart ran over her hand when she was trying to block one of the wheels; she has had, in other words, an *accident*. This disruption in the natural order of things sends Brobdingnag into profound despair. Before this he had felt himself a necessary agent in the cruelties that life metes out to people and had even wondered if he might not be "a secret agent of Fate" (*WB* 294). Now that Julie has suffered a kind of beating in his absence, he confronts the terrifying question: "*Had Fate acted without him?*" (*WB* 294). In the story's closing paragraph, the narrator speculates that the couple's "nocturnal rites" will grow more savage, but also more desperate, as Brobdingnag vainly tries to recover his place in the cosmic mechanism.

The vaguely condescending tone of both "Inferior Religions" and "Brobdingnag" implies that while ordinary people need the "refuge and rest" of patterned behavior (*WB* 316), the exceptionally creative individual will choose to dispense with the assurances provided by religion, inferior or otherwise. Arghol, the hero of Lewis's closet drama *Enemy of the Stars*, would seem to provide us with just such an example. He inhabits a cubist landscape near the Arctic Circle, where the forces of nature manifest themselves as undifferentiated violence. Even the impossibly distant heavens threaten those below, the stars shining madly like "machines of prey" (*CPP* 100). Arghol instinctively responds to his predicament by asserting the autonomy of the self against all restraint. Lewis had been reading

Nietzsche before the war (*RA* 128), and undoubtedly Arghol's radical individualism owes much to his portrait of the *Uebermensch*. Further traces of
Nietzsche's thought appear throughout *Enemy of the Stars*. In the midst of a
fight between Arghol and an embittered disciple named Hanp, the
anonymous narrator observes:

> To break vows and spoil continuity of instinctive behaviour, lose a prize
> that would only be a trophy tankard never drunk from, is always fine.
> Arghol would have flung his hoarding and scraping of thought as well
> now. (*CPP* 110)

But Lewis is not Nietzsche, and Arghol is not Zarathustra. Arghol's
"instrument of thought," the narrator continues, weighs too heavily upon
him and resists the "swift anarchist effort" that would have accomplished
this liberating gesture (*CPP* 110). He suffers, in other words, from the
disease of consciousness that allows a man to step outside the moment and
see his life not as an eternal present but as a paltry tale with a beginning and
an end. Finding the knowledge of his own death unbearable, Arghol
catches himself taking comfort in "words coming out of caverns of belief"
and the possibility of transcending this life instead of having to live it.

Despite Arghol's intelligence and sophistication (he has lately returned
from "the great city of their world" [*CPP* 108]), he differs from a Breton
peasant only by the degree of awareness that attends the performance of his
rituals. The narrator's speculations supply Brobdingnag with the possibility that he might be a secret agent of Fate; but when Hanp asks Arghol why
he submits to nightly beatings from a sadistic relative (a wheelwright, no
less, maker of closed circles), he himself explains: "Here I get routine, the
will of the universe manifested with directness and persistence" (*CPP* 101).
For Lewis, *both* the peasant *and* the superman must locate themselves
within a larger pattern of cosmic forces. The word *Arghol* itself tells the
story: we can hear it as a corruption of *Algol*, the name of a famous variable
star, which, like other objects in its class, performs a never-ending pirouette
with an invisible companion to the beat of gravity.[3] Arghol is merely another instance of what he seeks to oppose: a star, a mechanism, an inferior
religion.

For Lewis, the question about religion was not "whether?" but "what
kind?" since all men and women live within systems of limits. An "inferior"
religion implies the possibility of a superior alternative. This might mean

simply a larger, more public body of ritual and belief, the "big religions," such as Christianity, that offer "refuge and rest" for humanity at large (*WB* 316). Or the distinction between inferior and superior could be strictly qualitative. Brobdingnag and Arghol seek routine not only to affirm their place in the cosmic order, but to reassure themselves that this place is somehow meaningful. As we have observed, however, Lewis was dubious of any scheme that presented man (or a particular group of men) in a flattering light. It seems reasonable to assume, therefore, that this critique of satisfaction would apply to religion as well as to aesthetics and social relations. A superior religion would be one that acknowledged the boundaries of man's freedom without justifying these constraints as a necessary element in the eventual conquest of his environment. A superior religion would offer no "refuge and rest" and might, on the contrary, assert that man's appearance in the cosmic dance had no lasting significance at all.

To the extent that Lewis thought about religion early in his career, he inclined toward heterodox beliefs, which did not share with Christianity a commitment to historical progress and the final redemption of man. By the late 1920s, however, when religious issues engaged him more directly, Lewis's language became increasingly orthodox. This resulted not from a fundamental change in outlook, but from an awareness that the radical in religion (as well as in art) could be as smug and self-satisfied as the hoariest conservative. In the remainder of this chapter, we will examine the nature of Lewis's heterodoxy, consider his eventual withdrawal from this position, and describe his somewhat reluctant attachment to a Christian (and specifically Catholic) theology.

The Ancient and Valuable Principle of Duality

In 1927, Lewis brought out a book of short stories entitled *The Wild Body*. All the stories in this collection save one had been published by various little magazines in earlier versions. The single exception was "The Death of the Ankou." Curiously, in a passage cited earlier, Lewis identified this as the first story he had ever written, having composed it from material that he could not assimilate into a portrait he was doing of a blind beggar. The evidence suggests that the story must have lain unfinished for nearly two decades before Lewis decided to refurbish it for *The Wild Body*.[4] This long hiatus tells us two things: first, that the story had an enduring fascination for its author, and second, that the material must have presented him with serious difficulties. At all events, "The Death of the Ankou" is among the finest of Lewis's shorter works, both for its evocation of the starkness of Breton life, and for its skillful manipulation of the boundary between the natural and the supernatural.

The story opens in a small Breton town at an inn where the narrator, a young Englishman named Ker-Orr, sits among the noisy patrons reading a guidebook to the local antiquities. He finds himself lingering over the history of the Ankou, the ancient Armorican god of death. The god had once been worshiped throughout Brittany, but over the centuries, his altars had gradually fallen before the images of a gentler god. Not long ago, according to the guidebook, one could still find a statue of the Ankou at the church in Ploumilliau; but a local sorceress had made an embarrassing fuss over it, and the priest had it consigned to a storage room. "So one of the last truly pagan images disappeared," muses the narrator, "wasting its curious efficacy in a loft, dusted occasionally by an ecclesiastical *bonne*" (WB 107).

The guidebook also included an anecdote about the blinding of the Ankou. It seems that one evening as he traveled along the roads looking for people whose hour had come, the god of death saw a man and his master working in a field. When the man noticed the god's approach, he broke into song. This display of insolence scandalized the Ankou, who shouted over the hedge that the man had eight days to live, no more! By chance Saint Peter happened to be in the vicinity. Enraged at the Ankou for interfering with a man at his labor, he struck the Ankou blind on the spot, thinking to himself afterward that by doing so he had earned man's eternal gratitude.[5] Blindness did not prevent the Ankou from continuing his rounds, however, and fretful men still calculated the number of years or days left to them from various signs and portents attending their nocturnal encounters with the god.

Having persuaded himself that he must plan to visit Ploumilliau, Ker-Orr looks up from his reading and, through the haze of tobacco smoke and Celtic daydreams, sees the blind face of the Ankou passing almost in front of him: "It was noon. I said to myself that, as it was noon, that should give me twelve more months to live. I brushed aside the suggestion that day was not night, that I was not a breton peasant, and that the beggar was probably not Death. I tried to shudder. I had not shuddered" (WB 110). In actuality, he had seen a "garbled version" of the god, a blind beggar called Ludo, to whom a Breton friend of Ker-Orr's introduces him later that afternoon. A brief conversation shows Ludo to possess a wit and haughtiness equal to that of the original Ankou.

Two days later, Ker-Orr shoulders his rucksack and heads for another town. Along the way, he stops off at the cave where Ludo resides. At first, Ludo receives his visitor hospitably, even offering to share his meal. Although he now begins to feel more comfortable with the beggar, Ker-Orr is still a little haunted by his first impression of Ludo as the death-god. The blind face, the *deadest* part of Ludo's body, he thinks, betokens some unfathomable mystery within. Mystery aside, Ludo does not look well this day, and questioned on this point, he admits to being "indisposed." This prompts the following exchange:

> "Perhaps you've met the Ankou." I said this thoughtlessly, probably because I had intended to ask him if he had ever heard of the Ankou, or something like that. . . .
> "Who has been telling you about the Ankou, and all those tales?" he suddenly asked.
> "Why, I was reading about it in a guidebook, as a matter of fact, the first time I saw you. You scared me for a moment. I thought you might be he." (*WB* 114)

Ludo becomes instantly withdrawn. Soon he arises and, holding his side, reenters the cave, slamming the door behind him. The beggar's dog growls, and Ker-Orr knows that it is time to leave. He speculates briefly but inconclusively on the reason for Ludo's change of mood: "Perhaps I had put myself in the position of the Ankou, even—unseen as I was, a foreigner and, so, ultimately dangerous—by mentioning the Ankou, with which he was evidently familiar. He may even have retreated into his cave, because he was afraid of me. Or the poor devil was simply ill" (*WB* 115). The story ends abruptly with the report of Ludo's death later that summer.

While "The Death of the Ankou" can be read as an elegy for a dying culture and its beliefs, the strange affinity between the narrator and his subject makes the story more than a successful exercise in local color writing. When the Ankou dies in the end, we are led to believe that his death resulted from his meeting with Ker-Orr, who now seems to have inherited the Ankou's office; and so the story can also be interpreted as the account of an apostolic succession. Like its biblical and classical antecedents in this regard, "The Death of the Ankou" focuses upon the transfer of supernatural powers associated with prophecy. Ludo's unexplained blindness hints at a relationship with the gods, and although he never looks into the future per se, his status as an "embodied calamity" and his willingness to "enter into every door he found open" shows a man who, like Oedipus or Teiresias, has nothing to fear from the unknown (*WB* 110). The story's abrupt ending prevents us from saying exactly how Ker-Orr grows in knowledge and power after his encounter with the Ankou. But if we consider that the sequence of tales in the 1927 *Wild Body* culminates in a revised version of Lewis's essay "Inferior Religions," then this episode can be seen as another stage in the narrator's understanding of the supernatural order.

"Inferior Religions" and *Enemy of the Stars* describe a closed system in which nothing transcends the cosmic dance; "The Death of the Ankou" elaborates this scheme by showing that two imperfectly balanced forces— life and death—oppose one another within its confines. Death here is not merely the absence of life but a distinct power with its own identity; and whatever it lacks in vitality, it makes up for in having a sharper, more "acetic" identity than life (*WB* 110). Perhaps because the narrator comes from a world where the requirements of civilization proscribe impulsive self-expression, he finds himself naturally drawn to the primitive god of death. An alliance with death also forestalls the inevitable process of aging and decrepitude that one day erases personal identity.

This sentiment, at least, is reflected in the epigraph that Lewis chose for the story, "And Death once dead, there's no more dying then." The line concludes Shakespeare's sonnet 146, and while it might seem to announce the Christian's victory over death and consequent entry into the riches of everlasting life, the poem in fact describes the illusory nature of life's satisfactions and urges the mortification of the flesh as a way to preempt the surrender of personal identity to death. When Ker-Orr is transformed into the Ankou, he thus becomes the model for a long line of Lewisian heroes (Pierpoint, the Bailiff, Kell-Imrie, and eventually the Devil himself) who side with the forces arrayed against man rather than accept the sham existence that passes for life in the civilized world.

The presence of the Ankou at the beginning of Lewis's literary career (according to his own recollection of it) reminds us of Lewis's debt to the romantic tradition, which defined the hero as the opponent, rather than the defender, of the community's moral and ethical standards. This romantic transvaluation of good and evil originates in the political consciousness associated with the French Revolution and proceeds upon the assumption that the community possesses no greater insight into moral questions than does the individual. This does not mean that the individual is suddenly free to do whatever he or she pleases, only that the static opposition between good and evil has been superseded by one that is dynamic and dialectical. When Blake and Shelley identified Satan as the true hero of *Paradise Lost,* they were claiming not that Satan rightfully occupied the authoritative position held by God, but that the poem's energy derives from the struggle of cosmic forces it describes. Nothing can transcend this dialectic: if Satan had succeeded in displacing God, God would then have become Satan, the focus of whatever energies cannot be subsumed within any practical system of rule.

Shelley wanted to abandon Christianity altogether and explore mythologies that more readily acknowledged the dialectical relationship of good to evil. In classical Greek religion, Shelley found Prometheus, who once gave wisdom to Jupiter, but later turned on the Olympian when he proved as arrogant as his Titanic predecessor. Shelley also looked eastward for his mythic materials, and under the influence of his friend Thomas Love Peacock, discovered Zoroastrianism and its derivative, Manicheism.[6] In his "Essay on the Devil and Devils," Shelley comments directly on the appeal of this exotic religion:

> The Manichean philosophy respecting the origin and government of the world, if not true, is at least an hypothesis conformable to the experience of actual facts. To suppose the world was created and is superintended by two spirits of a balanced power and opposite dispositions is simply a personification of the struggle which we experience within ourselves, and which we perceive in the operations of external things as they affect us, between good and evil.[7]

Shelley's philosophical loyalties were ultimately more Neoplatonic than Manichean: in *Prometheus Unbound,* he looks forward to a resolution of the antinomy of good and evil.[8] More determined, perhaps, in his appropriation of dualistic cosmologies was Friedrich Nietzsche, whose *Gay Science* and *Thus Spake Zarathustra* owe an obvious debt to Zoroastrianism. Like Shelley, Nietzsche had only contempt for Christianity, which he saw as a conspiracy designed to validate the despair of the masses and undermine the courage of a healthy, creative minority. He particularly despised the self-satisfaction of Christians with their vision of a static, categorical truth embodied in the person of a supreme being, and in Zoroastrianism, he found a religion "that did not present its believers with an omnipotent and omniscient God."[9]

While we know that Lewis read Nietzsche during his early years on the Continent, he need not have relied entirely upon *Zarathustra* for his awareness of dualistic religion. The work of such philologists as Nietzsche's friend Paul Deussen pointed to ancient Persia as the homeland of Indo-European, the supposed progenitor of all European languages, and this commenced a flurry of scholarly interest in the region. Indeed, the number of texts, translations, and commentaries indicates, in the words of Peter Caracciolo, "an intellectual climate so extensive that it could be argued Lewis found many Zoroastrian ideas in the air."[10] Caracciolo goes on to note, however, that the evidence of Lewis's personal library shows a more direct engagement with the subject. Two books, Isaac Taylor's *The Origins of the Aryans* (1906) and, more importantly, James G. Frazer's *Folklore in the Old Testament* (1918) seem to have provided Lewis with many specific details that went into the design of his own mythological world in both *The Childermass* and *The Human Age*.[11]

While Nietzsche and Frazer did not cause anything resembling a conversion in Lewis's life, they did provide him with a vocabulary for expressing a particular religious sensibility. This sensibility, shaped by his acquaintance with Zoroastrianism, went on to inform his outlook in areas other than religion. In *The Art of Being Ruled*, his long and somewhat disorderly essay into political science, Lewis defines his method with reference to a religious principle:

> In our society two virtues are badly contrasted, that of the *fighter* and *killer* (given such immense prestige by nineteenth-century darwinian science and philosophy) and that of the *civilizer* and *maker*. But the ancient and valuable iranian principle of duality is threatened. We confuse these two characters that we violently contrast. The effort in this essay is to separate them a little. It is hoped that certain things that have flown a grey and neutral flag will be forced to declare themselves as Ozman or Ahriman, the dark or the light. (*ABR* 25–26)

Even in the 1950s, as he drifted closer to Christian orthodoxy, Lewis still adhered to this dualistic approach, seeing the world as a gladiatorial arena for an endless series of battles between good and evil (though by this time he also recognized that he had underestimated the difficulty of separating the two).

Lewis's Zoroastrian leanings account not only for the method of his polemics but for their argument as well. Consider again *The Art of Being Ruled*. As we might surmise from its title, the book counsels against active involvement in politics. Lewis believed that the desire for power would only corrupt the objectivity of the artist and intellectual.[12] Yet the book was written in the aftermath of the same war that moved Eliot to invoke, via Hermann Hesse, the horrific image of "those hooded hordes swarming / Over endless plains, stumbling in cracked earth."[13] Making a more direct address to postwar Europe's impoverished condition, Lewis declared: "whatever the reason may be for this, you cannot, unless you are a heartless fool, do nothing" (*ABR* 299). He went on to cite Pierre-Joseph Proudhon's remark that revolution was the only way to solve the problems of nine-teenth-century Europe and concluded: "The answer must be the same today" (*ABR* 299).

But exactly what sort of revolution did Lewis have in mind? "In the abstract," he wrote, "I believe the sovietic system to be the best. It has spectacularly broken with all the past of Europe: it looks to the East, which is spiritually so much greater and intellectually so much finer than Europe, for inspiration" (*ABR* 320). This seems an incredible statement, given Lewis's staunch opposition to communism in the 1930s and beyond, but several factors account for this anomaly. First, Lewis simply did not know much about the realities of communism at the time, as evidenced by his remark that "all marxian doctrine, all *étatisme* or collectivism, conforms very nearly in practice to the fascist ideal" (*ABR* 321). Secondly, Lewis's favorable disposition toward Zoroastrianism and other non-Western reli-gions led him to accept the innate superiority of a Russian-born revolution, since it has been a dogma of European historiography, at least since the eighteenth century, that the Russian psyche owes as much, if not more, to the East as it does to the West. And finally, by the "sovietic system," Lewis understood the establishment of syndicalist state comprised of various guilds within society. Although Lewis may have picked up a smattering of syndicalist theory through his association with *The New Age*, his primary source seems to have been the writings of Proudhon, who, in *The Art of Being Ruled*, is often compared favorably to Marx ("that colossal bulk of venom and vanity" [*ABR* 305]). Proudhon differed from Marx in one fun-damental respect that made his thought almost irresistibly attractive to

Lewis. In his book *Justice in the Revolution and the Church*, Proudhon offers a critique of dialectical materialism that makes him appear as the Zoroaster of socialist thought:

> If my *System of Economic Contradictions* is not, as regards its method, a completely satisfactory work, it is because I had adopted Hegel's view of the antinomy. I had thought that its two terms had to be resolved in a superior synthesis, distinct from the first two, thesis and antithesis. This was faulty logic as well as a failure to learn from experience, and I have since abandoned it. FOR THERE IS NO RESOLUTION OF THE ANTINOMY. This is the fundamental flaw in Hegel's philosophy. The terms are in a state of BALANCE, either with each other or with antinomic terms, and this is what produces the desired result. But balance is not synthesis as Hegel understood it and as I too had supposed.[14]

Upon the rock of "THERE IS NO RESOLUTION OF THE ANTINOMY," Proudhon built a system of political economy, which, though profoundly socialistic, sought to protect the diverse interests of people engaged in various occupations. But this "correction" of Hegel had broader world-historical implications, and Lewis had ample time to meditate upon them when he was reading Proudhon on the French-Belgian border in 1917, overlooking one of the worst unresolved antinomies in history.[15] Proudhon's dictum, distilled from his vision of a fundamentally antinomic universe, serves as a useful reference point in our thinking about Lewis, too: it accounts for his "implacable lifelong opposition to Marxism," despite the anticapitalist momentum pulling him in that direction;[16] his aesthetics of stasis that led to the construction of novels in which characters move from point A back to point A; his disdain for romanticism with its dialectical movement toward a redemptive synthesis (rooted in the same Christian theology that had also flowered in Hegelianism); and, in contrast, his desire to turn to the East for aesthetic and spiritual inspiration.

Beyond politics, Lewis's Manicheism further illuminates the uneasy relationship between his careers as writer and painter that we noted in the first chapter. Lewis once described himself as "a writer who never had had a half-finished canvas far away from the desk at which he wrote—who possesses a twin brother in another art" (*WB* 373). These twins, however, were on the order of Shem and Shaun in *Finnegans Wake*, opposites who complemented rather than mirrored one another. Unlike the other major poet-painter in English letters, William Blake, Lewis never practiced his two arts in tandem. With the exception of a few dust jackets and internal devices, he did not illustrate his works and almost made a point of not doing so. His insistence that while painting the Breton beggar who later became the Ankou he "squeezed out *everything* that smacked of literature from [his] vision" bespeaks an almost Levitical passion, as if the mixing of this milk and meat of art would destroy the delicate binary opposition that defines the purity of both (*WB* 374).

Indeed, painting and writing *are* antinomies in one significant respect, which may explain why so few have pursued double careers, much less achieved parallel successes. Northrop Frye in his study of the Bible, *The Great Code*, makes an observation relevant to Lewis's practice. Commenting on the Hebraic uneasiness with visual images, he writes: "The word listened to and acted upon is the starting point of a course of action; the visible object brings one to a respectful halt in front of it."[17] Words lead one into the vortex of history; images enable reflection upon it. Throughout his working life, Lewis was of two minds about the artist's degree of involvement with the world; like others of his generation, he was heir to conflicting traditions of Victorian social activism and aestheticism. While this does not explain *why* Lewis chose to pursue both, it does suggest that the one art (painting) served to express his estrangement from the world, while the other (writing) provided an outlet for the angry young man who demanded a program of complete social reconstruction.

Given Lewis's temperamental affinity to Zoroastrianism, it's surprising that this exotic religion does not play a more significant role in his work than it does. In no single work does the *Avesta*, the sacred text of Zoroastrianism, function thematically or structurally, as do the *Upanishads* in *The Waste Land* or the writings of Confucius in the *Cantos*. Zoroastrianism does supply some of the mythological trappings of *The Childermass*, but Lewis's one novel that actually employs an Oriental setting—*Snooty Baronet*, which Hugh Kenner describes as "a joint parody of D. H. and T. E. Lawrence"[18]— does so in part to mock the public's fascination with the superficially exotic.

No doubt several aspects of the Eastern worldview, as Lewis understood it, prevented a more radical "conversion." The *contemptus mundi* of most Eastern religions, for example, makes Christian asceticism seem tame by comparison. Orthodox Christianity never accepted the idea that brute matter was a positive evil, since God had created both spirit and matter; in fact, the early Christians spilled a considerable amount of blood suppressing heresies from the East that asserted the contrary. While Lewis's evidently casual reading of Eastern texts gave him another instrument for the dissection of the West's obsession with material power, as a plastic artist, trafficking in paint, canvas, and visual imagery, he could not altogether forsake the mundane. Even in his hostile analysis of Joyce, which at one point denounces *Ulysses* as "the very nightmare of the naturalistic method" (*TWM* 91), Lewis eventually comes around to fault modern literature for its "ineradicable abstractness," which comes from "the parched deserts of the Ancient East," and concludes with the unequivocal statement of principle: "I am for the physical world" (*TWM* 113).

Besides a vocational commitment to a philosophy that allowed the value of material things, the same conservatism that had originally drawn Lewis to the East and its unresolvable antinomies discouraged him from renouncing the Western religious tradition altogether. Throughout the twenties, when he was composing *The Art of Being Ruled, Time and Western Man, The Apes of God*, and *The Childermass*, Lewis undertook a serious reevaluation of the modernist enterprise.[19] People were "bound back" in ways that the prewar avant-garde, not to mention their bourgeois adversaries, had not figured into their calculations, and it was in the spirit of wanting to face about and confront the grinning shadow of these limitations that Lewis turned to religious questions or, more precisely, began to explore the religious dimension of his own work. And if he chose to remain within the framework of a myth, many of whose primary elements were uncongenial to his dualistic sensibility, it was because he recognized *BLAST*'s announcement, "END OF THE CHRISTIAN ERA," as premature, if not downright sophomoric.

Protestant Means

On the basis of Lewis's upbringing alone, one would never have expected him to be responsible for the most astonishing mixture of literature and Christian theology since Blake's *Milton* (wherein the mental traveler perceives all time and space winding into that quintessentially Lewisian figure, a vortex). Unlike Joyce, who inhaled the pungent atmosphere of Irish Catholicism from the day he was born and could never breathe it out again in all his years of exile, Lewis seems to have had no important religious experiences as a child or adolescent. His biographer has little to say on the subject beyond the fact that he was born of an American

Protestant father and an English Catholic mother (the latter never practicing her faith, but retaining a strong sentimental attachment to it). And yet, although there is no evidence to indicate that Lewis felt torn between loyalties to his parents' respective faiths, time and again we notice that the peculiar conflicts and contradictions in his thinking have the appearance of sectarian disagreements between the Protestant and Catholic faiths. Indeed, Lewis, who liked to think of himself as exceedingly independent, can almost be said to have been his own one-man Reformation and counter-Reformation: in short, he had the temperament of the new faith and the ideology of the old, a tension that often showed itself as a division between the medium and the message of his work.

To begin, Lewis shared with the romantics a basic sense of the artist as prophet, an idea that although not original to Protestantism was invigorated by Luther's claim that God more reliably spoke through individual conscience than through the protocols of the church. The artist-prophet appears in Lewis's work as early as "Les Saltimbanques," which culminates, as we have earlier noted, when a young boy, "with all the character of a vision," suddenly recognizes "the comedy of existence" in the struggle between the resentful circus performers and their amused but uncomprehending audience (WB 247). His awakening to the absurd is a myth about the origins of Lewis's own art, and indeed, at one point the narrator describes the boy as a "poet"; but as the story closes, religious language dominates the text and encourages us to see the boy as heir to Jeremiah and Ezekiel: "He would no doubt have met death with the exultation of a martyr, rather than renounce this transfigured image of an old and despondent mountebank—like some stubborn prophet who would not forego the splendour of his vision—always of the gloom of famine, of cracked and empty palaces, and the elements taking new and extremely destructive forms for the rapid extermination of man" (WB 247).

A more direct affirmation of the link between art and prophecy occurs, oddly enough, in a chapter from *Time and Western Man* entitled "Pure Poetry and Pure Magic," where Lewis attacks the mystical element in modern art and philosophy. Near the end of the chapter Lewis writes:

> I will state very briefly my own belief as to the true character of artistic creation. The production of a work of art is, I believe, strictly the work of a visionary. Indeed, this seems so evident that it scarcely needs pointing out. Shakespeare, writing his *King Lear*, was evidently in some sort of trance; for the production of such a work of art an entranced condition seems as

essential as it was for Blake when he conversed with the Man who Built the Pyramids. . . . If you say that creative art is a spell, a talisman, an incantation—that it is *magic,* in short, there, too, I believe you would be correctly describing it. That the artist uses and manipulates a supernatural power seems very likely. (*TWM* 192–93)

Lewis wanted to distinguish this position from the irrationalism of disillusioned postwar artists and philosphers who *"by means of art* . . . wish to lead us down and back to the plane of magic, or of mystical, specifically religious experience." He asserts to the contrary that although the artist "is certainly not devoid of religious emotion, it is exercised personally, as it were; and he is in temper the opposite of the religionist" (*TWM* 193). The fine distinction here rests upon the claim that the artist keeps his religious emotions to himself, while the religionist (priests, ministers, and orthodox apologists) and the mystic seek to collectivize spiritual experience. Once again we note the Protestant element in Lewis's thinking, for he insists upon both the freedom to speak to his God in his own way, and the right to a direct relationship with the absolute, undiluted by either conventional forms of worship or by some vague notion that divinity permeates the world indifferently. (In Lewis's view, the priest and the mystic occupied the same theological position: although the latter was perhaps more spiritually democratic than the former, both sought to mediate the overwhelming power of God, and thus effectively blur the distinction between human and divine.)

Strictly speaking, Lewis was not a theologian because he rarely inquired into the nature and activity of God, but his philosophical system still required an absolute otherness—a divine presence, absent and unknowable—who would serve as a sort of dialectical guarantor of our identity as human beings. Anything less spiritually rigorous only compounded the problem of preserving the integrity of the self in a technological age. (World War I and the behaviorists Watson, Yerkes, and Yoakum had already redrawn the boundary between man and machine [*TWM* 330–31].) Lewis's very Protestant attention to *personal* religious experience thus not only indicates a commitment to freedom of expression, but also a desire to conserve individual identity.

A more radical Protestantism, concerned not only with defining the self but also assaying its moral condition, is manifest in part of a letter that the twenty-eight-year-old Lewis wrote to his friend and mentor, the painter Augustus John:

My weaknesses and vices are quite patent to me, and I live with them with alternate irritation and bonhomie that I suppose everybody else bestows on similar anomalies chez lui. I believe with a Calvinistic uncompromisingness that one cannot be too hard on the stupidities of one's neighbors; and I thank you quite unaffectedly for having knocked a good deal of nonsense out of [me?], and am only sorry that I was not able (owing to my tender years and extravagant susceptibilities) to have rendered you a similar service. (L 45)

The word "Calvinistic" alongside the claim that "one cannot be too hard on the stupidities of one's neighbors" suggests the intensity of Lewis's ethical convictions and looks forward to the appearance of the "Enemy," the persona that Lewis used in his nonfiction of the twenties and thirties to denounce what he found objectionable in modern culture. The Calvinist parallel also provides insight into the problems that Lewis had in his adversarial role since, to the degree that Lewis's uncompromising attitude *was* theologically grounded, it shared with Calvinism the same internal contradictions.

Calvinism's tenets include a belief in the absolute power of God, the total depravity of man, and God's unconditional right to predestine men to Heaven and Hell. Upon this theological foundation arises a social and political philosophy that is decidedly "other-oriented" in its account of evil and unhappiness. If a man numbers himself among the elect and righteously affirms God to be benevolent and all-powerful, then other people—specifically, the damned—must be the source of all the world's troubles. Early Calvinist communities were distinguished by religious intolerance and persecution; short of these expedients, however, the faithful must conduct their lives in a kind of satiric mode: confirmed in the knowledge of their own sainthood, they must endure (and denounce) the evil ways of a world where the damned serve as ever-present reminders of how not to behave.

The problem with this arrangement is that if God has a monopoly on wisdom, then a man cannot know for certain whether he is counted among the elect. Upright living and good works might be outward signs of election, but what is pleasing to man will not necessarily be pleasing to God. Thus, the putative saint's denunciation of the sinner in this world may well be the text of his own indictment in the next. This seed of doubt could lead both individuals and communities into the most wrenching of self-examinations, thereby transforming a cold and categorical faith into a moody and introspective one.

Lewis's uncompromising view of the world shares with Calvinism a coterie of the elect (artists), a mass of sinners (nearly everyone else), a satiric approach to daily life, and an underlying sense that peace and harmony had reigned before the Fall (the French and industrial revolutions). As Jameson observes, Lewis's critique, like all conservative critiques, "takes as the basic object of its diagnosis the consciousness of *other people.*"[20] (Not surprisingly, the climactic chapter in *Time and Western Man*'s attack upon modern literature is entitled "An Analysis of the Mind of James Joyce.") But since he aimed to disabuse modern man of his pretensions, Lewis himself could never be absolutely certain that he was one of the elect. Thus, while the Lewisian critique of satisfaction attempts to function within categories of otherness, it eventually "engage[s] a peculiar dialectic of mirror images which does not in the end leave the place of the judging subject unscathed."[21] Indeed, the many failed or untalented artists and intellectuals who star in Lewis's fiction—Arghol, Kreisler, Zagreus, Pierpoint, the Bailiff, and a series of others, culminating in the Devil himself—indicate that Lewis was continually nagged by doubts that he had misapprehended the distinctions between sacred and profane, between good art and bad, and worried that he himself might be one of the damned.

But whatever his private uncertainties, the famous darkness that has enveloped modernist works since Conrad never dominates the atmosphere of Lewis's writing. Lewis persisted in the belief that one could transcend the self and acquire knowledge of the absolute—an entity that he sometimes reluctantly named God but more often refers to as an impersonal force called the "Not-self."

Lewis spoke of the Not-self as one of the "contradictory realities" that checks the natural tendency of the ego to choose things only for their "flattering pleasantness" and to indulge itself in a romantic "false unity and optimism" (*TWM* 10). While the Not-self would certainly include the stone that Dr. Johnson kicked to confute Bishop Berkeley, Lewis also equated it with the intellect whose potential for objectivity seemed to set it apart from the person it inhabited. He explains this division between the self and Not-self as it is manifest within the individual during an analysis of Oswald Spengler's philosophy of history, which Lewis considered highly romantic and self-serving:

> The "time" of Spengler is sensation, that we have now learnt. And *sensation* is what is *us* . . . whereas what we *think* is not us, or is the Not-self; what is not personal to us. And what is merely "thought" or the material of

the intellect—that part of us which reflects what is not immediately us—is cold and unreal compared with what is us. It is a *dead portion* of us, as it were. It is not susceptible of *sensation*, else it would be us; for anything that is sensation is us. (*TWM* 262)

Lewis's point here (which rehearses in philosophical language the aesthetic argument of *Tarr*) is that the cold, dead, unreal part of us should be valued precisely for its alien and unsensational quality. To the Not-self, in its way as remote and indifferent as Calvin's God, we must turn for redemption. Only the Not-self could rescue us from the solipsistic dungeon conceived by the philosopher F. H. Bradley and dramatized by Eliot ("We think of the key, each in his prison / Thinking of the key, each confirms a prison"), which the modern industrial system, with its fixation upon the satisfaction of human desire, had created.[22]

The loss of the Not-self lay behind the unhealthy state of modern letters (most notably, *Ulysses*, which for all its "scientific 'impersonality'" everywhere gravitated "to the ego of the author" [*TWM* 262]) and signaled a radical break with an ancient tradition of creative and intellectual accomplishment:

the Not-self, and especially the physical, is almost the patent and property of the Western genius. The "natural magic" of Western poetry owes its peculiar and penetrating quality to the intense relations of this Western mind to this *alien* physical world of "nature." It is in the detaching of himself from the personal that the Western Man's greatest claim to distinction lies, from the Greeks and early Celts to the present day. It is non-personal modes of feeling—that is in *thought*, or in feeling that is so dissociated from the hot, immediate egoism of sensational life that it becomes automatically intellectual—that the non-religious Western Man has always expressed himself, at his profoundest, at his purest. (*TWM* 263)

Lewis's reference to "non-religious" man seems once again an effort to distance his conception of the supernatural from that of the mystic or the orthodox priest, since elsewhere in *Time and Western Man* he sets the Not-self in a distinctly theological context. The first chapter of the book, for example, concludes with an offhand remark that practically defines this aspect of religious sensibility: "It was the keen awareness of the Not-self, and the consequent conception of 'righteousness,' that Matthew Arnold pointed to (in his *Literature and Dogma*) as constituting the originality of the ancient jewish people" (*TWM* 10). Lewis shared a taste for this kind of originality not only with Arnold (and behind him, Milton and Blake) but also with the Protestant reformers who often preferred the sublimities of the tooth-and-claw world of the Old Testament to the more sentimental sensations of the New.

The imposing presence of the "Not-self," the Prime Mover in Lewis's critique of human self-satisfaction, seems to have dictated the literary practice behind such works as *Tarr* and *The Apes of God*. This is at once a simple and complex topic: simple because Lewis's thinking about language can be reduced to the idea that words are inadequate to express the wonder of material creation, complex because this idea manifests itself in nearly every corner of Lewis's work.

In this way, Lewis dissented from what might be called the modernist celebration of the text. The turn from message to medium (evident in the plastic arts as well) had its origins in the individual artist's responses to a society whose values were increasingly those of the marketplace—speed, efficiency, dynamism, innovation, profitability, perhaps even equality. The prototypical modernist heroes who emerge by the middle of the nineteenth century—Kierkegaard's knight of faith, Dostoevsky's underground man, Poe's amateur detective—recoil from participation in the commercial hurly-burly and choose instead to exercise their significant intellectual powers only for the purpose of sharpening and better understanding those powers. Indifferent to the prizes of European civilization, the modernist hero (and his creator) finds the contemplation of the artistic process its own special reward.

Besides this, nineteenth-century scholarship in philology, archaeology, and anthropology suggested that language was not a static and eternal gift from the gods but rather a social institution that, like all institutions, reflects the needs and interests of its human creators. Many writers soon came to see language as a machine that skillful users could modify to carry out a wide range of tasks. James Joyce, who sometimes thought of himself as a Victorian engineer, positively delighted in the power and flexibility of this newly discovered "machine" and believed that he could do just about anything with words.

But despite his obvious willingness to experiment, Lewis adopted an increasingly skeptical view toward contemporary claims about language. In *Time and Western Man*, for example, he criticized Joyce for having no concerns beyond "technical processes," implying that books such as

Ulysses that indulged their own textuality were typical products of, rather than protests against, industrial society (*TWM* 90). For Lewis, the artist was at best a Dr. Frankenstein, the god of *a* creation, perhaps, but certainly not in the same league with the God who created the visible universe (as Stephen Dedalus seems to believe in *A Portrait*). If philology and the other social sciences had shown the extent of man's contribution to the making of this marvelous instrument called language, they had also demonstrated how creaky and limited this device was, how like any machine it performed its task by segmenting and quantifying what was seamless in nature. The artist's task, therefore, was not to capture experience in words but to gesture toward it by constantly exposing the inadequacy of his language. The extreme volubility of *The Apes of God*, which leaves the reader groping to understand what's really going on, was thus a deliberate strategy on Lewis's part, calculated to show that even a book ten times its enormous length could hardly do justice to the woof and warp of experience.

Lewis's Calvinistic, postlapsarian approach to language also shapes his conception of a radically fallen reader. By adopting an agonistic style in which words seem to struggle against one another to achieve meaning, Lewis makes his reader work, and work hard, to understand him. This inherent difficulty in communication further implies the remoteness of persons from one another in space and time, contrary to the claims of much romantic literature. *Enemy of the Stars* is set near the Arctic Circle, not in more familiar London, because it assumes, at least at the outset, that artist and audience have almost nothing in common: "Such a strange thing as our coming together requires a strange place for initial stages of our intimate ceremonious acquaintance" (*CPP* 96). The awkward rhythms of this sentence and hundreds more in Lewis's work through the late 1920s make us feel as though we're reading translations from some ancient language as distant from English as Chinese or Greek. Indeed, Lewis's writing often shares something with Victorian translations of Greek plays, which by sticking closely to the original syntax and diction, and making few concessions to idiomatic English, make the reader reckon with all that must have been lost in the twenty-odd centuries between himself and Aeschylus.[23] (Not surprisingly, Lewis himself never produced any translations and attacked his old ally Ezra Pound for trying to collapse the distance between past and present in his colloquial re-creations of ancient and medieval poetry [*TWM* 69–74].)

Catholic Ends

Having said this, we should also say that Lewis never produced the kind of minimalist art that might be expected of a man committed to a Calvinist aesthetic. For all their avoidance of the chattiness of more conventional novels, *Tarr* and *The Apes of God* still seem luxuriant compared to Samuel Beckett's *The Unnameable* or the French *nouvelle roman*. What I have loosely defined as Lewis's Calvinism was a response to aspects of modernity unfavorable to artistic creation (advancing technology, revolutionary politics), not the expression of an aesthetic ideal. Just as Calvin intended the sublimity of his God to restore a sense of mystery to the Renaissance humanist world, so Lewis administered the Not-self as a corrective to a romantic era in which imagination now obscured nature (the basis of all art), including human nature. After all, even modern selfhood was something of a fraud, less a triumph of the ideas of Locke and Rousseau than a consequence of industrial development: anxious for new markets, capitalists converted workers into consumers by rigging up every man, woman, and child with a unique "personality" that could only be "realized" by the endless consumption of mass-produced goods and services.[24] For Lewis, the modern self was not a true or natural self at all.

Moreover, the critique of satisfaction tacitly assumes a time when men *did* possess natural selves and *did* establish equitable relationships with the world around them, a time when men willfully acknowledged their limitations without having to be shown the chilly expanses of the Not-self. The critique also implies that some few men, the genuine artists among us, may never have lost this paradise in the first place.

Here we can draw a parallel between Lewis and Eliot, the other important modernist with whom Lewis remained on the best terms over the years and the one with whom he shared the strongest temperamental affinity. From Eliot's early poetry emerges the persona of a man who knows perfectly well how to get on in the world, but who finds the comfortable life of the office and the drawing room a stale illusion. Why, after all, should Prufrock listen to women talking of Michelangelo when he has heard the mermaids sing to one another? Eliot wanted to communicate his peculiar sense of wonder without reducing or falsifying it, and toward this end, he created an idiom that in many respects stands as a poetic equivalent to Lewis's vorticist prose. His language eschews the "small fry" of adjectives and adverbs and manifests itself on the page in discontinuous fragments that gesture toward the meaning that is impossible to say.

But despite his apparent success in this medium, Eliot always regretted not having been born in a time when language generally, and poetry in particular, expressed the reality to which it could only allude now. To account for what had happened, Eliot invented a myth of lost innocence which located our linguistic Fall sometime during the Puritan revolution. With the collapse of the old Anglo-Catholic order and its replacement by the liturgically spare Puritan church, the channels between heaven and earth had been reduced to one: individual conscience. As a consequence of this spiritual attenuation, the major work of the period, *Paradise Lost*, showed the "dissociation of sensibility"—a divorce between sound and sense, emotion and intellect, body and soul—that would hobble English literature for the next two hundred years.[25]

Lewis, too, believed that something unique and irreversible had occurred with the advent of Protestantism. A few pages into *The Art of Being Ruled*, he wrote:

> The modern "soul" began, of course, in the Reformation. . . . When Luther appealed for the individual soul direct to God, and the power of all mediating authority was definitely broken, God must have foreseen that he would soon follow His viceregents. The individual soul would later on, had he been God, have known very well that when he abandoned God, he would before long himself be abandoned. The mediator should have known that too. In any case, this necessary triad has vanished. The trinity of God, Subject, and Object is at an end. (*ABR* 27)

In the Reformation, "of course": Lewis here traces the origins of modernity to a religious revolution, a fundamental change in man's awareness of his place in the cosmos. While today we can point to a variety of social, political, and economic forces responsible for this transformation, Luther remains the pivotal figure. As Lewis observes, Luther radically personalized the relationship between man and God that until then had been mediated through a universal church. Henceforth the power to define reality, long the prerogative of a fairly stable institution, now devolved upon the individual.[26]

For the modern artist increasingly alienated from his bourgeois environment, this was the beginning of the end. Nietzsche, for example, saw Luther as the evangel of a certain vulgarity latent in the Judeo-Christian tradition. As he explained in *The Genealogy of Morals:*

In eastern Asia are found small inconsequential pagan tribes which might have taught [the] early Christians a lesson or two in tact; those tribes, as Christian missionaries have told us, do not permit themselves to use the name of God at all. Such conduct, it seems to me, shows a great deal of delicacy; but it is altogether too delicate, not for the primitive Christians only, but for many who come after. To get a clear sense of the contrast, think of Luther, the most eloquent and presumptuous of German peasants; think of his manner of speaking, especially when he held converse with God! Luther's militant attitude toward the mediating saints of the Church (especially "that Devil's sow, the Pope") was, in the last analysis, the truculence of a lout toward the Church's etiquette, that reverent etiquette of a hieratic taste, which would admit only the most discreet and consecrated into the holy of holies, and would exclude the louts. The latter must never be allowed to speak there. But the peasant Luther would have it otherwise; the traditional practice was not German enough for him. He wanted to be able to speak directly, in his own voice, "informally," with his God. . . . Well, that's what he did.[27]

In sum, Nietzsche denounces Luther for having ushered in the humanist phase of European culture, for when men began to address the omnipotent "informally," it was only a matter of time until God was brought down to human scale. Conversely, Luther's attention to the inner life of the ordinary Christian gave value to a part of experience—and a class of men—that had always been more or less ignored. Luther could not have known it, but he conferred a kind of transcendental legitimacy upon the crass material interests of a rising middle class, a loutish blunder for which Nietzsche never forgave him. (Never mind the fact that the decline of the Roman Catholic priesthood would some day open up a space for the new priesthood of romantic art, or that Nietzsche's own prophetic style owed a debt to Luther's highly personalized rhetoric.[28])

Nietzsche's argument with Luther looks forward to the ironies of Lewis's quarrel (and those of other modernists) with modernity. Inspired and iconoclastic, Lewis feared that the same conditions that allowed him to be the artist he was would render meaningless the art he wanted to create. A book or a painting ought to be important for more than fifteen minutes, and so despite his natural sympathy with the avant-garde, Lewis became a vocal proponent of conservative social and political values; or, to speak again in theological terms, we can say that he adopted the confrontational style of a Protestant reformer while urging a return to the traditional values of the Catholic church.

Lewis did in fact have more than casual sympathy with Catholicism at different periods of his life. While training as an artillery officer in July 1916, he wrote to Ezra Pound: "I have adopted the Roman Catholic category in my siege battery. This will eliminate one of the chief nuisances of life in the army, those dreadful English churches. I can think of nothing on earth as imbecile as the music and words of those English hymns. The Mass is a function I shall not object to."[29] Of course, saying that one "shall not object" to a "function" is hardly an affirmation of faith, and no doubt Lewis, who made a career out of gravitating toward the margins, welcomed the opportunity to identify himself with the religious minority. His comments on the imbecility of English hymns also reflect the aesthetic prejudices of a writer who eschewed popular taste (he had recently completed *Tarr*).

Less easy to gloss over, however, is what Jameson facetiously calls Lewis's "fellow-traveling adherence" to Roman Catholicism during World War II and, we might add, the dozen or so years before the war.[30] In 1927, for example, Lewis published in his short-lived journal, *The Enemy*, an extract from a treatise by Henry John, a son of Augustus John then studying for the priesthood, which bore the long and involved title: "*Towards Reintegration*. Section III. The Reintegration of Experience. A. *The De-intellectualization of Experience*. Sensation and Sex. B. *The Supernaturalization of Sensation*. Rimbaud and the Mystical Way." That Lewis should have allotted several pages to this dry tome is in itself remarkable, given the fact that he usually wrote the bulk of the material that appeared in his journals. He explained his decision in an introductory note: "This is the third section of a long essay. It is by a young catholic student. I propose to print further sections in forthcoming numbers of *The Enemy*. In relating the argument of *The Art of Being Ruled* to the catholic thought a service has been rendered, incidentally, to that book, and some misunderstandings should, as a consequence, be dissipated" (*E* 2:115).

For our purposes, the content of John's essay, which rehearses rationalist arguments against romanticism, is less important than Lewis's desire to have someone illustrate the relationship between his own cultural criticism and that of Catholic writers. Only rarely did Lewis admit to alliances with contemporaries in arts and letters. What then were the reasons behind this "Catholic connection"?

One important consideration was political. Although Lewis always insisted that political entanglements destroyed the necessary objectivity of the artist, he recognized that the success of a work of art was often determined by factors other than intrinsic merit. The public was a fickle beast and the squadrons of polemical essays that Lewis deployed to soften up resistance to his creative work were not always sufficient to ensure an appreciative response.

During the 1920s, many Catholic writers espoused principles close to Lewis's. This was particularly so in France, where Charles Maurras's *Action française* exercised considerable influence over intellectual life. Lewis had come into contact with Maurras during his early years in Paris, and although he never embraced the movement's monarchism or rabid anti-Semitism, he agreed with Maurras's emphasis on the need for classical order in everything from art to religion, remarking in *The Art of Being Ruled* that "any little organization that Europe has ever had has been centred in France, and symbolized by her classicist culture" (*ABR* 313).[31]

While there was no comparable Catholic movement in Protestant England for Lewis to support, he did cultivate a friendship with the Oxford Jesuit M. C. D'Arcy, the most important English Catholic theologian of his day. Lewis sent him a copy of *Time and Western Man* and, after receiving a favorable response, wrote back calling D'Arcy the spokesman for "the more intelligent portion of the catholic interest [?] in England" (*L* 173). For his part, D'Arcy praised Lewis (and Maurras) in his 1931 book *The Nature of Belief* for defending the distinction between the two spheres of good and evil, light and darkness, which he called "the inspiration and virtue of Western thought."[32] D'Arcy believed that the reign of humanism was coming to an end and that modern theologians were moving "from the conception of an immanent to that of a transcendant God."[33] Turning to the argument of *Time and Western Man,* he went on to say that "Wyndham Lewis is but repeating in his own way under the titles of Space and Time the old distinction."[34]

A subtler but perhaps stronger link to Catholic doctrine may have been forged by Lewis's reading of Georges Sorel, whom Lewis described in *The Art of Being Ruled* as "the key to all contemporary political thought" (*ABR* 119).[35] Sorel was a revolutionary socialist with a passionate commitment to the heroic ideals of classical civilization, which he hoped to see realized in climactic battle between the proletariat and the bourgeoisie. (His recognition of the political value of historical myth anticipates the fascist appropriation of the heroic past and partly accounts for scholarly uncertainty over whether to call him left-wing or right-wing.)

Like Marx, Sorel saw a revolution arising from the dialectical movement within capitalist economies, which would bring about an "absolute and irrevocable transformation" of society.[36] But although revolution was inevitable, workers still needed to prepare themselves for the event. Surprisingly, in an appendix to the second edition of *Reflections on Violence*, Sorel urges workers' syndicates to model themselves upon the organization of the Catholic church. "The present situation of Catholicism in France," according to Sorel, "suggests sufficiently remarkable similarities to that of the proletariat engaged in the class struggle, for the Syndicalists to have a real interest in following attentively contemporary ecclesiastical history."[37] Just as the true socialist had to combat revisionist elements within his own movement that would accommodate themselves to, and work within, the bourgeois parliamentary system, thus delaying the revolutionary Armageddon called the General Strike, so too had the pious Catholic to battle liberal elements that would weaken the absolutist and unworldly position that for two millennia had ensured the survival of the faith. Sorel also admired the church's internal discipline, not because it imposed a monolithic order on its adherents, but, on the contrary, because it preserved factional divisions, which were the source of its institutional strength. Commenting on the role of monastic orders, he wrote:

> The majority of Catholics has thus been able to remain alien to the pursuit of the absolute, and yet collaborate very efficiently in the work of those who, by conflict, were maintaining or perfecting the doctrines; the elite, which bore the assault to the enemy positions, received material and moral assistance from the masses which saw in it the reality of Christianity. . . . Rather similar observations may be made with regard to workers' organizations, they ought to vary with infinity as the proletariat feels itself more capable of cutting a figure in the world.[38]

If the proletariat failed to abide by the example of the church, with its functional oppositions and balances, it would risk becoming "an inert mass destined to fall, as democracy, under the direction of politicians who live on the subordination of their electors."[39]

This concern for an orderly system of opposites recalls the political philosophy of Proudhon (to whom Sorel was much indebted) and further underscores his importance to Lewis. Indeed, Lewis saw Sorel the man in antinomic terms, "a highly unstable and equivocal figure . . . composed of a crowd of warring personalities," to which only the heroic ideals engendered by a certain kind of religious militancy lent order and coherence (*ABR* 119). Although his experience in the Great War led Lewis to reflect upon the vanity of the violent measures preached by Sorel, this latter-day soldier of the counter-Reformation continued to fascinate Lewis for his claim that spiritual and heroic ideals could be translated into direct political action, a temptation Lewis could never quite wholly renounce.[40]

Beyond politics, Lewis was drawn to Catholicism because he believed that only contemporary Catholic thinkers still practiced philosophy in the classical sense of the word: a dispassionate, rigorous inquiry into the moral and metaphysical nature of things. This contrasted sharply with the work of notable academic philosophers such as William James and Henri Bergson, whom Lewis accused of succumbing to the same anti-intellectualism that had established a cult of the primitive before the war and soon after had given rise to dadaism.

In the chapter entitled "God as Reality" in *Time and Western Man*, Lewis argued that from a theological perspective anti-intellectualism was another form of the egoism that had its historical roots in Protestantism. For the Catholic, precise knowledge of the world was important because only through an understanding of Creation could a man come to know God. The Protestant, however, wanted a shortcut to God through direct personal experience. Criticizing James's advocacy of such an approach to divinity, Lewis wrote:

> It is the manner of the protestant Reformation, of course, the direct plunge to God, not only without meditation or by means of reason (with all the dangers of that confusing exercise), but with a debased reliance upon some kind of semi-philosophical, half-rational image. . . . About the wish to seize and mingle with the supreme Reality in a passionate attack there is something lunatic and egoistic. . . . The intellect has been given us as the appointed and natural path on which to make our approach to God. The emotional is too indiscriminate, and it is in any case unlikely that then God would be encountered. Rather our hungry Self would waylay us. (*TWM* 375)

It is at once ironic and fitting that this passionate denunciation of egoism came from a man who by most accounts was as notorious for his selfish behavior as Byron or Shelley. Also curious is his seemingly uncritical faith in the capacity of the intellect to apprehend the divine Other. In *Time and Western Man*, Lewis wanted to demystify various intellectual postures and show them for the ideological products that they were. Why then was the Lewisian intellect exempt from this same critique? In short, Lewis became uncritical at the point where the Catholic position spoke directly to the sort of artist he wanted to be: "Scholastic rationalism was (and is) bound up with the pagan 'materialism'; with the 'concrete' and its objective, external ordinance. *Matter,* for it, was the path to God, that *between* God and the individual" (*TWM* 374). "Concrete" and "objective" were the buzzwords of 1912, recalling the principles of T. E. Hulme, Ezra Pound, and the other imagist poets who demanded "direct treatment of the thing." But no matter how strong the desire to transcend language, the poet remained committed to a system of verbal abstractions. Concreteness in any but a metaphorical sense is the prerogative of the plastic artist, the painter brushing pigment on canvas, the sculptor cutting stone. For this reason Hulme eventually shifted the focus of his criticism from poetry to the visual arts. Lewis, despite his prolific literary output, always seems to have thought of himself as a painter first and a writer second. From *Tarr* and *Enemy of the Stars* through *The Apes of God,* he tried to carry over something of a painting's tangible quality into each of his works. The Catholic emphasis on material creation lent this aesthetic additional legitimacy.

But the real key to the passage in *Time and Western Man* lies in the appearance of the word "pagan." Pound, too, had been favorably disposed toward Catholicism for its custodianship of a pagan heritage. This preference reflects a half-conscious awareness that the arts occupy a more secure position in a pagan culture than in a monotheistic one. Paganism describes the world rather than moralizing upon its injustices.[41] The pagan represents the world as a convergence of natural forces; pagan religion, like art, names these forces and gives men a way to talk about and perhaps influence them. (As Lewis himself said, "art is the civilized *substitute* for magic" [*TWM* 193]).

Monotheists—and monotheistic thinkers within paganism, such as Plato—tend to see the visible world as an illusion orchestrated by a superior mind whose wisdom transcends human understanding. "The world we live in is a mistake, a clumsy parody," goes the theology of a radical Islamic prophet in a story by Jorge Luis Borges. "Mirrors and fatherhood, because they multiply and confirm the parody, are abominations."[42] The monotheist, whether he is named Plato or Jeremiah, sooner or later adds art to this list. Indeed, the Bible has no category for art because it cannot in the end admit the existence of plurality. The diverse forms that the world presents to the eye are but a temporary condition masking the essential unity. Art can only "multiply and confirm" that condition and therefore has no reality.

Lewis, however, remained too deeply in love with the productions of time to accept this monotheistic syllogism. "The Sistine Chapel Ceiling," he says in a rare moment of genuine reverence, "is worthy of the hand of any God which we can infer, dream of, or postulate. We may certainly say that God's hand is visible in it" (*TWM* 386). Behind this casual pantheism is a thesis that transcends ethics or aesthetics; it is a religious thesis because it addresses the question of man's limits and boundaries, of what (if anything) distinguishes him from the things with which he shares this life.

Yet Lewis's remained a reluctant pantheism. In this same chapter, he proposes a sort of contest between conceptions of the world as an "ultimate Unity" on one side and a "Plurality" on the other. If you had, he says, "a picture of a multiplicity of wave-like surface changes only, while all the time the deep bed of Oneness reposes underneath," and then contrasted this with "the idea of an *absolute* plurality, every midget existence, every speck and grain, unique (for what such 'uniqueness' was worth)," there could be no question that "the hypothesis of Oneness is the profounder hypothesis, and must, if it lay thus barely between those two, be the real" (*TWM* 387).

At this point Lewis's argument takes an unusual turn, one that enlarges our understanding of why this skeptical thinker should have developed such a fascination with chaotic modernity. He says that even though Oneness may have it all over plurality in the contest for the real, this hardly matters for us as human beings, because *as* human beings, we live only amidst plurality and are not, in that sense, real: "We are surface-creatures, and the 'truths' from beneath the surface contradict our values. It is among the flowers and leaves that our lot is cast, and the roots, however 'interesting,' are not so ultimate for us. For the ultimate thing is the surface, the last-comer, and that is committed to a plurality of being" (*TWM* 387).

Lewis's argument here is neither peculiar nor original, for he repeats, in effect, the claims of nominalism against realism. This speaks to his continuing interest in scholastic thought ("Constantly in our criticism we march with the 'thomist' [*TWM* 371]) and also accounts for the eventual emergence of the philosopher George Berkeley as the nonfiction "hero" of *Time and Western Man*. "Nothing, in a certain sense, more flippant has ever been invented than the gimcrack world of facades of Berkeley," wrote Lewis; nonetheless, he thought a system founded upon the doctrine of *esse est precipi*, which proscribed the category of stable, continuous existence as not so much wrong but irrelevant for beings like ourselves, "one of the best of all possible philosophic worlds" (*TWM* 462–63). Lewis even reaches the point of saying that God is so real and man is so nominal that we have to ignore the possibility of God: "if anything, the speculative reason seems to us to point to a One. But on the One we must turn our back in order to exist. Evidences of a oneness seem everywhere apparent. But we *need*, for practical purposes, the illusion of a plurality" (*TWM* 388).

In the last analysis, Catholicism provided a theological grounding for Lewis's art because it charted a middle course between unity and plurality—between the inhuman absolute of the Calvinist Not-self and the "greasy incense to Mr. Everyman" of modern humanism (*BB* 102). Indeed, if there were to be encounters between the human and the divine, these would occur in the intermediate space inhabited by pagan gods and Christian saints, where the One began to differentiate into the Many. In a long essay entitled "The Dithyrambic Spectator," published a few years after *Time and Western Man*, Lewis defined religion as

> the separation of the Subject from the Not-Self. It is this first sundering of the subject from its surroundings that produces it. It is something arising to fill in the gap caused by that separation. Just as the sequence of animal gestation is in this order, namely that two beings by mingling produce a third, so a "god" is produced but in an opposite manner, namely by their *separation*. This god however is not an amalgam of man and his environment: rather he is a new environment created to correspond to needs transcending the scene of his earlier magical operation. It is all that is (1) terrestrially the Not-self, and yet (2) that to which no visible Not-self properly corresponds. (*DPDS* 204)

Despite Catholicism's willingness to harbor the mediating saints and angels (not to mention the classical divinities) that Luther banished from the earth, Lewis remained as critical of the church itself as any reformer. His discussion of scholasticism, for example, begins with this unequivocal denunciation of the church's religious orthodoxy:

> It is incurably "conservative": it is forever the "old" against the "new"; it is "anti-modern" in a, to me, stupid, "historical" manner. . . . It is surely not a bad thing to remember that that system was unified, too, into a tyrannic orthodoxy, with every theological sanction; and that it was impossible then, as it is now, to think except in one way, and according to an intolerant unique and jealous standard. (*TWM* 372–73)

He then proceeds to criticize two well-known Catholic polemicists, calling Jacques Maritain "a frantic, hallucinated, 'soul'-drugged individual," and G. K. Chesterton a "dogmatic Toby-jug" (*TWM* 373). Luther himself could not have put it more bluntly.

Such internal tensions would have been fatal in the work of a philosopher; for the novelist, they made life difficult but also provided the inspiration for one of the few modern works that actively invites comparison with Dante and Milton. Having decided that man was *not* the measure of all things, Lewis turned his attention directly to the supernatural, whatever that had come to mean in the twentieth century.

5

The Childermass

Modernist Apocalypse

The Complete Work

"A novel—if you can call it that—'The Childermass' . . . is about Heaven: the politics of which, although bitter in the extreme, have no relation to those of the earth, so they do not concern us here" (*RA* 214). With this summary dismissal in his 1950 autobiography, *Rude Assignment*, Lewis moved on to other matters, adding only that despite its unfinished state, *The Childermass* had often been called his best book.

Actually, *The Childermass* is very much concerned with events on earth. The book's title comes from Herod's massacre of the innocents in Matthew 2:16–8, but it more immediately refers to the thousands of young men who died in battle during World War I and whose souls now crowd the gates of Heaven. The story opens as an anonymous voice describes a desert landscape that recalls the harsh subarctic environment of *Enemy of the Stars*. In the midst of this vast plain, we see a city whose totemic skyline includes bulky ziggurats, speckled cones, and a variety of shapes suggesting some kind of zoologic symbolism. (Similar images appear in Lewis's paintings of the 1920s and 1930s.[1]) Across a river running beside the city lies an encampment where the newly deceased await (we presume) final judgment.

Soon we encounter the two human principals of *The Childermass*, James Pullman, a famous writer, and Satterthwaite (or "Satters"), a childish bourgeois who had been Pullman's fag at Rugby. After meeting by accident on the margins of the camp, this unlikely Don Quixote and Sancho Panza begin an unauthorized tour of their new surroundings that leads to a series of harmless misadventures. About a third of the way through the book, trumpets announce the arrival of the Bailiff, a Saint Peter–like figure who presides over a court dedicated to "the adjusting of the niceties of salvation" (*CM* 131). The Bailiff dominates the remainder of the book, making long-winded speeches, examining individual appellants, and arguing abstruse philosophical points with an old Greek named Hyperides, who, with a small band of followers, constitutes an organized opposition to the Bailiff's authority. The original version of *The Childermass* ends inconclusively as a Hyperidean lieutenant named Polemon begins to debate the Bailiff on the question of whether or not he is real. In early 1928, Lewis signed a contract with his publisher to write parts two and three of *The Childermass*, but he did not return to the book until the early 1950s, by which time he had changed his whole approach to the project.[2] Although the substantially unrevised *Childermass* later became book one of *The Human Age*, because it was completed so many years before books two and three (*Monstre Gai* and *Malign Fiesta*), I will postpone discussion of the sequels until the next chapter.

A simple plot summary gives little idea of how it really feels to read *The Childermass*, a book in which the description of every gesture and thought process is so overdetermined that the narrative comes close to the absolute stasis demanded by *Tarr's* aesthetics of deadness. Readers usually find themselves struggling to see the forest for the trees. In a 1952 BBC radio talk on *The Childermass*, I. A. Richards asked the question, "What, after all, *is* going forward?" Richards's own tentative answer was not very heartening:

> I think everyone who has tried to write or talk about *The Childermass* has found himself in the same hole—the very deep and dubious hole Wyndham Lewis craftily keeps us in. We don't know—to an agonizing degree we are not allowed to know—what it is all about. That very ignorance may be, of course, what it *is* all about. From the advent of the Bailiff "this great administrative officer" to that puppet's last crack (about worms *it is*) we are in the same bewilderment. The more it all changes the more it is the same.[3]

Although it is facile to say that the book is about the reader not knowing what the book is about, this tautology probably reflects difficulties that

Lewis himself encountered when he sat down to compose the work. It is hard to imagine that anyone who had criticized *Ulysses* for obscurity could have been altogether satisfied with a book as bewildering, and occasionally just plain muddled, as *The Childermass*. This was a book that Lewis *had* to write, not necessarily one he *wanted* to write.

To better understand what *is* going forward, we will first consider *The Childermass* in the context of Lewis's literary activities during the 1920s, the busiest decade of his career. As we shall see, the book has a very specific relationship to other of Lewis's works published at that time. We will then look at the ways that four writers who were important to Lewis (two contemporaries, two predecessors) influenced the composition of the book. Finally, having situated *The Childermass* in Lewis's career and among a small grouping of similar works, we will turn to the narrative itself, focusing on the character who seems to hold absolute power in this imaginary world: the Bailiff.

In June of 1920, Lewis described the current status of his career in a letter to the American art collector John Quinn: "I should be the last person to claim for my finished work anything more than a character of essay, and unfulfillment. I will ask you in five years' time, when I am forty years old, to have another look. These coming few years should be my first years of *complete* work" (*L* 120).[4] Although Lewis had mainly the state of his painting in mind, his words apply equally to his progress as a writer. "It will be sufficient to say that I still had to learn a lot of things in my two professions," he remarked in *Blasting and Bombardiering* (*BB* 213). By the early 1920s, he had a first novel, a dozen short stories, and a handful of essays to his credit; but his friend and rival, James Joyce, born the same year as Lewis, had already entered the final stages of *Ulysses*. So Lewis went "underground" (as he described it) for the next several years, ceding his role as impresario of the vortex to Pound and others, and devoting himself to the composition of works delayed by the war.

What begins to emerge in the next couple of years is not *a* complete work, but *the* complete work—or at least, a serious effort in that direction. In the fall of 1923, he gave a progress report to T. S. Eliot, who had been urging him to contribute something to *The Criterion*: "My little treatise 'The Man of the World' has taken longer even to get on its legs than I had expected. I work incessantly at it. I am never in bed before 2, or often later; and for the present dine alone to get it done" (*L* 136–37). In fact, Lewis would not complete this project until the end of the decade, by which time sheer bulk had forced him to abandon the original conception. "A satirico-fantastico-polemic omnium gatherum," Hugh Kenner has called "The Man of the World": "As though bolts of lightning had melted together *Gargantua and Pantagruel*, the *Critique of Pure Reason* and the collected works of Thomas Nashe, this grotesque cumbersome pantechnicon filled up his work-room, unpublishably long, irrepressibly vigorous" (*MF* 231). The entire work would have run to well over two thousand pages; broken down into marketable segments, it yielded several major works, including *The Art of Being Ruled*, *Time and Western Man*, *The Lion and the Fox* (an analysis of Shakespeare's politics, very close in style and substance to *ABR*), *The Apes of God*, and *The Childermass*.

Behind the composition of Lewis's proposed summa lay a totalitarian ideal that also informed the *Cantos*, *Finnegans Wake*, and a host of other modernist works. The totalitarian ideal, in literature as in politics, is born out of the frustrations of life in a changing world; it expresses a desire to recreate in mass society the intimacy shared among oneself, other people, and the natural world that is presumed to have existed before the scientific, commercial, and political revolutions of the eighteenth century. It almost goes without saying that in the years after World War I, both European masses and elites were consistently drawn to schemes that promised to abolish "the separation between public and private life" and restore "a mysterious irrational wholeness in man."[5]

As we should expect, the origins of totalitarian thinking are contemporary with the early visible effects of modern revolutions. Rousseau, for example, whose philosophy provided a starting point for Lewis's thinking about the alienated condition of the artist in *Tarr*, promulgated the idea of the "general will" on the eve of a period in French history that showed the near impossibility of achieving such a consensus among the emerging classes. Similarly, his writings on the harmonious relationship between man and nature, a central theme in romanticism (and another of *Tarr*'s preoccupations), appear just as the terms of that relationship are undergoing a momentous change from the necessity of ecological cooperation to the possibility of industrial exploitation.

The English romantics of the early nineteenth century welcomed the demise of the ancien régime and explored ways of constituting a new postrevolutionary order within their works. This usually involved a claim that art transcends classical aesthetic boundaries: for Shelley, the poet was a legislator, for Byron, a political activist, for Blake and Wordsworth, a prophet. An heir to this tradition, Lewis himself once remarked that in secular and commercial ages such as our own, "the productions of art [assume] somewhat the role of sacred books" (*TWM* 193).

But two important features distinguish Lewis's attitude toward the creation of new "sacred books" from that of the romantics and, indeed, from that of his contemporaries. First, Lewis rejected the idea that the world could be re-created through an individual consciousness, even if that individual were a genius. As we noted in the preceding chapter, Lewis saw the romantic preoccupation with the self as part of the disease, not the cure. Romantic selfhood was a symptom of alienation, which ironically had contributed to the growth of a homogeneous consumer culture and the decline of true individualism. If the modern artist's goal *was* to forge the conscience of his race, he would do this not through a covert act of self-assertion (what Lewis found in *Ulysses*), but by a strategic withdrawal from subjectivity that would expose values common to all men.

Secondly, Lewis doubted that *any* attempt to put the world back together again was possible. For example, the tremendous verbal energy expended upon such trivial subjects as appear in *The Apes of God* seems only to mock Lewis's own encyclopedic aspirations. Of course, the impossibility of the restorative task did not excuse one from trying. Lewis sounds decidedly Arnoldian in *Rude Assignment* when he looks back upon *Time and Western Man* as a "substantial fortress, once full of vigorous defenders, but now silent," which had been set there to protect nothing less than "the Western World" (*RA* 207). And he no doubt would have scorned the sophisticated impishness of such writers as Borges and Nabokov, who revel in the ultimate meaninglessness of words and deeds. Despite this strain of high seriousness, however, Lewis remained less susceptible than Pound or Joyce to the idea that a twentieth-century artist could do for his world what Dante or Homer, respectively, had done for theirs.

Lewis's skepticism toward the totalitarian ideal undermined his ability to produce a contemporary summa and probably contributed (along with the economics of publishing) to the eventual breakup of "The Man of the World" into smaller parts. Indeed, looking back at the individual books that emerged between 1926 and 1930, we can see a kind of dialectical progression that would have made almost impossible the publication of a stable and coherent whole.[6]

Seeking to establish for himself the kind of authority as a culture critic that Matthew Arnold once commanded, Lewis with *The Art of Being Ruled* pursued the comprehensive study of modern society that he had begun in *The Caliph's Design*. Motivated by the admittedly selfish concern over what role, if any, the arts were to play in a mature industrial nation, Lewis carried out his analysis in chiefly *political* terms. For example, he explained the preoccupation of Joyce, Gertrude Stein, and other writers with the unconscious as an ideological product of socialism, which interpreted the traditional rule of the conscious over the unconscious mind as a parallel to the oppression of the working classes by the bourgeoisie.

But Lewis also recognized the limits of political analysis. Machiavelli, acknowledged by Lewis in *The Art of Being Ruled* as the master in this field, focused almost exclusively on what people *did*, not what they said or thought. Politics was an arena of brute and calculable force; abstract ideas were irrelevant, or of interest only as they operated in the *post facto* legitimization of a ruler's actions. Lewis, however, went on to criticize Machiavelli for assuming that the accumulation of material power could be the *sole* interest of *every* person. As an artist, Lewis claimed to have no interest in either power or action; he was instead a detached (though not disinterested) observer, a veritable scientist of culture. Like a theoretical physicist observing the fall of an apple, Lewis deduced the laws behind the exercise of power that went beyond the conclusions of empirical study. (Here we might recall Lewis's attacks on the behaviorists and their mechanistic assumptions about human nature.)

Accordingly, Lewis moved on from the *political* analyses of *The Art of Being Ruled* to the *philosophical* investigations of *Time and Western Man*. The transcendental bias of this latter work is obvious from Lewis's preface.

> Every one, I am persuaded, must to-day fit themselves for thinking more clearly about the problems of everyday life, by accustoming themselves to think of the abstract things existing, more distinctly than ever before, behind such problems. Where everything is in question, and where all traditional values are repudiated, the everyday problems have become, necessarily identical with the abstractions from which all concrete things in the first place come. And the everyday life is too much affected by the speculative activities that are renewing and transvaluing our world, for it to be able to survive in ignorance of those speculations. (*TWM* viii)

Unable to locate the cause of the postwar malaise in the mere facts of the situation, Lewis proposed a "rough ascent into the region of the abstract," which exerted an almost supernatural control over ordinary events (*TWM* vii).

A similar connection exists between the two fictional components of "The Man of the World." Just as the political pragmatism of *The Art of Being Ruled* gives way to the abstract philosophy of *Time and Western Man*, the naturalistic satire of *The Apes of God* develops into the theological fantasy of *The Childermass*. A brief comparison of the narrative structure of these works will clarify this relationship.

In the first half of *The Apes of God*, Dan Boleyn, the young Irish "genius" newly arrived in London, begins a tour of bourgeois bohemia under the guidance of Horace Zagreus, a highly ambiguous figure who takes his orders from the even more mysterious Pierpoint. When the picaresque phase of the narrative concludes, Lewis removes his characters to the country estate of Lord Osmund Finnian-Shaw, where he continues to expose the vanities and pretensions of the English art world. This exasperating second half is at once static and entropic: while there is an almost complete lack of narrative momentum, the seemingly random shifts from one group of revelers to another tax the reader's ability to follow whatever it is that's going on. Some continuity is provided by occasional glimpses of Zagreus, who has come to the party not only to play Virgil to Dan, but also to show off his skill in legerdemain:

> "He is a magician now," said O. with rounded eyes, to welcome magic. "They say he can walk through walls. He learnt to do so in the Orient where he has spent many years—he is an adept of afghan magic."
> "Is he going to put us under some spell this evening?" S. made haste to ask.
> "No, he will not this evening," O. disappointed S. "He says it is not worth while. He has promised however to cut one of his assistants in half: also he will make a flagstone float upon the surface of the bath-water—that will be only for members of the family." (*AG* 377)

In fact, Zagreus accomplishes neither of these things; he does, however, undertake a disappearing act, as if to satisfy the need of this assortment of jaded artists, intellectuals, and aristocrats for the supernatural. But the trick fails to work properly, and at the end of party, we are still wondering whether Zagreus is anything more than the clever charlatan he appears.

The Childermass proceeds along similar lines. In the first hundred pages, Pullman and Satters explore a region where cultural phenomena of the world they left behind have been distilled into a variety of symbolic objects. For example, what Lewis saw as postwar Europe's romance with the past (and unwillingness to deal with the horrors of the present) becomes still-life dioramas of earlier centuries, which Pullman and Satters stumble into on one occasion. At the conclusion of these rambles, the narrative settles down to describe events in the open-air court where the Bailiff adjusts "the niceties of salvation."

But this flippant expression jars against our Sunday school picture of Heaven, and we soon realize that Judgment Day in this universe has almost as much in common with a country house party as it does with a church service. While the nameless official known only as the Bailiff can grant or deny admission into the Heavenly City, unlike one of Kafka's dour gatekeepers, he gives the appearance of being jolly and lackadaisical about the whole affair, like a teacher who tells his students that although he must hand out A's and F's, he doesn't believe in the grading system any more than they do. In a moment of exasperation, the Bailiff tells his petitioners: " 'I do my duty that is all any one would think the way some people behaved that I was at the bottom of the whole business! I'm not. Nothing to do. On the contrary I use myself up day in day out trying to lighten the lot of you chickens. I know things are not ideal God knows—life is life I can't help it— I'm in it too aren't I?' " (CM 238). This announcement is followed by a "murmur of sympathy" from the audience. The Bailiff seems as concerned with staying in the good graces of his petitioners as he does in passing judgment upon them. To return to the parallel with *The Apes*, the Bailiff reprises the role of Zagreus, though blessed with supernatural powers, he is a far more accomplished performer: "his spirit dances upon this mesmeric sea, he bobs buoyantly in his appointed box. He is the arch trick-performer, the ideal Impostor of Impostors, surrounded by his most sensational properties: a star turn is in preparation, he continually winks at his assistants . . . " (CM 258).

Still, the Bailiff has his limitations. He claims only to carry out the will of God, an invisible being who occupies the same place in the structure of this work as Pierpoint did in *The Apes*. And if Zagreus (under Pierpoint's direction) seems to prosecute folly, while the Bailiff (acting for God) seems to promote it, it is also true that the Bailiff tends to confuse his positions with those of his opponents, just as Zagreus was doing by the end of *The Apes*. The Bailiff freely admits this; at the conclusion of a lengthy exchange with a spokesman for the Hyperideans, he shouts: " 'My God, I shall be down there soon beside you, with the rest of them, spitting up at this box! Quite without knowing it I've become your disciple, but you'll repudiate me!'" (*CM* 318).

In *The Childermass*, Lewis wanted to transcend the boundaries of the visible world he had explored in *The Apes* so as to discover "the abstractions from which all concrete things in the first place come"(*TWM* vii). Imaginatively speaking, this entailed his departure from earth for a parallel universe, where he would find the ideas from which such cultural phenomena as Zagreus received their identity.

Wells . . . Joyce

Although Lewis prided himself on the originality of his work, *The Childermass* was not written in a literary vacuum. Lewis suffered the usual vanities of his profession and was always looking over his shoulder. In this regard, two of his contemporaries deserve special mention, not only because they are alluded to in the text, but because their work represents two extremes between which *The Childermass* falls.

When Pullman and Satters enter the "Time-space" on their tour of the camp's environs, they notice that while everything looks real, nothing moves. A ploughman and his horse encountered along the way stand "transfixed in the act of ploughing" and offer no response to Pullman's salutation, causing him to remark: "'When the sleeper wakes, you'd say! It's quite uncanny. It's the most lifelike waxwork I've ever seen'" (*CM* 91). A few pages later, Satters worries about what would happen if all these figures were suddenly to come to life: "'They might be rather objectionable—*When the Sleeper Wakes*—possibly some would run amok!'" (*CM* 98).

These passing references to a well-known work of H. G. Wells suggest that *The Childermass* can be read as a work of science fiction, or a "fantasia of possibility," to use Wells's term, which extrapolates from our current state of scientific and technical knowledge to imagine what the world will be like in the future.[7] Lewis was genuinely interested in scientific developments and believed that science was at the root of all changes in the modern world. In a passage from *The Art of Being Ruled* that could almost have been written by Wells, Lewis explained how science and technology had now established the paradigm for other activities:

We instinctively repose on the future rather than the past, though this may not yet be generally realized. Instead of the static circle of the rotation of the crops, or the infinitely slow progress of handiwork, we are in the midst of the frenzied evolutionary war of the machines. This affects our view of everything; our life, its objects and uses, love, health, friendship, politics: even art to a certain extent, but with less conviction. (*ABR* 23)

Wells's effort to understand the human dimension of science and technology distinguishes him from lesser practitioners of the genre who use science fiction to titillate the reader's desire for a certain kind of novelty. Perhaps for this reason he responded favorably to *The Childermass* when Lewis sent him a copy, announcing his "glowing appreciation" for the book, and allowing Lewis to reprint his letter in his pamphlet *Satire and Fiction* (*L* 180). In his return letter, Lewis praised Wells for trying to articulate a coherent social vision in his fiction (he specifically mentions *The World of William Clissold*, a 1926 work that, like *The Childermass*, mixes fiction with cultural criticism), and also for dealing with "the questions of war and Peace" in occasional articles (*L* 180). Both writers shared a belief in the heuristic value of fantasy, seeing their work as a means to discover the unforeseen effects of contemporary ideas. Also common to both is a wavering faith in what Lewis called "the general educated man or woman" (*TWM* vii), whose actions could influence the course of history. Wells and Lewis often present a terrifying vision of the future, but they also wanted to believe that the intelligent reader can learn from his or her potential mistakes. Despite the nightmarish quality of the respective worlds they envision, both *The Childermass* and *When the Sleeper Wakes* can be seen as admonitory rather than apocalyptic works of fiction.

Still, there were important differences between Lewis and Wells, which may account for why they never became more than polite correspondents. Wells was nearly a generation older than Lewis and exhibited a faith in the power of reason, which aligns him more closely to the Victorians than the moderns. A classic nineteenth-century liberal, he viewed the social and political order as a serviceable machine that might require occasional tinkering but not replacement through revolution. Moreover, because Wells inhabited an essentially rational world, he was not particularly concerned with the aesthetic questions that exercised the artists of Lewis's generation, most notably questions about the status and meaning of language.

In this respect, Lewis is much closer to James Joyce, who was well along with the composition of *Finnegans Wake* when *The Childermass* appeared in 1928. The relationship between the two writers, which has been alluded to previously, found a literary outlet in the pages of these works.[8] Responding to the attacks upon him in *Time and Western Man*, Joyce caricatures Lewis on at least two occasions in the *Wake*: once as the pedantic "spatialist" Professor Jones, and later as the sanctimonious Ondt, who upbraids the artistic Gracehoper for wasting his time on such works as *Ho, Time Timeagen, Wake!*—to which the Gracehoper replies: *"Your genus its worldwide, your spacest sublime! / But, Holy Saltmartin, why can't you beat time?"*[9] For his part, Lewis gives certain Joycean attributes to Pullman, including a concern with the medium of an utterance at the expense of its message. Joyce also appears toward the end of *The Childermass* as Belcanto, a famous writer whom the Bailiff counts as one of his friends (the "moron" in the following sentence is Gertrude Stein, whose style Lewis consistently bracketed with Joyce's): "He lives by himself and never speaks, except for a few disjointed phrases in ice-cream English or counterfeit Latin with a sprinkling of tinker and Greek, in fact he's made up a cant of his own which is founded upon the stuttering of a particular moron that for some time we kept before destroying hoping she might get better—she never did . . . " (*CM* 278).

If a faith in the conscious mind separated Lewis from Wells, then a love of the unconscious divided him from Joyce. Still, in the final analysis, the distance between Lewis and Joyce seems to be more a matter of degree than of kind. Both *Finnegans Wake* and *The Childermass* represent efforts to transcend what Stephen Dedalus in *Ulysses* called the "nightmare of history"; both works recognize the need to replace history with myth, and both understand that the change to myth will have a profound effect on the way writing gets done, that is to say, on language itself.

History in this context means not only specific events (the struggle for Irish independence, the First World War), but the idea that events have a rational narrative structure, unfolding in accord with some obscure but ultimately discernible plan. In the latter part of the nineteenth century, Nietzsche had shown that such "plans" were convenient fictions serving the interests of a dominant class. Stephen Dedalus reaches a similar conclusion as he listens to the Orangeman Dan Deasy explain Irish history in *Ulysses*, and the whirlwind tour of the "willingdone museyroom" in *Finnegans Wake* further emphasizes Joyce's awareness of the fictional element in all histories.[10]

But what would take the place of history when history ended? Eliot, perhaps Joyce's most important early reader, noted in his famous review of *Ulysses* that the transcending of history would involve a return to myth, or rather, that the myth of history would have to be replaced by a myth that more accurately reflected the chaotic experience of life in the modern world.[11] In *Finnegans Wake*, Joyce attempted to complete the project he had begun in *Ulysses*, replacing the teleological history of a struggle between good and evil (culminating in the triumph of the good), with a dialectical history that allowed for the interplay of "good" and "evil" (nonmoral forces that he understood, after Blake, as energy and restraint).

Such a myth could not be conveyed by an insufficiently dialectical language where one word meant only one thing (suppressing the opposing term upon which it depended). And so in the *Wake*, Joyce created a language out of puns, which forces the reader to acknowledge the quintessential modernist insight, articulated by Nietzsche, Eliot, Ferdinand de Saussure, and others, that every member of a system has its meaning only in relation to every other member; that every part, in this sense, refers to the whole.

Because of Lewis's doubts that one could actually write a sacred book in the twentieth century, *The Childermass* is overall a less ambitious work than *Finnegans Wake*: it is a book *about* the world (or at least, about *a* world), not the book *as* world. Yet Lewis shared with Joyce a commitment to discover the artistic and conceptual forms appropriate to modernity. He, too, found untenable the notion of history as an orderly progression of events, though instead of replacing progress with an almost playful dialectic, Lewis envisioned a stalemate between opposing forces. Of the first meeting between the Bailiff and Hyperides, he writes: "They are the oldest opposites in the universe, they eye each other: all this has been enacted before countless times, on unnumbered occasions all these things they are now about to say have been uttered, under every conceivable circumstance" (*CM* 153).

Lewis had also recognized since the writing of *Tarr* and *Enemy of the Stars* that any change in sensibility must be reflected in one's language, and in *The Childermass*, he continues the stylistic experiments of these earlier works. Two general features evident in the preceding quotation contribute to the atmosphere of stalemate, of energy without direction: first, Lewis employs a paratactic structure within paragraphs that frustrates the forward movement of the narrative; and secondly, he leaves out punctuation and/or conjunctions between independent clauses in a manner that conveys a sense of extreme restlessness.

These similarities between their works aside, the fact remains that Lewis disliked *Finnegans Wake*. Although he no doubt appreciated the effort to invent new artistic forms, the book represented to him a kind of naive modernism, a throwback to aestheticism with its unstated premise that a revolution in language leads the way to a revolution in consciousness. *Finnegans Wake* argues for the radical interrelatedness of all things and makes a mockery of conventional notions of identity. But while in theory twentieth-century man no longer has his meaning alone, he still acts and thinks as if he does. That was the modern world, too, as Lewis wanted *The Childermass* to remind us.

Milton . . . Swift

While Lewis occasionally nods to the work of his contemporaries, he really hoped that *The Childermass* would invite favorable comparison to the classics. The original three-part plan announced in 1928, for example, leads us to think that Lewis had Dante in mind when he began the project. Although Dante does seem to have been an important influence on the two later volumes, little of the *Divine Comedy* shows through *The Childermass*. Two other masters, however, have left their mark on its composition: Milton and Swift. (Several critics have noted this in passing since Kenner first drew the parallels in the 1950s.[12]) Milton's presence here can be felt in the book's curious mixture of political and theological concerns, while Swift's spirit is manifest in the continuing preoccupation with the question of how cultural values affect basic human nature.

Jameson has done the most with Kenner's insight, showing that *The Childermass* shares with *Paradise Lost* (and other postliterate or "artificial" epics) a tendency to focus not on events, but on the *describing* of events.[13] Since the writer of artificial epic does not belong to the heroic world he seeks to re-create (he belongs instead to a "civilized" world), what he lacks in Homeric immediacy he tries to make up for with Virgilian polish. Jameson goes on to observe that this task becomes nearly impossible under the conditions of industrial capitalism, where every figure of speech has been so thoroughly appropriated to the business of buying and selling that a language such as Milton's can be handled only with irony. This accounts for Lewis's tendency to degrade whatever epic splendor survives in his Heaven, as when a mirage that rises up across from the city is said to have "the consistency and tint of a wall of cheese."[14]

Besides the problems of artificial epic, other features of *The Childermass* reenforce the parallel with *Paradise Lost*. Both Lewis and Milton allow an extraordinary amount of historical data to seep into their transcendent domains. Indeed, they seem committed to updating a mythological tradition in light of recent social and political developments and the technological changes connected with them. Milton's angels, for example, behave much like soldiers in a seventeenth-century army, right down to their predilection for platoon and squadron formation; their leaders, God and Satan, command material power in ways the Bible could never have imagined (Satan mines sulphur and other chemicals and produces gunpowder). Similarly, the "emigrant mass" collected outside the walls of Lewis's Heavenly City suffers from much the same malaise that afflicted Europeans after World War I's failure to make the world safe for democracy; and *their* leader, the Bailiff, has the ability to manipulate space and time, such as could not have been conceived before Einstein.

Lewis's decision to stick with an old mythology instead of creating a new one, or dispensing with mythology altogether, also shares something with Milton. Specifically, both men labored in the wake of failed revolutionary movements and felt the need to come to terms with these respective failures. The story of Milton's loyalty to the protectorate and his brief imprisonment at the outset of the Restoration is widely known; the events of Lewis's life were less dramatic, but in his 1937 autobiography, he speaks of himself, along with Joyce, Pound, and Eliot, as the vanguard of an artistic and intellectual revolution that never "came off," having been snuffed out by the war and the disillusionment with modernity that followed it (*BB* 256). Two problems confront the writer in this predicament: he must account for the success of the reactionary forces, and he must deal with the personal trauma caused by knowing that he has been rejected by history.

In *Paradise Lost*, Milton justifies the defeat of the rebellious angels by showing us that Satan, for whom he feels an undeniable sympathy in the early books, is the real tyrant of the poem, not God. The historian Christopher Hill, while cautioning against a reading of the poem as a roman à clef, suggests that "one possible source for Milton's conception of the rebel angels is the people he had encountered, whose activities had done (in his view) harm to the cause he believed in, although their ideas started from premises alarmingly close to his."[15] In this scenario, Satan appears as a revolutionary leader who had been corrupted by pride and ambition, thus explaining the failure of the protectorate to establish lasting rule. But Milton's implied criticism of the revolution did not extend to an abandonment of its ideals. The Stuarts, he knew, were the real usurpers in seventeenth-century England, having fundamentally altered the constitution by their assertion of divine right; indeed, for Milton, monarchy itself was usurpation.[16] Still, the fact remains that *Paradise Lost* appeared shortly after the Restoration, and it is hard not to see the tragedy of fallen angels and men as a public confession that the great experiment had failed. (The romantics, of course, were very disturbed by this conservative message, Blake insisting that Milton "wrote in chains" when he took the side of God against Satan.)

Lewis also faced the dilemma of a history that seemed to have repudiated the great plans that he and his friends had made for it. If the claims that artists and intellectuals assert for themselves have any substance, then creative genius ought to play a dominant role in society. The confidence of the young modernists that they *would* dominate is reflected in the first issue of *BLAST*, which half-jokingly, but only half-jokingly, called for the conversion of George V to vorticism ("A Vorticist king? Why not!" [*B1* 8]). They foresaw a world where the enlightened few would raise the cultural standards of the many who were increasingly free to attend to the arts in an age of labor-saving machines. To the extent that this elite could shape the tastes of the nation, artists would also guarantee themselves an audience whose vastness their predecessors could not have imagined.

Of course, this future never "came off," an event, or nonevent, for which Lewis offered two explanations. The first repeats Nietzsche's argument that the herd has simply overwhelmed genius by sheer force of numbers. In *The Childermass*, Lewis goes as far as to suggest that God's omnipotence has lately been undermined by the accumulating mass of humanity He has brought into being. Walking through the outer precincts of Heaven, Pullman and Satters occasionally meet "peons," members of a vast automaton-like proletariat, which Pullman explains thus: "It is the multitude of personalities which God has created, ever since the beginning of time, and is unable now to destroy" (*CM* 37). Lewis here implies that if God has been overwhelmed by mass society, genius can hardly expect to fare better.

Yet this answer begs the question of the natural superiority of the avant-garde; after all, stupidity should be no match for intelligence under any circumstances. Lewis therefore offered another theory, reminiscent of Milton's in *Paradise Lost*, which in various forms surfaces in all of his work from *Enemy of the Stars* to *Self Condemned*: since genius could not be defeated by numbers, genius must have defeated itself. In *The Childermass*, we see the highly intelligent James Pullman, the greatest writer on earth, applaud the alternately tyrannic and demagogic acts of a nameless functionary, acts that undermine the position of thoughtful men like himself (the Bailiff promises immediate gratification and at one point exclaims, " 'Le mob c'est moi!' " [*CM* 268]). To make matters worse, the Bailiff himself admits, " 'I *always* behave "beneath my dignity," it is my most settled policy, I would not be my own equal for worlds' " (*CM* 287). The Bailiff thus emerges as both a prideful and ambitious Satan, and one of those whom Nietzsche called "ascetic priests," sensitive but spiteful men who minister to mediocrity when they find themselves outnumbered by the ranks of the mediocre.

Lewis's deep suspicion of the intelligentsia may account for the most peculiar feature of *The Childermass*, its adherence to the essential terms of Christian mythology. Unlike Milton, Lewis was not compelled by his times to some profession of Christianity; the times in fact seemed to militate against it. Yet the reader of *The Childermass* enters a fairly conventional Heaven that exhibits a walled city, a gate, a gatekeeper, multitudes of sinners, and some talk of another place that no one cares to think much about. Neither Milton nor Bunyan would be lost here. Lewis's trenchant choice impresses me, therefore, as a reminder to himself and others who had had revolutionary aspirations that the old order is not so easily dismissed. *BLAST* had asserted the end of the Christian era; but the Christian era had not ended, and indeed, its cultured despisers had internalized the old Adam more than they cared to admit (Lewis's attacks on his former allies in the 1920s show them as bogus revolutionaries of one sort or another). By suggesting that when modern men die they go to a Christian heaven, Lewis was admitting that he and his friends had been naive about the world, that they had flattered themselves with the notion that one could bring about social revolution by writing manifestos, and perhaps a good novel every now and then. If we can believe for a moment that history does repeat itself, then let us call Wyndham Lewis a modern Percy Shelley (another of Milton's close readers) who lived to maturity and evolved into the Matthew Arnold who looked back upon the poet as an "ineffectual angel." Lewis never went the old Tory route of some disgruntled romantics, but he came to respect power structures that rightly or wrongly had lasted for centuries; and in the case of Christianity, he wondered if this persistence might not be connected to its fundamental validity.

While strategically *The Childermass* owes something to *Paradise Lost*, the writer who exerted the greatest tactical influence on Lewis was not Milton but Swift. One early admirer of Lewis's work also noted the connection. Soon after the book's publication in 1928, W. B. Yeats said in a letter to the author that there were moments in the first hundred pages "that no writer of romance had surpassed," and he went on to call this section "as powerful as 'Gulliver' and much more exciting to a modern" (*L* 181n). Lewis was immensely flattered by the comparison and wrote back to Yeats, requesting permission to use these comments in the promotion of the American edition of the book (*L* 182–83). (Yeats consented but insisted that the remark about *Gulliver* not be extended to cover the later parts of the work, whose dramatic dialogues reminded him little of Swift's novel.)

As we saw before, Lewis intended the first part of *The Childermass* to be a philosophical picaresque (complementing the sociological picaresque of *The Apes*), which, like *Gulliver's Travels*, allowed the author to survey a veritable rogues' gallery of ideas and ideologies. On at least one occasion, Lewis makes the parallel between Swift's work and his own explicit. While passing through one of the "Time-spaces" in the camp's environs, Pullman and Satters find themselves in a place covered with buildings five and six feet high and populated by little people who look like they stepped out of a Rowlandson print. When Satters begins to toy with one of these figures, the little man indignantly pulls himself away and addresses his would-be tormentor in these words: " 'We may be in Lilliput but you are not a gentleman as was Gulliver, it is evident, from whatever world you may have dropped, you may have been blown off some man but you are not one nor ever will be! You are a lout, as I have already said, and I say it again, sir, in spite of your dimensions' " (*CM* 107).

As with Swift's, Lewis's satire cuts in several directions at once. First, we are led to see the inadequacy of the observer and the system of cultural values he represents. Satters is a product of the middle-class family and the British public school, yet the only thing he can think to do when exposed to novelty is to use it for his own malicious amusement. (Pullman, the intellectual, objects to Satters's behavior, but with insufficient vigor to prevent him from trampling the Lilliputian into "an inert flattened mass" [*CM* 108].) Secondly, Lewis is pointing to a barbarizing trend in European history since Swift's time. Although the Whiggish Gulliver more often exploited than understood what he encountered (upon his return to England, he makes a considerable profit showing his Lilliputian cattle to "many Persons of Quality, and others"[17]), he was, at least, "a gentleman" and did not brutalize his hosts, though he occasionally felt tempted to do so. Satters's service in the Great War—for Lewis, the defining event of the modern period—also figures in this episode as well: soon after leaving the scene, Pullman tells his unruly ward, "'The Army had an unfortunate effect on you in some ways'" (*CM* 109).

Lewis's decision to send his heroes to Lilliput in the first place also has historical significance. A sign hanging in front of a miniature inn identifies it as the *Old Red Lion Tavern*, which Pullman remembers as the place where Thomas Paine wrote *The Rights of Man*; indeed, the Lilliputian harassed by Satters is apparently Paine himself, if we can judge by his "slight American accent." This Lilliput, Pullman concludes, represents England at about the time of the French Revolution. There is a nice irony here, given Lewis's feeling about the revolution and the romantic movement it fostered, drawn as he was to its apocalyptic promise, yet ultimately repulsed by its failure to acknowledge the consequences of revolutionary thought and action. From Lewis's standpoint, Thomas Paine's demise beneath the foot of Satters carries out the sentence of poetic justice: Paine dies beneath the heel of a creature who embodies the instinctive side of human nature first valorized by romanticism.

Besides this common concern with the relationship between ideology and culture, Swift and Lewis also share an interest in the effects of science on the life of the community. Throughout *Gulliver's Travels*, for example, Swift takes aim at the scientist's view of the world, as Hugh Kenner describes it in this brief summary:

> Gulliver knows nothing until he has had an experience, and what he knows then is the trace of the experience he has had. This was for Swift, apparently, the hallmark of the new barbarism, this subjection of the mind to sequences of physical evidence, since it undid the revolution Socrates effected in philosophy when he turned its attention to wholly moral questions. Socrates had rendered philosophy *useful*: moral determinations are useful, since they assist us to live. The discoveries which pertain to physical evidence are not useful at all, ministering as they do solely to idle curiosity (the distance of the earth from the sun in statute miles: who has a use for *that*?) So Gulliver's mind is busy in an idle way, like that of a Royal Society virtuoso, and it is no wonder that he is so ultimately helpless when talking horses challenge him to justify the ways of man to men.[18]

The operation and objective of Swift's satire can be seen in the well-known episode in which the Lilliputian officers report on the contents of Gulliver's pockets:

Out of the right Fob hung a great Silver Chain, with a wonderful kind of Engine at the Bottom. We directed him to draw out whatever was at the End of the Chain, which appeared to be a Globe, half Silver, and half of some transparent Metal: for on the transparent Side we saw certain strange Figures circularly drawn, and thought we could touch them, until we found our Fingers stopped with that lucid Substance. He put this Engine to our Ears, which made an incessant Noise like that of a Water-Mill.[19]

The small minds of these small people, subjected to sequences of physical evidence, and thus exemplary of the most advanced thinking of Swift's day, cannot manage to recognize the thing for what it is: a pocket watch. But the satire reaches beyond current intellectual fashion. An inability to know more than one has actually experienced reveals a profound selfishness—a selfishness that was becoming the norm in the increasingly commercial eighteenth century. Indeed, empiricism's domesticated *alter ego* is the common sense of the businessman, which directs him to seek only personal gain and conveniently blinds him to the consequences of his selfish acts, since the strictly empirical method teaches him to be skeptical of chains of cause and effect (as David Hume convincingly demonstrated) and wary of those traditionalists who argue for the interrelatedness of things. (Swift's Modest Proposer thus manages to persuade himself that butchery is a form of altruism.) The history of this shift in values was written in works from Hobbes's *Leviathan*, whose materialist author not surprisingly found life in the state of nature nasty, brutish, and short, to *Robinson Crusoe*, which, although appearing just a few years before *Gulliver's Travels*, takes us to the narcissistic antipode of the classical ideal of commonwealth.

Yet Swift's Lilliputians were not completely without insight into the meaning of Gulliver's watch. Unable to define the exact nature of his wonderful engine, they conjecture that "it is either some unknown Animal, or the God he worships: But we are more inclined to the latter Opinion, because he assured us (if we understood him right, for he expressed himself very imperfectly), that he seldom did any Thing without consulting it. He called it his Oracle, and said it pointed out the Time for every Action of his Life."[20] In the last analysis, the Lilliputians and Gulliver are equally victims of their own empirical methods. If the former cannot recognize the thing for what it is, the latter cannot see the significance of the thing for which he has only a name. The watch and the time it ticks away are perhaps the supreme creations of the Gulliverian mind, and Swift uses them to suggest the way that scientific efforts to make life more orderly and efficient were also rendering it fundamentally less human. A meaningful life depends upon a network of hard-to-define, even imaginary relationships; quantitative analysis, which demands exact measurement of the *thing*, has little patience for connections and contexts. Gulliver's watch, quantifying the flow of everyday life, was for Swift a dehumanizing instrument that encouraged men to think commercially, not morally, about existence and led them to ask the question "How much?" instead of "How good?" It is thus wholly appropriate that a timepiece should function as Gulliver's god, and that Gulliver should be unaware of, if not altogether indifferent to, his discipleship in this new, inferior religion.

But Swift recognized that science had political as well as moral ramifications. As science detaches a man from the immediacy of his surroundings, it weakens the ties that bind him to the community. The man who regulates his life according to the abstract units measured by his pocket watch has gained a degree of independence from his fellow men: he will eat at noon whether or not it accords with the wishes of others that he do so; the hour of noon may not even accord with his *own* wishes, inasmuch as we have all known people who ate when the clock, not their stomachs, told them to.

With this independence from man and nature, however, comes the specter of alienation. The historian Peter Laslett argues that although the England of Swift's lifetime was a grossly inequitable society, it was also an existentially secure one, no one suffering uncertainty about who he was and how he should act toward others.[21] Interestingly, this situation began to change around the time Swift published *Gulliver's Travels*, when the practical effects of the scientific revolution—industrialization, geographical mobility, and widespread literacy—started to become evident in England. Science was indeed an enemy of the world Swift wished to preserve, and the social consequences of a scientific approach to time were exemplary of the changes science portended. Gulliver must have been keeping his watch wound up in Lilliput, but why? The Lilliputians were apparently unacquainted with minutes and hours. Reference to his watch, marking the passage of abstract, asocial time, could have done nothing other than to further estrange Gulliver from the community in which he happened to find himself.

The Lilliputian conjecture about Gulliver's watch suggests that by Swift's time, men were becoming aware of the ways that science had altered our sense of that most elusive dimension of ordinary life. Time had become more fully comprehensible and, as such, more easily subject to the tinkering of the scientific mind. Indeed, not too many years before *Gulliver's Travels*, Sir Isaac Newton had turned the whole universe into a cosmic clockwork, methodically ticking away without divine assistance.

By the mid-nineteenth century, this once-radical concept of time had established itself as normative, even reassuring. Although time could be infinitesimally quantified in Newton's universe, it could not be otherwise altered: you could not shrink, expand, or make it go backward. Time remained an absolute, like the God since made redundant by Newtonian physics. But the scientific mind continued to be busy in its idle way. In the early years of the twentieth century, Einstein and others had shown that time was not absolute but rather was a phenomenon dependent upon the position of the observer. This new conception of time reflected a broader shift in scientists' understanding of the physical universe, from a deterministic arrangement of discrete blocks of stuff to a Heraclitean flux of process and probability where the boundaries between matter and energy were no longer distinct. Science had once led to certitude; now it was heading in almost the opposite direction.[22]

The French philosopher Henri Bergson, contemplating these developments in physics, transformed Einstein's mathematical categories into psychological ones; that is, Einstein's relative time became Bergson's *subjective* time. One would think that this reinterpretation of time might have pleased contemporary conservatives who, like Swift before them, objected to the mechanistic worldview on moral grounds. Indeed, Bergson's chief English disciple, T. E. Hulme, praised his master for dispersing the "nightmare of determinism" and restoring sovereignty to the perceiving self.[23]

But as we have seen, Lewis considered Bergson's idea of time to be the premier exhibit of contemporary intellectual decadence. In *The Childermass*, Bergson's position is represented by the Bailiff, who is completely obsessed with time. To a hostile appellant he shouts:

> *"Eternity is in love with the productions of Time!* The Eternal loves Time if you do not! The only motive for His weakness for you is in your capacity of *factor of Time*, that is your principal not to say unique claim upon His interest. Some of you disregard your debt to Time in a really unaccountable way. Time is the mind of Space—Space is the mere body of time. Time is life, Time is money, Time is all good things!—Time is God!" (*CM* 229)

Time here is understood not as an abstract entity but, after Bergson, as immediate subjective experience. (Thus Time *is* God in an age that worships the self.) To another appellant the Bailiff explains:

> "Things are bearing down on us from all directions which we know nothing about at this moment, when they shall have struck us we shall term that an *event* and it will possess a certain temporal extension. All the times of all these potential spatial happenings are longer or shorter paths that are timeless until they touch us, when they set our personal clock or proper measure of time ticking, measuring the event in question for us. You see the idea?" (*CM* 152)

Although Bergson may have given back to time a human face by making it contingent upon our perception of it, such perceptions were entirely idiosyncratic, in no way guaranteeing that a person would share his experience of time with that of anyone else. The problem with the Newtonian time that Swift satirized in *Gulliver*—that it is an amoral abstraction that alienates men from one another—simply reappears under a different guise as Bergsonian time, which further degrades the human condition while seeming to do just the opposite.

For Lewis, subjective time was another consequence of the anthropocentric worldview that developed in the Renaissance and culminated in romanticism. Subjectivity, of course, had also made possible the complex, postromantic personality (if not persona) of Wyndham Lewis; but as we saw in the preceding chapter, he seems to have recognized the fundamental egoism behind his posturings and sent each of his autobiographical protagonists to the scaffold after performing their duties as satiric hit men. The *Zeitgeist* itself—Lewis's shorthand for the "best" thought of the "best" men—rarely showed this degree of critical awareness. Twentieth-century man flattered himself with the idea that he could achieve anything he set his mind to. He had conquered space, first restructuring it in his mind, then reshaping it with his hands (with the advance of the industrial revolution); now he was going after the other dimension. Einstein and Bergson had made the necessary conceptual adjustments, and Lewis, drawing on a few stock conventions from Wellsian science fiction, imagined this technical accomplishment in *The Childermass*. Gulliver could only traverse the globe (aided by various marine and navigational technologies); Pullman and Satters can move back and forth across the centuries. Wandering somewhere between the seventeenth and eighteenth centuries, Pullman remarks smugly: " 'I delight in these time-spaces, they are passages really. You don't often come across them like this. Reversibility is the proof that the stage of perfection has been reached in machine-construction'" (*CM* 101).

The Hunchback of Heaven

The last two-thirds of *The Childermass*—the long Socratic dialogue that Yeats found too dull to praise—constitutes an inquiry into the desirability of the mechanically perfect world that our heroes have explored in the book's first hundred pages. The Bailiff completely dominates this final section, and if we are ever to get to the bottom of *The Childermass*, we will have to develop a clearer picture of him. Early in the narrative when Satters asks, " 'Who is he has he ever lived?' ", Pullman offers this speculation: " 'some say he is Jacobus del Rio some a Prince of Exile, I have heard him called Trimalchio Loki Herod Karaguez Satan, even some madman said Jesus, there is no knowing what he is. I believe he's just what you see, himself, he is the Bailiff simply. I don't understand the insistence on something factitive behind him or why he is not accepted as he is' " (*CM* 72). Pullman's reluctance to address Satters's question once again reveals what Lewis saw as the failure of his contemporaries to adopt a properly critical attitude toward their surroundings. For although Pullman may not think that the Bailiff's identity matters much, the Bailiff himself knows that it is the *only* thing that matters. Commenting on the limited right of petition in Heaven, he remarks, " 'This is not a despotic legislature, but it is also not a curia. However my personality is really the main factor in the whole thing, you need go no farther than me, I am your shepherd' " (*CM* 210). Our own efforts to understand this personality will proceed along three lines: first we will look at the Bailiff as a creature of his time, that is, the immediate postwar years; then we will consider him as an archetypal figure who transcends his historical period; and finally, we will note the biographical affinities between the Bailiff and his author.

Despite the quasimystical aura that envelops him, the Bailiff is very much a product of the 1920s. In his memoir of the period, *Blasting and Bombardiering*, Lewis often complains about the absence of cultural standards that allowed the dilettantism he attacked in *The Apes of God* to flourish, but the relative chaos in the art world during the postwar years could just as well be taken as a sign of creative vitality. The avant-garde impulse that had begun to mature about 1914 survived the war in surprisingly good shape and probably did not receive a mortal blow in England until the economic crisis associated with the General Strike of 1926. Lewis himself was back to his revolutionary ways by 1919, organizing the short-lived Group X, and although he soon went underground in an apparent effort to increase his productivity, he remained an artist committed to finding new ways of doing things.

Thus, one of the first observations we can make about the Bailiff is that he is an experimental character in an experimental work of fiction. Jameson observes that in Lewis's writing "the stable subject or ego" is frequently dissolved, allowing powerful subconscious impulses the freedom "to acquire their own figuration."[24] In his prewar closet drama *Enemy of the Stars*, Lewis dispensed with the canons of realism, presenting for our inspection persons who were more like embodiments of psychic energy than the people we meet in everyday life. Lewis invested *Tarr's* Kreisler with something of this quality, but only with the Bailiff does he create a narrative character (though an almost static one) who transcends most expectations of what a fictional person should be.

Another of Jameson's theses suggests why the work of Lewis and some of his contemporaries inclined toward this particular kind of experimentation. He notes that in Lewis's post-World War I fiction, a narrative system based upon psychological categories is replaced by an "energy model": "The logic of an energy model lies in its quantification of older qualitative components; in its attempt to reduce the heterogeneous substances and impulses of older kinds of models to the unified plus/minus system of a single force, whose increments then determine the variety and the conflicts of the world of phenomenal appearance."[25] The main idea here is that an event can be explained as either a successful or an unsuccessful application of force; nothing else really matters. Although Jameson is uncomfortable with "reflection" theories of history and literature, he implies that in Lewis's writing the Nietzschean view of the world as a place governed by a will to power (confirmed for Lewis by the war) has been translated into the novelist's formal understanding not only of events, but also of character. In this respect, the Bailiff resembles the protagonist of *Finnegans Wake*—the supremely experimental work of the decade—who was not conceived as a historical individual, but as an abstract paradigm of energy, represented by the symbol "⊓," which became a Dublin innkeeper or a Russian general or King Mark or Ibsen's Masterbuilder according to its shaping of the accidents of time and space. The Bailiff has the power to alter his physical appearance, and although we do not see him in as many guises as " ⊓ ," he, too, seems primarily the embodiment of a cultural energy that can just as easily show itself as Bacchus or Charlie Chaplin (*CM* 184).

Another contemporary analogy to this idea of character as force field can be found in Ezra Pound's favorite image of the mind as a magnet that draws iron filings into a coherent pattern: "the rose in the steel dust."[26] In greater or lesser degree, all of the beings that populate Lewis's afterlife behave like magnets, pulling the fragments of their earthly existence around them, though rarely into such attractive patterns. The ultimate source of energy for these various designs seems to be the Bailiff himself, whom Pullman calls, borrowing the phrase from Stendhal, " '*Professor of Energy* . . . that's what he is: he is really like Napoleon' " (*CM* 79). Lewis's Heaven is an effort to expose the first principles of modern life, and this conception of the life after death tends to confirm Nietzsche's dark vision: that in an industrial society, that is to say, one that single-mindedly devotes itself to the subjugation of nature, the only criterion of value is whether or not something facilitates the exercise of power. The reference to Napoléon and Stendhal is interesting in this connection because it locates the self-conscious origins of the "energy model" at about the time of the French Revolution, which itself represented the expression of new political realities brought on by technological progress. (This period also saw the appearance of William Blake's "giant forms," curious amalgams of material energy and spiritual vision that offer another precedent for the Bailiff.) The Bailiff even goes so far as to claim, while disputing with his enemies, that divinity is to be identified with power, and that to the degree that man commands unlimited power today, he is God:

> BAILIFF: "These subversive doubters call in question *everything*! All that marvellous edifice of Progress, those prodigies of Science, which have provided us moderns with a new soul and a consciousness different from that of any other epoch, that have borne man to a pinnacle of knowledge and of power—"
> (He licks his lips as though there were a great "sexual appeal" in the word "power" and gazes fiercely round the audience, allowing his eyes to rest especially upon the goggling round-mouthed countenances of the youngest, smallest, seated listeners, to his immediate left; then he continues.)

"—all that staggering scientific advance that has made modern man into a god, almost, dominating nature in a manner beyond the wildest dreams of Antiquity—all *that* these hot-heads you see here deny and call in question excited to insurgent zeal by that man who styles himself Hyperides—" (*CM* 261–62)

Besides the experimental form of his character, the political content of the Bailiff's addresses also marks him as a product of the 1920s, though this is often obscured by the medieval trappings of Lewis's Heaven, and the elapse of more than a half-century since the book's appearance. A comical reference to the decade occurs during one of the Bailiff's little disquisitions on the nature of social and political life in Heaven when he momentarily confuses an English poet with an American president: "'What is a gentleman' asked Samuel Taylor Coolidge—Coleridge, I mean" (*CM* 211). The Bailiff's slip of the tongue has much the same effect as the juxtaposition of classic and contemporary materials in Eliot's *Waste Land* and marks the precipitous decline of Western civilization, which Lewis claimed to be defending. Indeed, a reading of *The Childermass* in light of Lewis's polemical writings of the period makes it clear that the Bailiff (" '*Le mob c'est moi!* '" [268]) encompasses virtually all the cultural phenomena that Lewis identified as outward expressions of that decline: dadaism, feminism, homosexuality, communism, relativism, and, of course, "Time."

For Lewis, these movements of the postwar period represented variations on a single theme: "the loss of reality in modern life, or, if you prefer a somewhat franker version, the systematic undermining of the European White Male Will."[27] But while Lewis occasionally longed for an era when men such as himself exercised their prerogative without challenge, he was no common reactionary and generally accepted the social adjustments that accompanied technological progress. He would have thought any suggestion of a return to feudalism (as Ford Madox Ford advocated) absurd and conceded in *The Art of Being Ruled* that male dominance depended upon a reward system that no longer made sense in an age when technology had effectively erased a man's physical advantage. As far as Lewis was concerned, the day of the "White Male Will" was over.

To the extent that the "White Male Will" does persist as a category in Lewis's thinking, it functions as a kind of political reality principle. Lewis believed that authority was inescapable and considered arguments to the contrary both misleading and dangerous. This conviction lay behind

Pierpoint's analysis of contemporary literature in *The Apes of God*, which noted the peculiar conjunction of a cult of impersonality (ostensibly undermining the authority of authors) with a school of unabashed personal fiction (elevating the author to a status of a demigod) (*AG* 259).

A similar belief informed Lewis's analysis of postwar politics. In England, free enterprise and parliamentary democracy had created the illusion of popular government, while allowing big business interests to manipulate a complacent public. In Lewis's view, most Englishmen were no better off than they would have been in Russia or Italy, where repressive dictatorships had been established; indeed, at least communism and fascism had the virtue of *"frankness"* when it came to the exercise of power (*ABR* 74). Like many intellectuals disgusted with the false piety of bourgeois culture, Lewis seems to have concluded that in the modern world individual freedom varied *inversely* with the strength of a state's affirmation of that freedom.[28]

The Childermass dramatizes this political axiom, demonstrating that tyranny by any other name, including liberal democracy, is still tyranny. The Bailiff presents himself as hardly more than the equal of the petitioners upon whom he must pass judgment. His position of authority frankly embarrasses him, and he even alters his appearance for the worse lest his supernatural beauty offend anyone. (A few years later, Lewis observed these same characteristics in the man who would exploit the Weimar Republic's diffidence about power: "Adolf Hitler is just a very typical German 'man of the people.'... As even his very appearance suggests, there is nothing whatever eccentric about him. He is not only satisfied with, but enthusiastically embraces, his *typicalness*.")[29] But this egalitarian gesture only assuages in advance whatever guilt he might feel from the exercise of absolute power and actually encourages him in his arbitrary behavior, as when he suddenly orders the decapitation of a petitioner who had mildly insulted him. Every now and then, the Bailiff allows this mask of equality to slip in a way that none but the most secure and cynical of human despots would ever dare:

> BAILIFF: "Your rights, gentlemen, can be summarized in one word, *Petition*. You are *petitioners*, for better or for worse. I am ashamed to have to tell you that no appellant is entitled to his Habeas Corpus or to anything resembling it, there is no Rule of Law for us, you are absolutely without rights independently of my will: that is the situation: a sorry one, an un-

English one, one I am heartily ashamed to have to stand here and expose to you." (*CM* 209–10)

But though he may be heartily ashamed of the situation, the Bailiff does nothing to change it. The only thing that can be said for him (and Lewis was prepared to say this about Lenin or Mussolini or Hitler) is that he is not a hypocrite.

Despite these topical allusions, *The Childermass* aims to do more than dramatize the cultural criticism of *The Art of Being Ruled* and *Time and Western Man*. The preoccupation with art and politics continues, but the supernatural atmosphere of the narrative cannot be dismissed as mere decoration. While Lewis still employed the methods of satire in this work, he now had the goals of a romantic mythmaker. The youthful artist of "The Saltimbanques" who refused to forgo the splendor of destruction matured into a writer who wanted to fill the void his satire had created with a positive vision.

The mythmaking ambitions of *The Childermass* were readily apparent to Yeats, who in the same letter in which he compares *The Childermass* to *Gulliver's Travels* also notes the affinity between Lewis's book and his own *A Vision*. Yeats was particularly intrigued by the figure of the Bailiff, with whom, he believed, he had already become acquainted during his researches in automatic writing. Yeats amplified the point in a letter to his friend Olivia Shakespear: "The Baily is of course my Hunch-back—phase 28 [sic]—though L. does not know that . . ." (*L* 182). Lewis himself was both pleased and amused when he learned of the coincidence, writing to Yeats during a brief visit to Munich: "Since I have been away I have met nothing but hunchbacks—they have driven me in cars, blacked my shoes, served me with drinks at cafés, and sold me newspapers—so perhaps I may have disturbed by my activities here such figures as you mention" (*L* 182).

Yeats's recognition of the Hunchback in Lewis's work provides another clue to the identity of the Bailiff. The Hunchback occupies the twenty-sixth phase of the dialectical struggle between self and other that Yeats describes in *A Vision*. Yeats goes on to call this "the most difficult of the phases, and the first of those for which one can find few or no examples from personal experience."[30] The Hunchback seems, in fact, to be a relatively new phenomenon in the current gyre of European history, thus accounting for the paucity of examples. He represents the man who can no longer believe in the "old abstraction" of morality or religion. In the absence of an overarching structure of belief, he has no motive for action except his own selfish ambition; but as he finds selfishness ultimately unsatisfying, the Hunchback becomes jealous of others who believe themselves possessed of some larger purpose in life, or who feel the simple emotions that come with commitment to an ideal. Still, the Hunchback has a will like other men, and the will, Yeats tells us, must have an object. In the absence of a moral or religious abstraction, belief in which has become untenable, the Hunchback seeks a purely sensual object: Yeats gives, as an extreme example, "the Indian sage or saint who coupled with the roe."[31] One final point to note about the Hunchback: because he sees every individual life in relation to a "supersensual unity"—a purely physical universe stripped of all its abstractions—he becomes an exceedingly harsh judge of both other men and himself. Whatever terms men use to describe themselves will seem to the Hunchback a pretension, since he knows that man is nothing more than a random collection of atoms. Yeats does not specifically mention him, but one imagines the Gulliver of book four, trained by the strictly empirical "horses of instruction" to see his body for the *thing* that it is, as another example of a Hunchback. Indeed, the Hunchback is a natural-born satirist.

The Bailiff, more than others among Lewis's satirist-heroes, expresses that condition Yeats described as a "sinking-in of the body upon its supersensual source."[32] As befits a supernatural being, he has raised disillusionment with moral and religious abstraction (and the consequent preoccupation with the supersensual) to the level of a theological principle. We observe this tendency in his thinking on various occasions, as in this response to a youthful petitioner's question about the nature of the life after death:

"Substance, then, it is our aim to secure. But perhaps it may occur to you that my description of the especially concrete nature of what we seek to perpetuate precludes the idea of substance. I think that would be foolish, an effect of the snobbery of the old deep-seated dualism which attached disgrace to physical nature. When we set out to look for substance where else shall we find it but in the flesh? In the last analysis is not *substance* itself flesh?—as for that matter those excellent contemporary philosophers have shown who confound flesh and spirit to the advantage of the former and of physical law. . . . there is no mind but the body; and there is not singularity but in that. Every step by which you remove yourself from it is a step towards the One. As we interpret it, that is towards nothingness.—So to be unique—no one quite like us, that is the idea, is it not?—and for that substantial uniqueness, as well, to be solid, so that we can pinch it, pat it, and poke it—that is, there you have—am I not right?—the bottom of our desire." (*CM* 150)

Although the Bailiff says that he longs for the early days of Christianity (*CM* 162) and gives every appearance of occupying an important office in the bureaucracy of salvation, he no longer seems to subscribe to the doctrine of the soul's immortality. The Bailiff has been as much influenced by the advances of science and technology as an educated mortal, and he has adopted the metaphysic of "those excellent contemporary philosophers" such as Bergson, who, in a sort of last ditch effort to defend the soul against the encroachments of the machine, simply declared that the mind and body were one and the same. But how strong is the Bailiff's commitment to this new dispensation? The sarcastic tone of " 'no one quite like us, that is the idea, is it not?'" followed by the absurd image of someone pinching, patting, and poking his identity as if it were a kewpie doll recalls the figure of the Hunchback, who embraces the polar opposite of his ideal, finding in this gesture the only adequate expression of his disillusionment. So there we have the Bailiff's dilemma: he has an immense capacity, and an even greater need, to believe in something that transcends the visible world (the Hunchback is only one phase removed from the Saint in Yeats's scheme), but he cannot believe in the abstractions that science and philosophy have been systematically deconstructing since the Renaissance.

The Bailiff is without question the official villain of *The Childermass*. Historically, he incarnates what Lewis perceived as the cultural decadence of the immediate postwar years; mythologically, he expresses the particular spiritual dilemma responsible for this cultural decline. If the reader cannot discern the Bailiff's shortcomings for himself, he will have them pointed out to him by Hyperides, the leader of the opposition in the next world, who at times rehearses the arguments of *The Art of Being Ruled* and *Time and Western Man* almost verbatim.

Yet looking back on *The Childermass*, one cannot help feeling that Lewis had much the same relation to the Bailiff as Milton had to his arch-villain, Satan. Just as Satan was "the battleground for Milton's quarrel with himself,"[33] the Bailiff becomes an alter ego where Lewis dramatizes his own inner conflicts. On the one hand, Lewis wanted us to hate the Bailiff for having made the choice that many contemporary artists and intellectuals had made, a choice that Nietzsche had described in *The Genealogy of Morals* when he said, anticipating Yeats's Hunchback, that because man's will requires an aim, "it would sooner have the void for its purpose than be void of purpose."[34] The Bailiff suffers from the complete disillusionment of his ideals and ventilates his frustration on others through a series of nihilistic acts.

Nonetheless, whatever energy the latter part of *The Childermass* possesses belongs to the Bailiff. (Indeed, it almost seems as though his dynamic personality has drawn the life out of the surrounding narrative, rendering it the static dialogue that tried the patience of Yeats and most other readers.) While his forensic adversaries lecture, the Bailiff declaims, cajoles, pontificates, threatens, weeps, flatters, and, of course, broadcasts. When in response to one of Hyperides's lieutenants he says, " 'Let's cocker-up our answer under their noses and forestall them!' " (*CM* 263), he invokes the figure of Jonson's Volpone, thoroughly immoral in his protean genius but fascinating precisely on account of it. Here, too, we might also recall Lewis's portrait of the contemporary artist about 1914 as one who could satisfy an audience's demand "to be amused . . . By brilliant fellows like me. Letting off brilliant fireworks. Performing like dogs on tight ropes."[35]

But even if we reject this romantic interpretation of the Bailiff, which trusts the tale before the teller, and let ourselves be guided to a recognition of the Bailiff's essential villainy by the didactic presence of the author, it is still possible to see the Bailiff as the tragic hero of *The Childermass*, a rather sad figure deserving of our sympathies. Much like the traveling acrobats in "Les Saltimbanques," the Bailiff is compelled to perform before a marginally appreciative audience (from a bema "in the form of a lofty tapering Punch-and-Judy theatre" [*CM* 129]) without ever fully comprehending the reasons why. We hear a note of very human frustration through the ironic complaint quoted earlier, which ends: "I know things are not ideal God knows—life is life I can't help it—I'm in it too aren't I?" (*CM* 238).

The Bailiff can also be pitied as the victim of an unfortunate historical circumstance. Since 1789 (the date of the Lewisian Fall), Europeans have become progressively more hostile to the idea of aristocracy in all its forms, from the hereditary ruling classes to the creative minority of artistic and intellectual geniuses. Some of this animosity was justified, Lewis believed; much of it was not, however, particularly in those areas where an individual earned his claim to excellence. Now the Bailiff has an ugly hump in his back, and his head looks like the beak of a tortoise (*CM* 264). Since it is apparent that the Bailiff can take whatever form he wishes (man, beast, or god), it might be assumed that he has adopted these deformities to insult and perhaps intimidate his human charges. Hyperides accuses him of precisely this crime on several occasions. But the Bailiff responds that his ugly appearance has been forced upon him by the requirement of the liberal democratic state that all men become equal by a process of leveling down to the lowest common denominator. " 'From time to time as I stand here off my guard I find I am caught even now napping and once I allowed myself to be great for a whole day,' " the Bailiff explains to Hyperides, and he goes on to describe how he became the object of other men's suspicions and resentments, which left him isolated in a sort of "living death" (*CM* 282, 285). The Bailiff's lengthy narrative ends with this exchange:

> HYPERIDES: "What I understand you to say is that, given what men in the average are and their native hatred of excellence, then even a presentable human form symbolizes too much—that, called upon to be symbolic, the wise man would choose the most unpleasant body he could find?"
> The Bailiff assents by a smile. (*CM* 288)

That smile, however, belongs on the mask of tragedy. For the Bailiff has been driven to adopt a false identity in order to avoid the "living death" of ostracism from the human community.

What is interesting about the Bailiff's predicament is that it so closely parallels Lewis's. Lewis created the Bailiff as an example of the European intellectual who lacked the will to make difficult aesthetic and ethical choices. Yet Lewis himself was uncertain how to proceed in the postwar world, and his public persona during these years more closely resembled that of his villain than of his hero, James Pullman (who seems dramatically unworthy of the role). Lewis called himself the Enemy and wrote polemics and satires that if not intended to improve their readers (a project that assumes the liberal idea of human perfectability) might at least serve the marginally healthy as a prophylactic against further corruption. But Lewis's readers are often made to feel as though the decline in the human values the Enemy professes to defend has been so thorough and pervasive that virtually no one except Wyndham Lewis is capable of redemption. Lewis thus finds himself in a position not unlike that of the Bailiff, who, convinced that he inhabits a world of infants and morons incapable of affording him honor or companionship, figures that he might as well have the minor satisfaction of making the lives of his oppressors miserable. This impression of the Enemy as embittered Bailiff, permitting or denying admittance to a heaven that may or may not exist, is reinforced by Lewis's self-portraits of the period. Most notable among these is the early *Mr. Wyndham Lewis as a Tyro*, which depicts the artist as a toothy gangster.[36] (Interestingly, the Bailiff of the sequel volumes operates lucrative drug and liquor rackets inside the Heavenly City.) This same persona emerges in the narrator of *Snooty Baronet*, whose embittered romanticism is manifest when he quotes the opening lines of Keats's *Endymion* to describe the feeling of a rifle shot, which kills a man he has convinced himself is really a puppet. I suggested earlier that a work like *Snooty Baronet* should be read ironically, with an awareness that the author's true values lie just beyond the horizon of the text. Indeed, *The Childermass*, like *Snooty Baronet*, asserts its values by a satiric method that hearkens back to Apuleius's picaresque tale *The Golden Ass*, which presents such a horrific picture of the world as to throw us back upon our intuitive sense of the sacredness of life.

This may be an overly disingenuous reading of Lewis's work. Lewis usually does more tearing down than building up, and if he has an ideal vision in *The Childermass*, he never really lets us see what it is. While he leads us to expect some kind of revelation, some leap of faith at the end, none materializes. The penultimate line of the novel belongs to one of the Hyperideans who exclaims, pointing to the Bailiff, " 'Who is to be *real*—this hyperbolical puppet or we? Answer, oh destiny!' " (*CM* 320). But the idea that faceless destiny, and not the human intellect, should make decisions properly belongs to the Bailiff, not to Lewis's official spokesman. This brings us to perhaps the most troubling feature of *The Childermass*: it comes to no conclusion, nor did Lewis attempt to provide one for another twenty years. As an artist and intellectual, he seems to have been as lost and uncertain as the resentful Hunchback who had dominated the action of his supernatural morality play.

6

The Human Age

Favoring the Divine

In Scaled Invention

Polemon's cry at the end of *The Childermass*—" 'Answer, oh destiny!' "—marks the exhaustion of a millenarian impulse that extended back through *BLAST* and "Les Saltimbanques." Lewis's desire for social and political apocalypse weakened during the war (though *The Caliph's Design* still shows traces of it) and died with the British General Strike of 1926, which, instead of achieving Sorel's "Napoleonic battle" between classes, fizzled out after nine tense but peaceful days with little change in the status quo.[1] By the mid-1930s, Lewis sounded like a jaded old revolutionary, complaining about how the world had *"fallen back"* from the future he and his contemporaries had tried to create for it (*BB* 256).

An important sign of Lewis's change in temperament was the modified *scale* of his writing in the 1930s. While the surviving fragments of "The Man of the World" retain something of the grandiose conception of the original, his major works of the next decade (*Snooty Baronet*, *Men without Art*, *Blasting and Bombardiering*, *The Revenge for Love*, and *The Vulgar Streak*) have a narrower focus. Each of them is less concerned with metaphysics than with localized events. Although Lewis may have been forced to this position by disillusionment, he soon exploited the resources that this new literary territory afforded him, as we can see in what is often acknowledged as his most well-crafted novel, *The Revenge for Love*.

As several critics have noted, *The Revenge for Love* has many elements of a popular best-seller. While *The Childermass* showed the world in a glass darkly, and *The Apes of God* mocked an artistic coterie, *The Revenge for Love* spins a tale directly out of the headlines. The novel opens as Percy Hardcaster, an English communist agent, tries and fails to escape from a Spanish prison. After recovering from the bullet wound that cost him part of a leg, Hardcaster returns to England, where he is lionized by London's "salon-Reds," middle-class artists and intellectuals sympathetic to international communism. On the outer fringes of this group we meet Victor and Margot Stamp. Victor is a young, rugged-looking Australian artist whose modest talents have brought him nothing in the way of material success; Margot (not legally Victor's wife) is a quiet and perceptive woman whose being is determined by her absolute devotion to Victor. Unable to make a living as an artist, Victor becomes involved with two well-heeled fellow travelers named O'Hara and Abershaw, who first employ him in the "manufacture" of lost Van Gogh masterpieces and later send him on a gunrunning expedition into Spain. There he and Margot link up with Hardcaster, who, disgusted with the hypocrisies of his English admirers, is only too happy to return to the dirty but honest work of revolution. What none of these three realize is that O'Hara and Abershaw intend to use Victor as a decoy and have already betrayed him to the Spanish authorities in a move calculated to protect the real gun shipment. Hardcaster, who has developed a genuine affection for Victor and Margot, is captured once again as he attempts to warn them of the double cross; later, in his prison cell, he reads a newspaper account of how the couple perished in the mountains attempting to escape back into France.

If *The Revenge for Love* stands out from among his other novels for its "unaccustomed emotional resonance,"[2] it is because Lewis shows us the other side of his savage indignation, a pastoralism that the harshness of satire deliberately obscures from view. Here the angry prophet is moderated by the good shepherd, and the insistence upon a radically transcendent absolute is replaced by a willingness to accept an immanent one. In the lines below, Hardcaster experiences a kind of homely epiphany as he contemplates the face of the man who has just shot him in the leg:

> And as he idly examined the stern, traditional features under the warder's
> cap they began to dissolve into the stars around them, and Don Percy

became one with that vast and beautiful neutral system, of the objective universe of things, which cared nothing for the Social Revolution but flattered him into thinking—upon moonlight nights—that he was a Beethoven who had been forced into politics by poverty. And he hoped his mother would air his shirt against his return—for he was going home after this, to his mother in Edgbaston. Percy was definitely tired: so he thought he would go home. And the flash of the carbine a foot from his face and the tremendous roaring of it in his head made no difference at all to his plans for immediate withdrawal from these troublesome scenes—a man's world, yes, but he was through with the whole business. (*RFL* 43)

The passage is unmistakably Lewisian in its presentation of man as an object in a universe of objects. But here we find sympathy for the individual who almost hears the stars addressing him, and scant irony in the account of his desire to return to his mother's house in an industrial suburb of Birmingham.

A related sign of the changing emphasis in Lewis's fiction is the intensely *personal* quality of *The Revenge for Love*. Lewis had always been an autobiographical writer, but he kept a long emotional distance from his material. We know from external evidence, for example, that the events narrated in *Tarr* closely mirror his prewar experiences in Paris. He tells us in *Rude Assignment* that the figure of Tarr "may be seen [as] a caricatural self-portrait of sorts"(*RA* 165) and that Kreisler expresses not only the "melodramatic nihilism" of the typical young European intellectual of the period but also the brooding and self-destructive side of his own personality that he discovered through his reading of Nietzsche and Dostoevsky (*RA* 162). The novel's heroine, Bertha Lunken, was also drawn from life, having been based upon an attractive German woman named Ida, with whom Lewis had had a painful four-year affair.[3] Yet Lewis keeps *Tarr*'s people at a distance by rendering them as caricatures so extreme in their fidelity to an idea that they could not possibly be mistaken for persons one might actually have known. In this passage from *Tarr*, for example, Bertha seems to conform more to a universal paradigm than to a particular individual of Lewis's acquaintance:

Bertha's was the intellectually-fostered Greek type of German handsomeness. It is that beauty that makes you wonder, when you meet it, if German mothers have replicas and photographs of the Venus of Milo in their rooms during the first three months of their pregnancy. It is also found in the pages of Prussian art periodicals, the arid, empty intellectualism of Munich. She had been a heavy baby. Her body now, a self-indulgent athlete's, was strung to heavy motherhood. (*T* 51)

Similarly, the schematized presentation of the male protagonists leads us to see them more as archetypes than as unique persons. It is thus not surprising that Lewis qualified his remark that Tarr was a "self-portrait of sorts" with the claim that this applied to his physique "though not of course [to] his character or behaviour" (*RA* 165).

In *The Revenge for Love*, however, Lewis invests his characters with far more complex emotional and interpersonal lives. As Valerie Parker notes, this novel, in contrast to *Tarr*, "takes love seriously, and suggests that, like art, it demands loyalty and dedication."[4] Margot and Victor have nothing: no money, no security, no power. Victor wants to be an artist, but it is apparent that he lacks the talent to be anything more than second-rate; Margot has no visible talents, and worse, her head is filled with all sorts of romantic clichés about art and life, gleaned from her desultory readings in Wordsworth, John Ruskin, and Virginia Woolf (*RFL* 274–79). But Victor and Margot do love one another, and that love, though often sentimental, is absolute: it does not change according to the advantages or disadvantages their relationship brings them (and their love, in material terms, brings them only the latter). This immutable love gives them heroic stature in a world caught up in self-gratification, but it also makes them an object of resentment for those like the gunrunners O'Hara and Abershaw, who prostitute their humanitarian principles for wealth and power. In the last analysis, power will not give a man or woman value:

> It was *their* reality, that of Victor and herself, that was marked down to be discouraged and abolished, and it was *they* that the others were trying to turn into phantoms and so to suppress. It was a mad notion, but it was just as if they had engaged in a battle of wills, to decide who should possess the most *reality*—just as men fought each other for money, or fought each other for food. (*RFL* 158)

Modernity thrives upon change and abhors the presence of an absolute, as Margot seems to realize the moment that she appears in the novel:

> If she could have hidden her love away from fate, then fate would have turned elsewhere, have been kinder to Victor! She was the cause of all the ill-luck that came his way. It was because *she* was there that no pleasant thing

ever happened. It was *the revenge for love!* This, on the part of fate, was the revenge for love. There was no way out, unless she could kill love. And to do that she must first kill herself. But even then love would not die! Once to have been loved as she did Victor was enough—it was compromising to the *n*th degree. He was a marked man! Even if he did not return it, fate would never forget. Victor would always be, whatever happened to her, *the man who had been loved*, in the way she had done (it was *the way* that she had loved was at the bottom of the matter). She *knew!* But there was no help for it. (*RFL* 61)

Love makes this novel a tragedy, whereas the absence of love in *Tarr* and all the intervening works made them comedies that included occasional tragic episodes. Thus Tarr can explain the death of Kreisler with the assistance of a pet "theory":

I believe that all the fuss he made was an attempt to get out of Art back into Life again, like a fish flopping about who had got into the wrong tank. = It would be more exact to say, *back into sex.* = He was trying to get back into sex again out of a little puddle of art where he felt he was gradually expiring. = What I mean is this. He was an art-student without any talent, and was leading a dull, slovenly existence like thousands of others in the same case. (*T* 302)

Tarr holds forth on the subject to his girlfriend after having "waded through a good deal of food" at a favorite café. His treatment of Kreisler is detached, mockingly academic; the German is a species of vertebrate that has had an unfortunate mishap, not another human being like himself who has lived and suffered. Kreisler's corpse is hardly more real to Tarr than was Soltyk's (the man killed in the duel) to Kreisler.

The equivalent scene in *The Revenge for Love* occurs at the very end of the novel, when the imprisoned Hardcaster learns from a newspaper that Victor and Margot have been killed in their attempt to escape through the Pyrenees. Hardcaster is a seasoned professional in the business of sacrificing means for an end and shows no emotion at the loss of his two comrades, for whom he was more or less responsible. No *outward* emotion, that is:

But meanwhile a strained and hollow voice, part of a sham-culture outfit, but tender and halting, as if dismayed at the sound of its own bitter words, was talking in his ears, in a reproachful singsong. It was denouncing him out of the past, where alone now it was able to articulate; it was singling him out as a man who led people into mortal danger, people who were dear beyond expression to the possessor of the passionate, the artificial, the unreal, yet penetrating, voice, and crying to him now to give back, she implored him, the young man, Absalom, whose life he had had in his keeping, and who had somehow, unaccountably, been lost, out of the world and out of Time! He saw a precipice. And the eyes of the mask of THE INJURED PARTY dilated in a spasm of astonished self-pity. And down the front of the mask rolled a sudden tear, which fell upon the dirty floor of the prison. (*RFL* 340–41)

No amount of posturing or theorizing can mitigate the unbearable sadness that comes from remembering the deaths of Victor and Margot.

But the most radical innovation in *The Revenge for Love* is indicated by the feminine voice in this concluding passage. We have not heard the voices of women very often in Lewis's fiction; indeed, in his most purely imaginative work, *The Childermass*, women gain admittance to the celestial city through an entrance separate from that of the men, and they never appear in the narrative. A bitter and admonitory feminine voice *is* heard on one occasion in *Snooty Baronet*, when Snooty imagines the Shan Van Vocht, "snooty sibyl of the Gael," grinding out her ceaseless imprecations against a corrupt human race. But not until this novel does Lewis explore the love that underlies the outrage of the "poor old woman" of the Celtic myth. Because they were traditionally relegated to positions of inferior status in society, women were the ideal observers of the life of action, and the ideal mourners when foolish actions resulted in death. Throughout the novel, Margot has premonitions of the evil fate that awaits Victor and herself:

"I want to be in London again, with my Victor!" she began to cry, her voice growing stronger, and coming to sound more like his Margot's now. "Then I will die, my love—I will gladly die!"

"Why die?" he asked matter-of-factly and mawkishly at the same time. "There's no need to die."

"This place, Victor, is more than I can bear! You must come away with me too and leave it now before it is too late! *Too late!*" she whimpered, very sensationally, as if to herself. "Victor, my darling. Oh please, before anything happens."

"Happens! What can happen, Mar?" he asked, almost venturing upon a little sceptical laughter.

"I don't know, Victor. Listen to your Margot this once though, Victor. There's something wrong. I can't just tell you what it is." (*RFL* 271–72)

Margot's voice descends to melodrama on this occasion and others in the novel, for it has been informed by a "sham-culture" of the romantic clichés that Lewis sought to debunk in his satires and polemics. Indeed, from the standpoint of her development as a character, the climactic moment of her intellectual life comes in the very next chapter, when, lying by a stream in the Pyrenees with a volume of Ruskin and reflecting upon recent events, she realizes that nature is not the "sunny dream" implied in the works of her masters. But despite the encrustation of B-movie dialogue, Margot's expression of concern for her husband can be no more easily dismissed than the lament of the anonymous Great Mother at the end who calls out for the lost Absalom. When she leaves her copy of Ruskin lying on the grass and goes back into the village to advise Hardcaster that she and her husband want nothing more to do with international intrigue, she proves herself the sole hero of the novel. She alone sees that the emperor wears no clothes (that the gunrunning scheme is a plot to eliminate Victor, and that political idealism is another mask for brute force), and she alone has the courage to stand up to this encroachment of the unreal, though sadly her efforts come too late.

It is difficult to say what motivated Lewis's changed attitude toward women in this and subsequent novels, all of which feature a female character who occupies a privileged position of insight.[5] From *Tarr*, "Cantleman's Spring Mate," and his other early fiction, it is obvious that Lewis, like D. H. Lawrence, saw women as enemies of the transcendental aspirations of the modern artist. On the one hand, they stood for the instinctual aspect of life (sexuality), which threatened to dissolve the concentration required for the production of art; on the other, they were at the center of the bourgeois family (logical and biological outcome of sexuality), which could hardly accommodate the Odyssean wanderings of the creative mind. Marriage, the untimely death of his mother, and an extended period of illness may have contributed to Lewis's increased sympathy with what he would have perceived as the weaker sex. Whatever the reason, domesticity holds the place of honor in *The Revenge for Love*: Margot's tender concern for Victor's dignity and well-being emerges as the novel's highest good.

Lewis's latent hostility toward the grand designs of history in *The Revenge for Love* becomes explicit in his next important novel, *Self Condemned*, published almost twenty years later. *Self Condemned* tells the story of Professor René Harding, who decides on the eve of World War II that he can no longer in good conscience teach the record of criminal acts that passes for Western history and who resigns his position at a British university for an uncertain future in Canada. There he and his wife, Hester, occupy a one-room flat in a seedy Toronto hotel. Months of loneliness and a devastating fire that destroys the hotel finally drive Hester to suicide and René to a nervous breakdown. He recovers a semblance of mental health after a few months in a Catholic seminary and later returns to academic life, accepting a position at a major American university.

Oddly enough, though the setting of *Self Condemned* spans two continents, the action of the novel focuses so claustrophobically upon the lives of the two protagonists that we almost forget the world at large. When René Harding and his wife emigrate to Canada, they effectively banish history from their lives. While the Second World War rages across the Atlantic, the Hardings' world is completely contained within the hotel room—"twenty five feet by twelve"—that the two of them inhabit for almost the duration of their stay. Accordingly, small things in this world take on a value inconceivable in Lewis's earlier novels. The Hardings (whose experiences closely parallel those of the Lewises during the war) live in virtual isolation from their somewhat xenophobic Canadian neighbors, but perhaps because of this, the narrator is careful to register their gratitude for even the smallest kindness extended to them. This is apparent in their attitude toward the hotel manageress, Mrs. McAffie, whom Lewis describes in a way that shows how he could treat a character sympathetically when he wanted to:

> Mrs. McAffie was their favourite figure. They developed an affection for this flying wraith, with the faintly rouged cheeks, who dashed, flew and darted everywhere, as though she desired to get rid of every remaining piece of flesh on her bones. She was tall and still enjoyed, in the manner of an afterglow, a vanished grace. She was known as Affie in the Room, where she was a welcome apparition. (*SC* 203)

The refocusing of Lewis's interest from large- to small-scale problems, represented by René Harding's translation from history professor to hotel resident, was accompanied by an increasing concern with life (as opposed to art) and less inclination to attack others through satire. For example, the narrator observes that Affie endeared herself to René in an early conversation "by the sincerity of her horror at the new war," and that although occasionally nosey and mischievous, she was "not inhuman" (*SC* 203, 209).

From here he proceeds to a generalization that would have been highly uncharacteristic twenty years earlier: "What René objected to in the American system—a modified form of which exists in Canada—was its inhumanity. They had got involved in a violent and unintelligent dance, in which all reference to the happiness and interests of the human individual had been abandoned" (*SC* 209).

Although such sentiments might indicate a late conversion to humanism, Lewis continues to argue in *Self Condemned* that concern with the human must be rooted in an apprehension of the divine. Neither in this novel nor the ones that follow does Lewis adopt a humanist position, if we understand humanism as a philosophy that sees man as the ultimate measure of things. An old friend and disciple of René's says as much when he writes: "'Professor Harding's way of seeing the world is, then, analogous to the Vision of the Saints. But it is not necessarily in any way connected with saintliness. What this system amounts to, in reality, is a taking to its logical conclusion the humane, the tolerant, the fastidious'" (*SC* 95). "Fastidious" is a key term here, balancing "humane" with its suggestion of the continuing need for careful discriminations among the things of this world, and reminding us that Lewis's religious sensibility remains hieratic rather than mystical. If *Self Condemned* does represent a change in Lewis's outlook, it marks a stronger commitment to the belief that the divine exists not only for its own sake, but also as the measure of man's essential humanity (thus the "Vision of the Saints" need not be connected with "saintliness"), and that, conversely, the humane can serve as an opening to the divine.

Lewis was not alone among his modernist contemporaries in evolving toward this position. An interesting parallel to *Self Condemned* is offered by the *Pisan Cantos*, in which Ezra Pound counsels the reader to "Learn of the green world what can be thy place / In scaled invention or true artistry."[6] Imprisoned by the government for alleged treason at the end of World War II, Pound lamented history's failure to produce the paradise on earth toward which both the *Cantos* and Mussolini's fascist state intended. (Similarly, Lewis believed that everyone had ignored his visions and admonitions, a fact bitterly alluded to in the title of René Harding's last prewar book, *The Secret History of World War II*.) Having been repudiated by history and locked up in a steel cage, Pound now had ample opportunity to focus his attention on homelier things: an ant crossing the floor, the smell of mint, the design of a eucalyptus seed. Although he differs from Lewis in his attraction to a microcosm of natural objects and events (Lewis preferred a more civilized environment), he shared with his former vorticist colleague a sense that this scaled world provided an immanent expression of the divine. Indeed, nowhere does Pound seem to be on such easy terms with his beloved gods and goddesses as in these later *Cantos*.

René Harding does not survive his self-imposed exile intact. Although for a time he finds solace among the seminarians and replies "Yes" when asked whether or not he is becoming a Catholic, his restless intelligence eventually crowds out whatever spiritual sense allowed him to feel God's presence. ("He did not repudiate [the reality of God], but merely ceased to experience it" [*SC* 389]). René proceeds to dig himself in "with concrete and steel" against any future misfortune by becoming a respected citizen of academe, and by the time he accepts his professorship at a prestigious American university, he is little more than the "glacial shell of a man," who once proposed a new way of thinking about history (*SC* 400, 407). Still, the revaluation of the humane that has occurred in the wake of René's tragedy opens up for Lewis the possibility of a comic resolution to a work of fiction; and he began to exploit this possibility in the sequels to *The Childermass* that occupied the better part of his last years.

The Theology of Imperfection

Lewis finally returned to his magnum opus in 1951, after a successful radio version of *The Childermass* brought him financial support from the BBC. He completed two additional volumes, *Monstre Gai* and *Malign Fiesta*, and renamed the entire work *The Human Age*. Both Lewis and the world had changed in the twenty-odd years since the appearance of *The Childermass*, and so it is not surprising that books two and three of the series differ at many points from book one. Whereas *The Childermass* reads like a literary experiment, with its complex verbal manner and intellectual preoccupations, *Monstre Gai* and *Malign Fiesta* have a style as straightforward as that of a Graham Greene novel, and almost as much action. In *Monstre Gai*, we follow Pullman and Satters as they pass through the gates of what is now cryptically referred to as Third City, and once there, they find themselves increasingly caught up in the intrigue between demonic and divine powers for its control. By the end of the novel, the political situation has become so anarchic that they are forced to flee with the help of the Bailiff, who, to their chagrin, takes them not to Heaven but to Matapolis, his native city in Hell. Here, at the beginning of *Malign Fiesta*, Pullman comes to the notice of Lord Sammael, a cross between Milton's Satan and a modern corporate executive, who invites Pullman to become his chief counselor in a radical scheme to strip himself and his followers of their immortality and thus establish a "Human Age." Pullman believes that he has no choice but to advise the Devil, though he feels ill at ease about this, and increasingly finds himself looking to Sammael's ancient adversary, God. *Malign Fiesta* ends when two of God's angels burst into Pullman's flat to take him away, presumably to Heaven.

The final two volumes of *The Human Age* return us to the questions that have engaged us from the beginning of this study: how did a writer without strong religious convictions in the traditional sense find himself writing about God and the Devil? And what value should we assign to the heterodox Christian theology that emerges from these works?

One way to resolve these issues is to deny the religious content of *The Human Age* altogether. Fredric Jameson has adopted this approach, commenting that Lewis's "is an afterlife utterly lacking in transcendence. It is, indeed . . . a resolutely materialistic one: 'There is no such thing as the supernatural,' the Devil remarks authoritatively to Pullman" [*MF* 62].[7] We have noted before that as *The Childermass* goes along, the supernatural world does come to resemble life on earth. *Monstre Gai* and *Malign Fiesta* continue this tactic, acknowledging, for example, the emergence of a new international order at the end of World War II. As Jameson sees it, "God is . . . one powerful angel among many, and the conflicts in this afterworld are little more moral (but no less ideological) than those of the Cold War."[8] Perhaps Lewis intended his abstract vision of the afterlife as a laboratory where he could examine the zeitgeist away from the distractions of ordinary time and space; or he might have erected this theological edifice only to knock it down, thus proving Sammael's claim in *Malign Fiesta* that the supernatural is merely "one of the customary illusions" (*MF* 62).

The first and most obvious problem with this argument is its reliance upon the word of a Devil who consistently underestimates the position of his adversary and who, at the end of the trilogy, has been foiled by God in his attempt to humanize the divine. Sammael's failure in *Malign Fiesta* has already been anticipated by the collapse of the Bailiff's municipal regime in *Monstre Gai*.[9] The Bailiff had also operated on the assumption that nothing transcended power politics, setting forth his position at a lavish formal reception, the occasion of his first meeting with Pullman in *Monstre Gai* (" 'Ah ha, welcome Pullman—welcome to Eternity!' "), where he addresses an admiring audience on the subject of contemporary morality:

> " Well, let us get back to the great changes which have taken place. As we all know, and can see for ourselves, the *Good* and the *Bad* are blurred, are they not, in the modern age? We no longer see things in stark black and white. We know that all men are much the same. An amoralist . . . such is the modern man. And in the same way in these supernatural regions. It is a terrible come-down all round. What was once the Devil (to whom one 'sold one's soul' and so forth) well today, he is a very unconvinced *devil*, and our Padishah, as we call him, he is a very unconvinced Angel. I know *both*, so I know what I am talking about." (*MG* 112–13)

But the Bailiff abandons Third City for Hell when factions opposed to his corrupt practices drive him from power; in this instance, right does seem to have been a match for might. And Sammael loses Hell itself by assuming that God has no more concern for right and wrong than he does. Both of these events oblige the reader to at least consider that there *is* such a thing as the supernatural.

Secondly, although Lewis no doubt believed that force usually directed the course of history, Pullman's development in *Monstre Gai* and *Malign Fiesta* shows that force per se was without value. Like every successful artist, Pullman had a nose for patronage, and upon arrival in Third City, he thinks to himself, " What had to be discovered was where the true power was to be found. . . . the point of maximum power had to be located, and those possessed of this maximum were the only safe circles to have any truck with" (*MG* 86–87). The locus of power *within* the city is not the only issue; certainly, no one could ignore the mysterious blitzes directed against Third City from both Hell and Heaven, which bear a ghastly resemblance to atomic bomb blasts:

> The bottle [Pullman] had been holding in his hand whizzed away, and, in the total blackness of the room, it might as well have flown out of the window. He lay where he was, half-stunned. There was a series of deafening reports—like blows upon a gigantic gong, accompanied by explosions of light similar to a photographer's flash bomb, and then a crack so loud that Pullman could hear no more for some time. . . . he looked up and saw in the sky a fiery cross. It exactly bisected one of the large panes of the window. It was blood-red, and quivered upon the blue-black of the sky. . . . then a shock,

as elemental as that of an earthquake, picked him up and hurled him through the air. (*MG* 150)

But while acknowledging the reality of force, Pullman is not a man easily intimidated by the threat of personal harm, often facing dangers that cause others to run and hide. Besides this, Pullman's earliest efforts to rationalize his alliance with the Bailiff (which precede the apocalyptic rumblings noted above) imply serious misgivings about the relationship:

> As unattached as the "lone wolf" man, of the fierce modern "genius" type, believing not in God, in class, in party, but solely in himself, it was all one to him who it was supporting Pullman; anyone who did so was a good man. He was not, of course, so utterly faithful to the god Pullman as that suggested. Solipsistic he was in principle, but no man is so watertightly an ego as all that. He had started life a devout Catholic, for instance: and that first self haunted him to some extent. (*MG* 146)

As the narrative progresses and the inhumanity of his demonic patrons becomes clear to him, Pullman feels increasingly guilty—that is, he recognizes that one day his actions will be measured against a standard higher than that of power. Pullman's crisis first comes to a head as Third City descends into chaos and he finds himself in a huge plaza filled with partisans of the city's four primary factions (including the Bailiff's), roughly corresponding to what Lewis saw as the major ideologies of the twentieth century: liberalism, communism, fascism, and Christianity. Pullman again reflects upon his situation:

> simply in order to be as comfortable as possible in Third City, I accept [the Bailiff's] patronage. I come here from Earth, with a Big Name, and I sell my Big Name to the highest bidder. The values behind that Big Name either were of a trivial kind on Earth, or, if they were real and important values, I now betray them in this spectral life—spectral life—as such I think of it. But there is my big mistake. This is no more a spectral life than the life on Earth. (*MG* 221)

Although he would prefer to maintain what he thought of on earth as a godlike artistic detachment, Pullman now becomes aware that he will have to make a choice among these competing positions sooner or later: "He had known that there was such a thing as the Right and the Wrong; that there was no such thing, for a man, as 'Beyond good and evil.' That was merely the self-advertising eccentricity of an intellectual" (*MG* 220–21).

With this confession on Pullman's part, we can begin to see the possibility of some positive values transcending the "nonmoral calculus of sheer power" that Jameson believes governs Lewis's system.[10] The operative expression here is the brief prepositional phrase "for a man." From the beginning of his career, Lewis presented himself as an artist more interested in ideas than in people. He subscribed to T. E. Hulme's theory that the cultural crisis leading to World War I stemmed from Renaissance humanism, which, despite claims to the contrary, thrust man into the position once occupied by God. As a human being, man could accomplish good works, but as a god, he could be depended upon to abuse his fellow man and his natural environment. The function of art and philosophy thus became, in Lewis's view, the recalling of man to the status of human being. Practically speaking, this meant that the artist should turn away from his culture's preoccupation with the self and toward a study of the "Not-self," broadly defined as all the forces that resist and transcend selfhood.

By the late 1920s, however, Lewis realized that the strategy was backfiring or at least was practiced by others in a spirit alien to his own. To some extent, European intellectuals had redirected their attention from men to the impersonal forces that mold them, and in that sense, art and science were more objective, more oriented toward the Not-self than had been the case at the turn of the century. But Lewis also observed that this ostensible change in subject matter had *not* been accompanied by a fundamental change in consciousness. Rather, it seemed that modernism was yet another chapter in the post-Renaissance history of man's increasing satisfaction in the exercise of his intellectual powers. The arts and sciences had created abstract systems of thought that functioned as masks behind which men could indulge and advance their self-interests with impunity as never before. In the 1930s, therefore, in reaction against the abuses of the impersonality he had once championed, Lewis turned from the universal to the particular. As noted before, the domestic began to take its place alongside the philosophical and the political; instead of focusing upon overarching ideas, he concerned himself more directly with the persons who often became the instruments of those ideas.

A parallel movement in his visual art will further clarify the logic of this transformation. By the eve of the First World War, Lewis had assimilated the lessons of cubism and was producing highly abstract compositions.

Indeed, many years later, in a letter to the art critic Charles Handley-Read, where he briefly outlined his artistic development, Lewis drew his correspondent's attention to "Mr. W. L.'s complete divorce from the external sensuous reality in 1913–14" (*L* 504). Within a few years of this early abstract work, however, Lewis began to readmit living persons into his art. This was already evident in the pictures of his *Guns* exhibition in 1919. Lewis commented in *Rude Assignment* that "though decidedly angular," these pictures "were naturalistic" (*RA* 137); and in the letter to Handley-Read, Lewis affirmed that his career from this point on could be viewed as "Mr. W. L.'s return to nature" (though the fact that some of his later paintings are executed in "the mixed idiom of pure-abstraction-and-stylized-nature" suggests that the "nature" he returned to was less Newtonian than the one he had once left behind).

This return to nature and the human figure was not a celebration of man; rather, Lewis came to believe, no doubt because of the relative ease with which the abstract style had established itself in a bourgeois culture that should have rejected it, that it was as silly and presumptuous to think that you could banish nature from a painting as to think that you could reproduce it in every detail. "I never associated myself with the jejune folly," wrote Lewis in the foreword to the *Guns* catalog (which he quotes in *Rude Assignment*), "that would assert one week that a Polynesian totem was the only formula by which the mind of man—Modern Man, heaven help him!—might be expressed: the next, that only in some compromise between Ingres and the Chinese the golden rule of self expression might be found. . . . " (*RA* 137). He now saw that the modern abstractionist occupied exactly the same position as the nineteenth-century naturalist in the sense that both believed in the power of man to reshape the world or himself according to his own preconceptions. Lewis still wanted to acknowledge a world he had not (and could not have) created. At the beginning of the century, one dissented from humanism by producing abstract art; now that the abstract style was becoming normative and, in effect, the vehicle for expressing man's domination of the world, one dissented by becoming a naturalist in art.

Paradoxically, then, the return to the particular, the domestic, and the naturalistic had a religious motivation: the recognition of limits, the awareness that one is always "bound back." This outlook was implicit in his earliest artistic and polemical work but becomes wholly explicit in some of his late paintings (many on religious themes, including *Jehovah the*

Thunderer and *Small Crucifixion Series I–IV* [11]) and of course in the major work of his old age, *The Human Age*.

Lewis's renewed appreciation for the efforts of such inherently flawed human beings as Victor and Margot Stamp, René Harding, and James Pullman emerges in *The Human Age* as a theological doctrine that holds that man should be valued not because he can be godlike but because, on the contrary, he is imperfect. His imperfection obliges him to exercise the faculty that makes him interesting and occasionally admirable: intelligence, that is, an ability to discriminate among alternatives. As Pullman explains to an acquaintance in *Monstre Gai*:

> "Just for one moment attempt to imagine yourself as an archangel like our friend the Padishah. What would it feel like to be that? If you were a young Catholic as I was once, before my English public school, your Thomist instructor would inform you that angels were spiritual intellectual substances. Their purity is equal to that of God, only it is limited of course. But we do not inhabit a world of artifice and even verbal icing. For *me* the archangel nicknamed by you and your friends 'Padishah,' for me he is an athletic, perfectly ignorant entirely unphilosophic young man. He is a big baby, who does not know the ABC of life. If he were willing to have a free conversation . . . he would turn out to be naif to an unbelievable degree, a mass of little conventional clichés, and with a basic incapacity to think. . . . Now to be a real angel, and, just on the same principle, to be God, you must be entirely stupid. We are compelled deeply to admire such perfections. And it is in no way to take away from the splendid pre-eminence of God—in no way to diminish one's awe of His might—if one said one did not desire to *be* God, or to be an angel. . . . Perfection repels me: it is (it must be) so colossally stupid. Here—in Third City—we are frail, puny, short-lived, ridiculous, *but* we are superior, preferable to the Immortals with whom we come in contact." (*MG* 139–40)

In some ways, this represents quite a turnaround for a writer who had spent most of his career as a practitioner of satire, that fine art of gibbeting human beings after you have held them up to high standards and found them wanting, as you inevitably will. On the other hand, Pullman's thesis can also be seen as the logical conclusion of the satiric worldview: the satirist never really expected man to be perfect and, in fact, tries to warn against men who believe that they are.

This new theology (or anthropology) of imperfection offers Lewis certain practical advantages. To begin, it solves the long-standing problem of how to see man as a limited creature without seeming to hate him for his limitations. By dispensing with satire's necessary (and covert) fiction of an ideal, Lewis has less immediate reason to express disillusionment with mankind. Moreover, the thought of intelligent but frail men arrayed against infinitely powerful immortals sharpens the tragic vision that lay behind Lewis's best work. Until *The Apes of God*, Lewis seriously entertained the idea that a character could avoid tragedy by means of his commitment to art. Yet such figures as Ker-Orr, Tarr, and Pierpoint remain the most dimly realized in Lewis's fiction, while the failures (Brobdingnag, Kreisler, and Zagreus) command our attention. As early as *Snooty Baronet*, and certainly by the time of *Self Condemned*, it must have dawned on Lewis that the artist was interesting not because he differed from other people, but because, though an artist, he shared their failings.

The theology of imperfection is also connected with another change in Lewis's worldview during the post–World War II period: a moderation in his political sentiments. Lewis the satirist had demanded that his reader accept two premises: first, that the past was nobler than the present, and second, that *other* people (that is, not the satirist and his reader) were responsible for this decline. An emphasis on the past and on the faults of others are the essential components of the classic conservative position. But conservatism had really been a kind of accidental by-product for Lewis, who simply wanted to point out the limited nature of the species, past, present, and future, in others and ourselves. (This goes some distance toward explaining Lewis's sometimes puzzling assertion that his sympathies lay with the Left, not the Right.[12]) Pullman's theology of imperfection achieves that goal, without insisting that the fault lies outside the self. Indeed, Pullman dogmatically asserts that he is as imperfect as anyone else. The onus of guilt having now been lifted from the other, it becomes possible for Lewis to demonstrate sympathy for those who are patently inferior or dull: their difference from the artist is only a matter of degree, not of kind.

Valuing the Human, Favoring the Divine

Despite Pullman's increasing disenchantment with the Bailiff, whom he finds less dogmatic than the leaders of the other factions, he follows the Bailiff to his exile in Hell. But this translation only sharpens the dilemma that confronted him in Third City. Now instead of having to deal with a petty Capone, who claims that good and evil have become passé, he finds himself uneasily drawn to the patronage of the Devil himself.

Not long after their arrival in Matapolis, the Bailiff tells Pullman, " 'I am going to take you now to see the Devil in person. . . . You must learn to think of him as Sammael. It was by that name that he was known when he lived on equal terms with God in the beginning of the world' " (*MF* 32). They proceed across town in a chauffeur-driven car to Sammael's headquarters:

> When they entered the room, which was a mediumsized office, a tall dark man rose from a swivel chair, in which he had been seated before a desk, and allowed his eyes to rest upon the stranger. Pullman cast his eyes down, and his mouth assumed those strict and staid lines, which were survivals of his religious youth. What he had seen, before he lowered his eyes, was a classically handsome, young middle-aged man, the regulation six-foot-three of the angel, heavy shoulders, of superbly athletic build. His head was thrown back; it was large, with thick, dark, well-ordered hair. His face was a pale mask, with strong black eyes which said nothing, but contained a conventionally amiable light, the lips smiled slightly. What he most looked like was an American of high managerial class, Indian blood, perhaps, accounting for an invincible severity. (*MF* 33)

This description unexpectedly returns us to the beginnings of Lewis's career. The exotic background and managerial status recall the Raza Khan of *Mrs. Dukes' Million*, who, like Sammael, had elaborate plans for changing the rules by which people played the games of art and life. Sammael's physique and deportment also resemble Lewis's in the early years of this century, when various combinations of wardrobe and coiffure succeeded in expressing both the aesthete and *Uebermensch* within him.

Indeed, the more fully acquainted Pullman becomes with Sammael, the more he appears an accurate caricature of the Wyndham Lewis responsible for all the works extending from *Tarr* to *Snooty Baronet*. He chiefly occupies himself, as did Lewis in his satires, with overseeing the "Surgery of Morals" upon sinners who "belonged almost exclusively to the European and American bourgeoisie" (*MF* 87, 42). The "Punishment Centres," where most of the damned receive their tortures, offer a final solution to human stupidity beyond the wildest dreams of a Sir Michael Kell-Imrie, who could only make his fellow men suffer one at a time. Pullman learns about these facilities in depth from the senior Administrative Officer of the Centre, Dr. Hachilah, who mixes in his person the refinement and butchery we associate with the Nazi doctors of Auschwitz and Dachau. Hachilah suggests to

Pullman that their tour begin with "The Inferno," a block of cells in which he takes special pride: "'They are a kind of caricature of Dante's Inferno,'" he explains to a silent but horrified Pullman, who himself had been a practitioner of satire during his lifetime. "'They are rather amusing, though terribly macabre, of course, as everything else here, for that matter. ... But you know where you are, of course. This *is* Hell'" (*MF* 81). The host and his visitor then proceed to a contemporary version of Dante's fifth canto:

> They went along the passage to a door marked 15. The official turned a key, and they both entered. It was painted over to represent a wild October sky, through which everywhere couples were represented as flying. The pressure of a quite powerful wind was felt as soon as one entered the room.—In the centre of the room were a man and woman strapped to one another. About four feet from the floor they were suspended from the ceiling, and arranged at an angle very near the horizontal, simulating flight.
>
> Dr. Hachilah went up to them, and slapping the woman upon the buttocks spoke in Italian.
>
> "Ah, Francesca, how is love?"
>
> He asked Pullman to approach and pushing aside a garment, revealed the fact that they were naked, and indecently glued to one another, the man exactly placed to facilitate sinful love. (*MF* 81–82)

After viewing this exhibit, Hachilah remarks to Pullman that he considers this Paolo and Francesca "'a great improvement on Dante's sentimental pair'" (*MF* 83). He believes that if sexual indulgence is a sin of the first magnitude, endangering the stability of the family and the state, it deserves a punishment more severe than simple transformation into a bird. Hachilah further implies that this cynical reduction of human affections to sex reflects the philistinism of the middle classes: "'we have fixed them as if they were in flight, but we have fixed them in a horrible rigidness—lips to lips and sex to sex. They may never move a fraction of an inch from that mockery of love'" (*MF* 83). The cult of sentimentality, Lewis always maintained, merely served to mask or distract from the actual object of modern life, the acquisition of things (including persons) and power. By symbolically strapping Paolo and Francesca together, the Devil forces the sinners to confront once and for all this ugly truth about their innermost desires. Other "vignettes" in the Punishment Centre cells are similarly designed to rub the noses of the bourgeoisie in their own materialism.

Given the efficiency of Hachilah and his staff, Sammael need rarely concern himself with the details of administering punishment, finding such work moderately distasteful. This does not mean that he feels pity for these sinners who lust after wealth and pleasure. Indeed, as the novel proceeds, Sammael, like other great satirists, emerges as an idealist of the spirit, with a corresponding contempt for matter. "The most fundamental thing about Sammael was his puritanism," the narrator remarks, going on to characterize him as a Cromwell, who though for political reasons ("this astute politician no doubt knew that the Puritan was not a popular fellow") affects a manner less severe than what was natural to him (*MF* 126). The more physical the nature of the sin, the more violent Sammael's reaction, and the greater his interest in seeing punishment administered. Of a beautiful adulteress Sammael remarks, " 'Her voice is redolent of the unreal life lived by the French bourgeoisie' "; minutes later, not trusting his assistants' power to resist her charms, Sammael personally tosses her to a band of Yahoo-like demons, who in no time rape, murder, and devour her. Eventually, he confides to Pullman, "On principle, I approve of punishing Man just for being Man" (*MF* 62). This statement captures the essence of the "metaphysical satire," of which Lewis once claimed to be the most accomplished modern practitioner.

Sammael is not altogether satisfied with his role, however, and feels that throughout history he has been misunderstood. During his initial interview with Pullman, he undertakes to explain the relationship between himself and God, beginning with the observation that neither he nor his adversary actually created the world. He continues:

> "But it was my old companion who had the bright idea of starting the race of men, by means of Eve. It was over that we quarrelled. For he was a very bumptious man and wanted me to applaud his handiwork. That was the last thing I could do. There was no *battle*, of course, as it is always represented. I simply left him, and many of my friends came with me. I consider that this race of pygmies, who, with their beastly women, live a clownish and sinful life—that to be responsible, in part, for the creation, and for the protection of this ignoble species, proves him whom you call God to be of an inferior nature. I told him so, and he shrank from me. He realized his base and unintelligent action.—But once I had established myself elsewhere he asked me to help (in a sort of scavenging capacity!). Ever since I have meted out punishment to man and to woman." (*MF* 35–36)

In a later conversation, Sammael amplifies upon the reasons for the long-standing opposition between himself and God:

"as far as the created earth is concerned, my origins are Mazdean, or shall we say Persian. The language which I, and all other angels, first spoke, proto-Iranian. Now, in speaking to a Christian I must tread warily, but the Jewish God (and subsequently the Christian God) came from Iran, too. The language we spoke when we first knew one another was Iranian: when the Hebrew selected God, his new God learned Hebrew: and that subsequently was the language we spoke—with a strong Persian accent. I have had no purpose in saying all this—I have no diabolic desires to debunk God—except to demonstrate how it came about that Christianity has a Counter-God, as it were, an Anti-Christ, a Devil. The fact is that the Iranian dualism is at the bottom of God's mind. . . . This piece of history in which I have been indulging may be summarised as follows. Into an essentially tribal, 'chosen people' religion, a phoney cosmic dualism has been introduced, in which I play a ridiculous part. I am where I am as a result of a disagreement with your God, not because I am a malignant promoter of disorder or because I was born bad. There are plenty of people who are by nature evil, but I am not one of those." (*MF* 129–30).

In Sammael's speech we have the ultimate defense of the ultimate satirist, as if the hero of *Snooty Baronet* were to apologize to the reader for abusing his girlfriend and murdering his literary agent. Because he resents coercion, and particularly resents having to play an *ethical* role imposed upon him by God (he claims to hate man just for being man), Sammael announces to Pullman a radical proposal: " 'I wish to cease to be [God's] Devil. It is my idea to send him a missive notifying him of my intention' " (*MF* 131–32). In the context of the Devil's career as we learn of it in Judeo-Christian mythology, this decision comes as quite a shock; the reader who has followed Lewis's career, however, can look upon it as the climax of a movement away from satire, which we have been observing in Sammael's creator since the 1930s.

Sammael's proposal involves two revolutionary changes. First, he and his followers would be reduced to human stature, a move that Sammael believes would also entail a loss of their virtual immortality. Second, women would have to be introduced into the community in order to ensure the propagation of the now mortal angelic species. Since Sammael has little experience with either mortality or sex and cannot trust his plans to any of his peers, he turns for advice to Pullman and a number of other intelligent human sinners (as a Roman emperor might choose a "learned captive" with whom to discuss matters of state [*MF* 131]), whom he establishes in a sort of Institute for Advanced Study called Haus Europa. Pullman becomes, in effect, a "Machiavellian counsellor" (*MF* 111) who helps Sammael bring dissident factions of angels around to his viewpoint. One of his major contributions toward this end is the holding of a fiesta:

> "Declare a holiday in two weeks' time," Pullman advised. "No. Better in one month. That will give me more time . . . call an emergency meeting of the governing body at once, at which your large majority will assure a victory. This Council Meeting will decree the transformation of certain points in the town, in preparation for the Fiesta. At the Sports Circle illuminated fountains must play; there must be places for bands. Confetti, masks, postiche noses, moustaches, fancy caps, etc., must immediately be manufactured. The sale of these and other things will help pay for the expense of the Fiesta." (*MF* 154)

Pullman intends the fiesta as a general aphrodisiac, during which the angels, whose sexual instincts have been dormant at least since their taking the daughters of men in the sixth chapter of Genesis, will feel attracted to the hundreds of beautiful women who will be scattered throughout the crowd. To further this objective, Sammael himself will appear with a "young American octoroon of surpassing beauty" whom he has personally selected:

> "this girl, with a white hibiscus in her oily raven hair, is just the thing for the occasion. We will dance the rumba together."
> "That is the idea!" Pullman applauded. "It will be terrific." (*MF* 155)

Initially, Pullman is very favorably disposed to Sammael's plans and his role in them, thinking not only of his personal security, but also of the advantages that it could bring to humankind. He tells his patron:

> "I desire a limited perpetuity for the Newtons and Plancks, and the human effort is, at present, directed to giving it to them. If you could surrender to them a little of your immortality, that would be wonderful. A superb Human Age could be built upon a suitable planet, where all the high activities could blossom. Your own ambitions, as you explain them to me, are going out to join the human ambitions."(*MF* 143)

The history of such a planet would match the history René Harding wanted to write for Earth, concerned only with creative works of creative men. Moreover, from a personal standpoint, Sammael's elevation of Pullman to the position of chief counselor fulfills the dream of all of Lewis's artist-heroes, and perhaps the dream of every artist since Shelley, who felt the modern world's lack of appreciation of his skills. Pullman, more than an unacknowledged legislator, is at last in a position to build a world almost from scratch, incorporating into it the highest principles of his own art.

Yet at the very moment when the conflicts in his life are nearing a resolution—the moment when the satirist is about to be reconciled to his victims and be allowed to participate in an ostensibly creative enterprise—Pullman is overtaken with remorse. This contrary movement begins three days after his initial meeting with Sammael, when he reflects that although Sammael appeared to be a polished and urbane gentleman, "at the basis not only of his mind but of his nature, was his hatred of the human race" (*MF* 39). Later that night, lying in bed in a hotel room provided for him by his new patron, Pullman

> unexpectedly . . . found himself with his hands covering his face, whispering a traditional supplication: he prayed for mercy and forgiveness, and for the intervention of God in the terrible ordeal in which he and his young friend found themselves. Satters, he insisted, had in no way shared in his sinfulness, indeed he was so simple that he was incapable of sin. He derived great comfort from his prayers, he slept, if not serenely, at least without mental shock. The next morning, it is true, he thought of what would be Sammael's reactions, could he have known about this. But he felt no alarm, he had been greatly fortified. (*MF* 40)

Despite Sammael's assurances, Pullman eventually concludes that the supernatural *is* real, and that the relative safety he enjoys, though ostensibly the result of the Devil's charity, really comes from God, to whom he now prays with such regularity that he fears the consequences of even an accidental interruption (*MF* 124). As in *Monstre Gai*, Pullman seems incapable of decisive action and resorts to a typical rationalization: "His way of accounting for his days, spent with His Majesty the Devil, was to say that he was, in reality, spying out the weakness of this evil personage. Every night he informed God of what he had done during the daytime" (*MF* 153). During the fiesta, however, Pullman witnesses the summary execution of an angel charged with circulating a damaging rumor ("Sammael inserted the point of the stiletto in the neighbourhood of the heart, and drove it home" [*MF* 180]) and realizes that neither his indifference nor the Devil's brutality can be explained away. Perhaps someone unaware that others have feelings cannot be charged with cruelty; but Pullman decides that even if this is true, "it isn't worth saying." He then experiences the pivotal revelation in *The Human Age*, one that Lewis has been leading his heroes to since *The Revenge for Love*: "God *values* man: that is the important thing to remember. It is this valuing that is so extraordinary. There are men who only value *power*. This is absurd, because power destroys value" (*MF* 181–82).

Pullman's remorse about participating in the Devil's scheme arises from the recognition of two specific evils that would follow from the successful merging of the human and the divine. First, Sammael's plan represents the fulfillment of modern man's fantasy of rendering the world a perfect reflection of the self, a nightmarish vision whose consequences were first perceived by the romantics. For Lewis, as for Blake, beauty derived from diversity and the conflict of opposites. Man's desire for complete domination of the world, however, expressed here in the Devil's proposed "Human Age," destroys the possibility of conflict. "Value can only exist with multiplicity," Pullman admits to himself near the end of *Malign Fiesta*. "The only value for Sammael is solipsistic. I, Pullman, am acting in a valueless vacuum called Sammael" (*MF* 182).

Secondly, when Sammael decides to annihilate the divine, to "mix it up with the pettiness and corruption of mankind," he destroys the standard against which man is measured and invariably found wanting (*MF* 168). Man's imperfection is the paradoxical source of divine grace because God values man for his perseverance in the face of failure, an exercise of virtue denied even to God Himself. Without the divine, Pullman realizes, the possibility of man's tragic dignity vanishes. God is, in a sense, man's enemy, but man needs God all the more for that reason. As noted earlier, T. S. Eliot once suggested that *The Human Age* was more "mature" than earlier works, that between *The Childermass* and its sequels there had been a "development in humanity."[13] While Lewis extends sympathy to his characters as he had not done before, it would be a mistake to see a wholesale conversion. If anything, Lewis has matured in his understanding of the role of Enemy. He has finally purged satire of its aesthetic and moral content and affirmed the religious function of the satirist as one who guarantees man's humanity by preserving a proper adversary relationship between man and God.

Lewis's eventual attachment to God seems to have caught even Lewis by surprise. The original radio script version of *Malign Fiesta*, which aired in May 1955, concludes when a gigantic angel, a follower of the Devil on his way to do battle with an invading army from Heaven, accidentally steps on Pullman and obliterates him. This would have been, as Hugh Kenner points out in his afterword to the novel, entirely consistent with the antihumanism that had earlier led him to abstraction and satire (*MF* 235). But his recognition that God values man for his failings seems to have made Lewis more favorably disposed toward his own kind, and in the published version of *Malign Fiesta*, which came out in October of that year, the angel narrowly misses Pullman and instead squashes a flower. Lewis apparently came to feel a certain pity for man and concluded that he deserved to inhabit something better than the debased "Human Age" the Devil was in the process of establishing. He therefore proposed to write a fourth volume, tentatively entitled *The Trial of Man*, that would describe Pullman's assimilation to the divine element and make him, in Kenner's words, "the first character in any Wyndham Lewis work to achieve a meaningful destiny" (*MF* 239). This additional volume, Lewis observed, would further demand a change in the overall title of the work that would indicate the supreme importance God had acquired in his mind. Writing to Kenner in August about the way he had come to see Pullman, Lewis remarked: "He favours the Divine. I favour the Divine" (*L* 562).

Not long before composing this letter, Lewis had written a draft opening of *The Trial of Man*. It begins with a brief account of God's invasion of Hell, which results in Sammael losing a leg to amputation and the unconditional surrender of his army. Sammael winds up in a hospital staffed by nuns, where one evening he receives a mysterious visitor who is occasionally seen around the wards:

> The Sister had by now become familiar with the magnificent geography of his superb face: the broad forehead, surmounted by heavy blue-grey hair, the light lines not seemingly drawn there by nature, but by the man himself—they had so voluntary an appearance; she knew by the soft compulsions of the deep grey eyes—and as to the expression of this stately countenance, she knew that in every emotion expressed there, a vast indifference must seemingly be mixed into any expression of feeling. (*MF* 218)

The visitor, of course, is God, and his appearance in the text marks the distance that Lewis has come from his earlier iconoclasm. While this God transcends the pettiness that characterizes so much of human existence, sympathy for the tragic condition of His creatures leavens His necessary indifference. The nun's thoughts linger over the problem of this delicate balance between transcendence and immanence:

> From her young days she remembered "Where there is nothing there is" ... oh, what was it that there was? Something like *this* ... something which was not zero, as she had always supposed this meant. No—that *nothing* of her early teachers meant somewhere where *nothing* oppressively human was to be found—nothing functional, that loved and hated, nothing that uncomfortably *willed* and wanted—something which *had* everything. But that was the reverse of nothing was it not? Yes, the reverse, the Sister thought, the greatest degree of the opposite of nothing which it is possible to imagine. (*MF* 218)

Lewis had begun years earlier with a negative theology of transcendence designed to protect life's irreducible mystery from the encroachments of rationalism, for without mystery there can be no artistic freedom. Whoever defines God brings Heaven crashing down to earth because language itself is a peculiarly earthly phenomenon. Lewis felt that definitions of the absolute too easily served selfish ends and thus ought not to be undertaken in the first place. Yet the logic of transcendence also leads to the conclusion that a perfect Being would lack nothing, divine or human. Indeed, in God's perfect sympathy for His creatures, He would come to value and even love man; and if God loves man, so then should a man love his fellow creatures, for their sake and for God's. The human now becomes the royal road back to the divine. Reviewing his career from this point, we might well say that Lewis had almost managed to reinvent Christianity on his own, recapitulating the sacred history that extends from the appearance of Jehovah the Thunderer on Sinai, an event that announces the paradox of immanence and transcendence (why should a transcendent God reveal himself at all?), to the resolution of this dialectic in the Incarnation of Jesus, which argues for the essential unity of the human and the divine.

Still, Wyndham Lewis should not be confused with that other writer of theological fantasy with whom, much to his chagrin, he shared a surname. One cannot ignore the fact that Lewis *rejected* this proposed opening and never returned to complete *The Trial of Man*, busying himself during his final months with less demanding projects. Among these was Lewis's last published book, *The Red Priest*, which serves as a further reminder of Lewis's uneasiness with anything resembling orthodox Christianity. This rather imperfectly realized novel follows the tragic career of Father Augustine Card, an Anglican priest, who sets himself the task of revitalizing his church through an improbable combination of Roman ritual and communist politics. (Card, for example, makes a great display of having Russian priests officiate with him at Mass; the fact that the Russians would have been Orthodox, not Roman or Anglican, and almost certainly would have been anticommunist seems not to have troubled the author.) This bizarre plot only begins to make sense when viewed against the backdrop of *The Human Age*: thus we can see Father Card as a mortal version of Lord Sammael, who, bitterly resigned to what seems the inevitable democratization (and thus vulgarization) of life in the modern world, seeks to exercise some control over the process by blending the human and the divine (here, communism and Anglo-Catholicism) on his own terms.

Of course, the introduction of politics into religion corrupts the absolute, and Card ends up as a man who simply uses God for his own selfish purposes: Jesus for him becomes "a stick of dynamite . . . the bomb of Jesus" (*RP* 244). When one of his curates challenges him with the assertion that "the man of God and politics are deadly enemies" (*RP* 240), Card kills him and, after a conviction for manslaughter, goes into self-imposed exile as a missionary in the Arctic, where he kills an Eskimo who attempts to steal his wallet and is finally murdered in revenge. This nihilistic conclusion is confirmed with the posthumous birth of a son, appropriately named Zero, who in the novel's closing words is "fated to blast his way across space and time" (*RP* 298).

Despite having been composed while Lewis was working out what Kenner describes as Pullman's "acclimatization to the Celestial environment" (*MF* 239), *The Red Priest* seems to demonstrate as a practical matter the difficulty of a Lewisian hero's finding a secure religious home. Perhaps Lewis the novelist felt that the obligations of narrative, which include conflict and suspense, made it impossible to write about the genuinely omnipotent God he had lately come to conceive. Indeed, the rejected draft of *The Trial of Man* ends with attention focused not on God or even Pullman, but on Sammael, who stomps out of a meeting with God, "his mind a tornado" (*MF* 227). In addition, although Lewis spoke on more than one occasion about joining the church, he never actually converted. His mature attitude toward orthodoxy can probably be discerned in the thoughts of René Harding as he recovers from his nervous breakdown in the Canadian seminary: "The peace of the scene, the restful monotony of the lives of these people, whose minds reflected the massively built Summa of all philoso-

phies (providing a static finality in which the restless intellect might find
repose), had proved in the end nothing but an irritant to René. His intelligence was too dynamic, his reason was too bitterly bruised, for a static
bliss" (*SC* 380). To paraphrase Blake on Milton, Lewis no doubt saw himself
as a true poet who was of the Devil's party and would always know it.

Sainthood, with or without God

Many of the changes in Lewis's art can be summarized in the following
observation: that in the decades between the works conceived for the "Man
of the World" project and the final volumes of *The Human Age*, Lewis
shifted his creative energies from social novels to what we might call novels
of individual crisis. Again, in some respects, the child was father to the man:
from the outset, Lewis claimed that he had rejected the tradition of the
English novel, which simply cataloged the features of an established social
order, and had embraced a more introspective tradition of Continental
fiction. Interestingly, this latter kind of writing had something of a resur-
gence in Europe at the end of World War II, partly as a response to the
behavior of many artists and intellectuals during the war. In France, this
movement, which Lewis acknowledged on several occasions and into
which *The Human Age* neatly dovetails, had gathered itself together under
the name of existentialism.

As with earlier "-isms" with which he found himself in partial accord,
Lewis took pains to distinguish the exact contours of his beliefs from those
of the latest Continental fad. In *Rude Assignment*, composed during the late
1940s, he offers this comment: "The ultimate value of existentialism ... is a
matter we are not called upon to decide. But such people as Sartre or
Camus—with books such as 'Etre et Neant', 'Huis Clos', or 'Miramolin'—
at least keep the place alive and keep the 'Neant' at bay." Unqualified praise
rarely appears in Lewis's critical writing, and this case is no exception; he
continues: "They do reply, whether well or ill, to the spectacle of social ruin
in which they find themselves, and invent a doctrine of hideous pessimism
to match the challenge of the diabolical Zeitgeist" (*RA* 187). Lewis indirectly
refers to the cause of his dissent from existentialist pessimism a few
pages earlier during a discussion of his early book on Shakespeare and
Machiavelli, *The Lion and the Fox*:

> Machiavelli was a prophet of action of existentialist type. Action he
> regarded as the only reality. It would be impossible to find a more single-
> minded advocate of the agent-principle. "Shakespeare," as I wrote, again,
> "differed profoundly from such a theorist of 'action' as Machiavelli . . . he
> was without that mechanical appetite for what he would regard as a useless
> and degrading performance of a series of (however logically perfect) tricks."
> And this would apply also to the Machiavellian obsession regarding power:
> for with him power was the highest end of action. (RA 175–76)

The existentialist, according to this view, looks foursquare into the abyss of
a secular universe dominated by material values and, eschewing any hope
for a spiritual relief expedition from Heaven, finds redemption in the bare
assertion of the individual will against the void. While Lewis could sympa-
thize with the tragic assumptions of this philosophy, he could hardly accept
the patently anti-intellectual response that he deemed a throwback to
romanticism. The exaggerated claims made for the rational faculty by
Enlightenment thinkers simply did not justify the romantic conclusion that
reason had no place in the lives of civilized men and women. Moreover, the
general argument that Lewis made in *Time and Western Man* against romanticism—that it reinforced the values it sought to undermine —could
just as well be made against the French existentialists: that by emphasizing
a program of action for its own sake, they demonstrated as strong an
attachment to a discredited notion of the will to power as had their Nazi
adversaries during the occupation.

Lewis, however, made some important distinctions among existentialist
writers. In *The Writer and the Absolute*, Lewis's last book-length study of
literature and politics, he remarks that "[Albert Camus's] books are probably the best that are being written in France today, of the new writers" (*WA*
66). What distinguished Camus was the fact that, like Lewis himself, he was
"a thinking animal . . . instead of a man-of-action animal" (*WA* 69). The
characters in his novels do assert themselves against the void, but only after
careful meditation upon the meaning of their actions. Specifically, Lewis
found Camus preferable to Jean-Paul Sartre, whose conception of the hero
Lewis found "somewhat theatrical" (*WA* 97). Camus's brand of pessimism,
on the other hand, allowed for the exercise of reason and intelligence:

> Far from welcoming "the tragic" as " heroic" material for the literary artist,
> [Camus] is against those things in men which produce it. Incidentally he
> produces great tragedy that way, as a literary artist, which Sartre does not.

He does not wish to see men living in terror—in the midst of massacres, bombardments, tortures, and *pressure*. We find him reacting as violently against those conditions, as Jean-Paul Sartre with a fatalistic gusto exploits them. (*WA* 82–83)

Indeed, when we compare the work of Lewis and Camus during this period, we find more than a superficial resemblance. Lewis admitted to being impressed with Camus's novel *The Plague*, writing to Dorothy Pound, "You should tell Ezra by the way to read *La Peste* by Camus and inform you what he thinks of it" (*L* 416–17). *The Plague*, like *The Human Age*, details the predicament of a thinking man in hellish and impossible circumstances when an outbreak of plague forces the authorities to quarantine the Algerian city of Oran. The record of events during the course of his period of quarantine is narrated by Bernard Rieux, a physician, who in the history also presents a kind of spiritual autobiography as he registers the effects of the plague and its consequences upon his moral being. Rieux's own story is closely bound up with that of his friend Jean Tarrou, a figure of obscure origins who emerges as the novel's hero in Rieux's narration. Tarrou arrived in Oran some weeks before the outbreak of the plague and seems to have no other interest than to observe and appreciate the rhythms of life in what would impress most visitors as a dull, commercial town. In fact, he keeps a notebook full of unremarkable observations and marked by a style of understatement. Rieux comments that "Tarrou had a habit of observing events and people through the wrong end of a telescope. In those chaotic times he set himself to recording the history of what the normal historian passes over."[14] Tarrou speculates somewhat idly on such matters as how a man might be fully aware of the passage of time and responds with a list of exercises: "By spending one's days on an uneasy chair in a dentist's waiting-room; by remaining on one's balcony all of a Sunday afternoon; by listening to lectures in a language one doesn't know; by traveling by the longest and least-convenient train routes, and of course standing all the way; by lining up at the box-office of theaters and then not buying a seat; and so forth."[15] He is, in short, an aesthete of the kind first identified by Kierkegaard, who, having decided that the sublime in modern life has been vulgarized beyond redemption, makes a complete turnabout and discovers the sacred in the hopelessly mundane. But like the true knight of faith, Tarrou advances beyond the merely reactionary stage. When the plague unleashes its full fury upon the town, he makes the necessary transition from the aesthetic to the ethical. Although he has no special medical training, he takes it upon himself to organize a voluntary corps of sanitation workers to fight the plague. The work is dangerous, and Rieux is frankly perplexed by anyone who would involve himself in such labors when he did not absolutely have to do so:

> "Out with it, Tarrou! What on earth prompted you to take a hand in this?"
> "I don't know. My code of morals, perhaps."
> "Your code of morals? What code?"
> "Comprehension."[16]

Tarrou expands upon this curious definition of morality later in the novel when he explains that people fall into one of two categories: carriers of pestilence and the victims of pestilence. (He admits the possibility of a third group, which he calls "true healers," but notes "that one doesn't come across many of them."[17]) Since there is little one can do to eradicate the disease itself, Tarrou resolves "to take, in every predicament, the victims' side, so as to reduce the damage done."[18] But this is an accomplishment of no mean proportion: " health, integrity, purity (if you like)—is a product of the human will, of a vigilance that must never falter. The good man, the man who infects hardly anyone, is the man who has the fewest lapses of attention. And it needs tremendous will-power, a never ending tension of the mind, to avoid such lapses."[19] Tarrou's willingness to side always with the victims reveals more than an ethical concern for his fellow man, however. He admits to Rieux that among the victims lies his only hope of discovering how one attains to the third category of true healers, "in other words, to peace."[20] He hopes to achieve an understanding, if that is the right word, with the powers that transcend temporal human relationships. This desire is indicative of Tarrou's final passage from the ethical stage to the religious, a passage that has become almost impossibly difficult in the modern world:

> "It comes to this," Tarrou said almost casually; "what interests me is learning how to become a saint."
> "But you don't believe in God."
> "Exactly! Can one be a saint without God?—that's the problem, in fact the only problem, I'm up against today."[21]

As if to underline the absence of God from the world, Tarrou remains healthy until it becomes apparent that the incidence of plague has begun to subside. As the city begins to breathe a collective sigh of relief, Tarrou manifests symptoms of the dread disease and dies after a short but valiant struggle. Initially, Tarrou's death leaves Rieux feeling empty and embittered; as he keeps vigil over the body of his dead friend, he "could not tell if Tarrou had found peace, now that all was over, but for himself he had a feeling that no peace was possible to him henceforth, any more than there can be an armistice for a mother bereaved of her son or for a man who buries his friend."[22] Later, however, he reflects that even if all that a man earned in his battle with the plague was "knowledge and memories," this would have to be accounted a victory in Tarrou's world, where knowing stands as the supreme virtue. The novel concludes on a positive note, as Rieux acknowledges the possibility of transcendence in his assertion that if men cannot become saints, at least they can think and act and, by virtue of this exercise, "strive their utmost to be healers" of the universal sickness Camus would have us identify with the human condition.

The precise degree of Camus's influence on Lewis in the 1950s is as difficult to gauge as the degree of Joyce's influence upon him two decades earlier. Although the world that Lewis created in *The Human Age* lent itself easily to the telling of an existentialist fable, he had, of course, established its general outlines long before anyone had heard of Albert Camus. Suffice it to say that Lewis interested himself in what he considered the major political and philosophical currents of his day and took careful note of his fellow artists' responses to these same currents. In *The Human Age*, Third City stands as an analogue to Camus's Oran, a purgatorial chamber in which men can either advance to Heaven or retreat toward Hell; and James Pullman, who as a professional artist and writer encompasses the roles of both Tarrou and Rieux, is above all a man who must make actual choices among mutually exclusive alternatives. During his climactic scene in the plaza, Pullman realizes, as Camus and Sartre realized in occupied France, that European intellectuals since Nietzsche have been whistling in the dark if they believe that they have in fact transcended the ancient contraries of Good and Evil; such a claim had no value beyond a "self-advertising eccentricity" (*MG* 221). Perhaps the Bailiff was correct when he said that the boundaries between the two have become blurred in modern times, but that only serves to make the issue more complex, not cause it to go away.

Unlike Tarrou, however, Pullman does not choose Good over Evil in *Monstre Gai* but instead elects to throw in his lot with the discredited Bailiff; moreover, when we come to the end of *Malign Fiesta*, we still cannot be sure that Pullman has exercised his own free will on behalf of what he acknowledges as the Good. This makes *The Human Age* a much less appealing and, inevitably, less popular work than *The Plague*, but it might also suggest Lewis's greater fidelity to a vision of the modern world. Lewis has in fact arranged a far more difficult purgatory for Pullman than did Camus for his hero. Ultimately, there could be little question of aligning oneself against the plague; the only question is whether or not one has the requisite courage to act. But Pullman faces an evil harder to recognize as such than a literal or allegorical plague. First the Bailiff and later the Devil possess sympathetic, even endearing characteristics, which is not the case with the enemy inside the walls of Oran; and secondly, while there is nothing more to be learned about the plague by promoting rather than fighting it, the same cannot be said about Pullman's potential adversaries. Both the Bailiff and the Devil are as interesting as they are evil, and Pullman, who at one point admits, " 'I esteem *knowing* immeasurably more than I do *being*' " (*MG* 140), can hardly turn down the opportunity of their acquaintance.

In a world where God is or may well be dead, both Lewis and Camus affirm the value of the man who has the capacity to know and to love despite his congenital imperfections: ignorance, selfishness, mortality. Indeed, whatever claim man has to immortality springs from his struggle with mortality; thus Tarrou achieves his sainthood in a world without God, and Pullman assimilates to the divine in a world with Him (or presumably would have, had Lewis lived). If *The Human Age* teaches a lesson, it is this: that only through this struggle to think and to act can modern men become healers of the universal sickness called the human condition that afflicts us while we wait to find out whether He is with us, or not.

Epilogue

Hulme was correct when he noted how difficult it was to introduce the word *religious* into critical discourse, admitting that the educated reader in the twentieth century will probably intuit some "sentimental reaction" in the use of the term. Although we customarily think about religion as a conservative force, I have tried to present Lewis as a writer who evolves toward a religious position that *because* it acknowledges man's limitations actually emphasizes his creative and dynamic role in the world.

While it would be a mistake to claim Lewis as a radical thinker, there was always an ideologically unstable element in his painting, fiction, and social criticism; Lewis himself was genuinely unsure whether he belonged on the Right or the Left. Indeed, one of the things that makes Lewis such an interesting writer is his way of arriving at a certain viewpoint almost in spite of himself. In *Time and Western Man*, for example, he says that while he personally prefers the idea of a Thomistic God—a rationally apprehended absolute Oneness—he recognizes that since no man can conceive the absolute except in terms of the self and thus reduce the divine to the human, we would do better to think of the cosmos in terms of multiplicity. As he explains in a passage quoted earlier, "We are surface-creatures, and the 'truths' from beneath the surface contradict our values. It is among the flowers and leaves that our lot is cast, and the roots, however 'interesting,' are not so ultimate for us. For the ultimate thing is the surface, the last-comer, and that is committed to a plurality of being" (*TWM* 387).

This credo closely resembles something that Nietzsche said in *The Gay Science* when he asserted that the world becomes infinite all over again as soon as modernity teaches us that all knowledge is in fact interpretation. Again reminded of our intellectual limitations, we return to a religious universe, but with the difference that we can no longer fool ourselves into thinking that the absolute is a mirror of the human desire for stability and order:

> Once more we are seized by a great shudder; but who would feel inclined immediately to deify again after the old manner this monster of an unknown world? And to worship the unknown henceforth as "the Unknown One"? Alas, too many *ungodly* possibilities of interpretation are included in the unknown, too much devilry, stupidity, and foolishness of interpretation—even our own human, all too human folly, which we know.[1]

Like his contemporaries Pound, Eliot, and Joyce, Lewis could never quite let go of the notion that art might be able to return interpretation to knowledge; but more violently than they, in his life and in his art, he kept bumping into the ungodly possibilities that made this impossible. This condition of infinite interpretations we now call the postmodern world; Wyndham Lewis, aesthete, satirist, and religious writer, may well have been its foremost modernist explorer.

Notes

1. Wyndham Lewis in the Modernist Canon: Dissent, Division, and Displacement

1. Jeffrey Meyers, *The Enemy: A Biography of Wyndham Lewis* (London: Routledge and Kegan Paul, 1980), 207.

2. Ezra Pound, "Wyndham Lewis," in *Literary Essays of Ezra Pound*, ed. T. S. Eliot (New York: New Directions, 1968), 424.

3. Meyers, *Enemy*, 207.

4. Pound, *Essays*, 428–29.

5. Hugh Kenner, *Wyndham Lewis* (Norfolk, Conn.: New Directions, 1954), xiv–xv.

6. Fredric Jameson, *Fables of Aggression: Wyndham Lewis, the Modernist as Fascist* (Berkeley: University of California Press, 1979), 1.

7. Many of the facts in the following account are drawn from Meyers's biography of Wyndham Lewis cited above. Meyers also observes the disruptive effects of American, English, and European influences upon Lewis's character and career (1).

8. Cited in Meyers, *Enemy*, 85.

9. Pound, *Essays*, 424.

10. Meyers, *Enemy*, 250–51.

11. Ibid., 4.

12. Aaron Scharf, *Art and Photography* (London: Allen Lane, 1968), 194.

13. Cited in Scharf, 197.

14. Though Lewis turned away from abstraction and back toward naturalism in the 1920s, he never abandoned his abstract manner altogether, holding it in reserve for subjects that resisted representational treatment.

15. Lewis reserved some of his harshest words of criticism for English aesthetes and German romantics who sought to demonstrate the underlying unity of the arts and thus to argue for an unalienated relationship between man and the world, a view that Lewis recognized as anthropocentric and potentially self-serving. In this robust passage from *Time and Western Man* (1927), he attacks Oswald Spengler, behind whom Lewis saw Walter Pater and Richard Wagner:

> Spengler sets "Plastic" and "Music" at each other's throats, in an eliminating contest. It is world power or downfall for Gothic Music as interpreted by this warlike professor; and the arts become weapons in his hands, which he wields with a picturesque barbaric clumsiness, brandishing them hither and thither. There is no room upon the same earth for two such *opposite* things as Plastic and Music. He insists characteristically on a *unity* in everything. So Music eats up the Plastic, dissolves it, and it streams out to "infinity." There is then *only* Music throughout the triumphantly Gothic World. (285–86)

Irving Babbitt, T. S. Eliot's teacher at Harvard and an important figure in the effort to define the spirit of the modern age, also argued for the recognition of distinct aesthetic boundaries in his *The New Laokoön: An Essay on the Confusion of the Arts* (Boston: Houghton Mifflin, 1910). Susanne K. Langer summed up this view of the matter when she remarked that "there are no happy marriages in art—only successful rape" (*Problems of Art: Ten Philosophical Lectures* [New York: Scribner's, 1957], 86).

16. T. S. Eliot, "A Note on *Monstre Gai*," *Hudson Review* 7, no. 4 (Winter 1955): 524.

17. Hugh Kenner, "*Mrs. Dukes' Million*: The Stunt of an Illusionist," in *Wyndham Lewis: A Revaluation*, ed. Jeffrey Meyers (Montreal: McGill-Queen's University Press, 1980), 87.

18. Stephen Kern, *The Culture of Time and Space 1880–1918* (Cambridge: Harvard University Press, 1983), 137.

19. Cited in Sanford Schwartz, *The Matrix of Modernism: Pound, Eliot, and Early Twentieth-Century Thought* (Princeton: Princeton University Press, 1985), 77.

20. Walter Michel, *Wyndham Lewis: Paintings and Drawings* (Berkeley: University of California Press, 1971), 48.

21. T. S. Eliot, " 'Ulysses,' Order, and Myth," in *Selected Prose of T. S. Eliot*, ed. Frank Kermode (New York: Harcourt Brace Jovanovich, 1975), 178.

22. Mark C. Taylor, *Erring: A Postmodern A/theology* (Chicago: University of Chicago Press, 1984), 33.

23. James Joyce, *A Portrait of the Artist as a Young Man*, ed. C. G. Anderson (1916; New York: Viking Press, 1964), 215.

24. Since Lewis's time, critics have become increasingly attuned to ironies in Joyce's text that warn us against taking his characters' words at face value. For discussions of the personal element in Joyce's "impersonal" narrative voice, see Jeremy Lane, "His Master's Voice? The Questioning of Authority in Literature," in *The Modern English Novel: The Reader, the Writer, and the Work*, ed. Gabriel Josipovici (London: Open Books, 1976), 113–29; and John Paul Riquelme, *Teller and Tale in Joyce's Fiction: Oscillating Perspectives* (Baltimore: Johns Hopkins University Press, 1983), 131–34.

25. T. E. Hulme, *Speculations: Essays on Humanism and the Philosophy of Art*, ed. Herbert Read, 2d ed. (London: Routledge and Kegan Paul, 1936), 16–17.

26. Ibid., 19.

27. *The Indispensable Rousseau*, ed. John Hope Mason (London: Quartet Books, 1979), 60.

28. John Stuart Mill, *Principles of Political Economy with Some of Their Applications to Social Philosophy*, ed. J. M. Robson (1848; Toronto: University of Toronto Press, 1965), 756.

29. J. Hillis Miller, *The Disappearance of God: Five Nineteenth-Century Writers* (Cambridge: Harvard University Press, 1963), 5.

30. Hulme, *Speculations*, 46.

31. T. S. Eliot, *After Strange Gods: A Primer of Modern Heresy* (New York: Harcourt Brace, 1934), 15–18.

32. Rudolf Bultmann was probably the most important and influential member of this school. See "New Testament and Mythology," in *New Testament and Mythology and Other Basic Writings*, trans. and ed. Schubert M. Ogden (Philadelphia: Fortress, 1984).

33. Hulme, *Speculations*, 71.

34. For a good overview of Kierkegaard's "stages of existence" and their various interpretations, see Mark C. Taylor, *Kierkegaard's Pseudonymous Authorship: A Study of Time and the Self* (Princeton: Princeton University Press, 1975), 62–78. Kierkegaard's most accessible treatment of the movement from the "aesthetic" and the "ethical" can be found in the various essays and fictions of *Either/Or*, vol. 1, trans. David F. Swenson and Lillian Marvin Swenson (Princeton: Princeton University Press, 1959), and *Either/Or*, vol. 2, trans. Walter Lowrie (Princeton: Princeton University Press, 1959); he analyzes the movement from the "ethical" to the "religious" in a meditation upon the biblical patriarch Abraham's near sacrifice of his son Isaac in *Fear and Trembling*, trans. Walter Lowrie (Princeton: Princeton University Press, 1959).

35. Jameson, 3.

2. In Praise of Life: The Aesthetics of Deadness

1. Walter Pater, *Selected Writings*, ed. Harold Bloom (New York: Signet, 1974), 60–61.

2. Alan Robinson, *Symbol to Vortex: Poetry, Painting, and Ideas, 1885–1914* (New York: St. Martin's, 1985), 56–57.

3. Timothy Materer, "Lewis and the Patriarchs: Augustus John, W. B. Yeats, T. Sturge Moore," in *Wyndham Lewis: A Revaluation*, ed. Jeffrey Meyers (Montreal: McGill-Queen's University Press, 1980), 60.

4. Materer, "Patriarchs," 55.

5. Meyers, *Enemy*, 27.

6. Wyndham Lewis, ts. Wyndham Lewis Collection, Olin Library of Cornell University.

7. Ezra Pound, "Ford Madox (Hueffer) Ford; Obit," in *Selected Prose*, ed. William Cookson (New York: New Directions, 1973), 462.

8. Donald Davie, *Ezra Pound* (New York: Viking, 1975), 15.

9. Meyers, *Enemy*, 27.

10. Joyce, *Portrait*, 169.

11. W. B. Yeats, "The Theatre," in *Essays and Introductions* (New York: Collier, 1961), 166.

12. Michel, *Paintings and Drawings*, 48.

13. Pound, "Wyndham Lewis," in *Literary Essays*, 426.

14. Robinson, 17.

15. Ibid., 18.

16. T. E. Hulme, "Modern Art: A Preface Note and Neo-Realism," in *Further Speculations*, ed. Sam Hynes (Lincoln: Bison-University of Nebraska Press, 1962), 119.

17. Wilhelm Worringer, *Abstraction and Empathy: A Contribution to the Psychology of Style*, trans. Michael Bullock (New York: International Universities Press, 1953), 13.

18. Ibid., 7–8.

19. Ibid., 14.

20. Ibid., 14.

21. Ibid., 15–18.

22. Hulme, "The Philosophy of Intensive Manifolds," in *Speculations*, 174.

23. Ibid., 211.

24. Robinson, 115.

25. Worringer, 15.

26. Victor Erlich, *Russian Formalism: History-Doctrine*, 4th ed. (The Hague: Mouton, 1980), 67.

27. Victor Shklovsky, "Art as Technique," in *Russian Formalist Criticism: Four*

Essays, trans. and ed. Lee T. Lemon and Marion J. Reis (Lincoln: Bison-University of Nebraska Press, 1965), 5.

28. Ibid., 6.

29. Ibid., 9.

30. Erlich, 34.

31. Ibid., 35.

32. Shklovsky, 10.

33. Ibid., 12.

34. Ibid., 12.

35. Christopher Pike, "Introduction: Russian Formalism and Futurism," in *The Futurists, the Formalists and the Marxist Critique*, ed. Christopher Pike (London: Ink Links, 1979), 3.

36. Richard Poirier, "The Difficulties of Modernism and the Modernism of Difficulty," in *Images and Ideas in American Culture: The Functions of Criticism*, ed. Arthur Edelstein (Hanover, N.H.: University Press of New England, 1979), 125.

37. Shklovsky, 12.

38. Marjorie Perloff, *The Futurist Moment: Avant-Garde, Avant Guerre, and the Language of Rupture* (Chicago: University of Chicago Press, 1986), 90.

39. Cited in Richard Ellmann, *James Joyce* (New York: Oxford University Press, 1959), 417.

40. Pound, *Prose*, 462.

41. Pound, *Essays*, 425.

42. Lewis had a highly ambivalent attitude toward Nietzsche. In *Rude Assignment*, he admits that *The Gay Science* and "those admirable maxims . . . which he wrote after the breakdown in his health" were among his favorite reading during his early years in Paris; on the other hand, he claims to have always disliked the idea of the "Superman," seeing it as "a sort of titanic nourishment for the ego" (*RA* 128).

43. Perloff, 121.

3. From Morality to Metaphysics: Lewisian Satire

1. Meyers, *Enemy*, 29.

2. Lewis's account of the episode, which consists of a few pages of notes to himself, is reproduced as "A Breton Journal" in *The Complete Wild Body* (191–99).

3. "Conscious of the fact that bourgeois society considers him nothing but a charlatan," observes Renato Poggioli, "[the artist] voluntarily and ostentatiously assumes the role of comic actor." Poggioli traces this image back through Rilke and Picasso to a prose poem of Baudelaire (*The Theory of the Avant-Garde*, trans. Gerald Fitzgerald [Cambridge: Belknap-Harvard University Press, 1968], 110, 142).

4. Meyers, *Enemy*, 27–28.

5. For a brief overview of Orage and *The New Age*, see Miriam Hansen, "T. E. Hulme, Mercenary of Modernism, or, Fragments of Avantgarde Sensibility in Pre–World War I Britain," *ELH* 47 (Summer 1980): 358–59.

6. Ibid., 359.

7. Meyers, *Enemy*, 36.

8. Michel, *Paintings and Drawings*, 68.

9. Ibid., 68.

10. Perloff, 36.

11. Michel, *Paintings and Drawings*, 88.

12. Quoted in Meyers, *Enemy*, 83.

13. Benjamin H. D. Buchloh, "Figures of Authority, Ciphers of Regression: Notes of the Return of Representation in European Painting," in *Modernism and Modernity: The Vancouver Conference Papers*, eds. Benjamin H. D. Buchloh, et al. (Halifax: Press of the Nova Scotia College of Art and Design, 1983), 81–115.

14. Meyers, *Enemy*, 105.

15. Michael Seidel, *Satiric Inheritance: Rabelais to Sterne* (Princeton: Princeton University Press, 1979), 11.

16. Poggioli, 116.

17. Ibid.

18. Typical is this exchange between two characters at the Lenten party:

> "But for some time it has seemed to me—I know it sounds absurd—that all the noise is proceeding from *those three people* over there"—she slid her eyes round, followed by those of Osmund "the ones with the steeple-hats, who look like three friends of Guy Fawkes," and the Sib lowered her blind-puppy eyelids, while Lord Osmund observed with attention the three masked mystery-men.
> "Do you know—!"
> "Yes!"
> "I had exactly the same impression Sib!"
> "No really?"
> "It was identical!"
> "I do think that was a coincidence!"
> "Wasn't it! I thought my ear must be deceiving me! It would not be the first time!"
> "Don't talk to me about one's ears! But I believe we must—"
> "We must I believe be right Sib!"
> "I don't believe our ears have played us false!"
> "In this matter—I believe they haven't!"
> "I am not positive—but I should be surprised if they had deceived us!"
> "For once I do believe that mine has [*sic*] proved trustworthy!"
> "It is a miracle if mine have!"
> "Not more so than with mine!" (*AG* 362)

19. To separate works of art from run-of-the-mill fiction, Lewis devised what he

called *The Taxi-cab-Driver Test*: "I believe that you should be able to request a taxi-cab driver to step into your house, and (just as you might ask him to cut a pack of cards) invite him to open a given work of fiction, which you had placed in readiness for this experiment upon your table; and that then *at whatever page he happened to open it*, it should be, in its texture, something more than, and something different from, the usual thing that such an operation would reveal" (*MWA* 237).

20. Robert C. Elliott, *The Power of Satire: Magic, Ritual, Art* (Princeton: Princeton University Press, 1960), 266.

21. Stanley E. Fish, *Self-Consuming Artifacts: The Experience of Seventeenth-Century Literature* (Berkeley: University of California Press, 1972), 1–4.

22. These are the judgments of Hugh Kenner and William Pritchard, respectively; cited in Timothy Materer, *Wyndham Lewis the Novelist* (Detroit: Wayne State University Press, 1976), 101.

23. Ibid., 101.

24. Ibid., 109–10.

25. Jameson, 25.

26. Kenner, *Wyndham Lewis*, 131.

27. See especially "The Origins of Myth and Ritual," in René Girard, *Violence and the Sacred*, trans. Patrick Gregory (Baltimore: Johns Hopkins University Press, 1977), 89–118. In *The Lion and the Fox*, Lewis wrote: "It is a commonplace that, pursued in its effects, far enough and deep enough, the most civilized canons lead to oppression and manslaughter" (*LF* 79).

28. Seidel, 21.

29. Elliott, 39.

30. Seidel, 6.

31. Elliott, 140.

4. Religious Sensibilities

1. D. M. Rosenberg, *Oaten Reeds and Trumpets: Pastoral and Epic in Virgil, Spenser, and Milton* (Lewisburg, Pa.: Bucknell University Press, 1981), 17–20.

2. Henri Bergson, *Laughter: An Essay on the Meaning of the Comic*, trans. Cloudesley Brereton and Fred Rothwell (New York: Macmillan, 1928), 10.

3. Kenner, *Wyndham Lewis*, 23.

4. Lafourcade does admit the possibility that bibliographers have overlooked an earlier appearance of the story (*WB* 106).

5. "The Death of the Ankou," as it appears in *The Wild Body* (the only extant version), reflects certain concerns of the post–World War I period. For example, this description of Saint Peter upholding the sanctity of work (proving him "a suppressed communist of an advanced type") is vintage *Apes of God* material.

But in general, the story's style and subject place it in company with "Les Saltimbanques."

6. Shelley's primary source of information about Zoroastrianism seems to have been Thomas Love Peacock's unfinished poem, *Ahrimanes*, the manuscript of which Peacock gave to the poet. Peacock, in turn, learned about the subject from a theosophist and vegetarian named J. F. Newton. *Ahrimanes*, through Shelley, also had an influence on Byron's *Manfred* (Kenneth Neill Cameron, ed., *Shelley and His Circle: 1773–1822*, vol. 3 [Cambridge: Harvard University Press, 1960], 234, 239).

7. David Lee Clark, ed., *Shelley's Prose, or The Trumpet of a Prophecy* (Albuquerque: University of New Mexico Press, 1954), 254.

8. Carl Grabo observes that Shelley's argument in *Prometheus Unbound* finds an analogy in the teaching of Zoroaster that "evil is something alien to the scheme of Ormuzd, an intrusion for which he is not responsible" (*Prometheus Unbound: An Interpretation* [1935; reprint, New York: Gordian Press, 1968] 23). But while Zoroastrianism does imagine a time when good will triumph over evil, it remains far less mystical in spirit than Neoplatonism.

9. Walter Kaufmann, *Nietzsche: Philosopher, Psychologist, Antichrist*, 3d ed. (Princeton: Princeton University Press, 1968), 198–99.

10. Peter Caracciolo, "'Demavend! recalling Zendavesta': Ancient Iranian Myths in *The Human Age*," *Enemy News* 15–23 (1982–86): 14.

11. Ibid.

12. Lewis's argument closely follows (and is much indebted to) that of the contemporary French writer Julien Benda; see Benda's book *The Treason of the Intellectuals*, trans. Richard Aldington (New York: Norton, 1969).

13. T. S. Eliot, *The Complete Poems and Plays 1909–1950* (New York: Harcourt Brace, 1971), 48.

14. P.-J. Proudhon, *Selected Writings*, trans. Elizabeth Fraser, ed. Stewart Edwards (Garden City, N.Y.: Doubleday, 1969), 229.

15. Meyers, *Enemy*, 80.

16. Jameson, 18.

17. Northrop Frye, *The Great Code: The Bible and Literature* (New York: Harcourt Brace, 1982), 117.

18. Kenner, *Wyndham Lewis*, 93.

19. Julian Symons remarks that book one of *Time and Western Man*, entitled "The Revolutionary Simpleton," amounts to "a declaration of divorce from some of the most notable experiments of literary modernism in his generation" (*Makers of the New: The Revolution in Modern Literature 1912–1939* [London: Andre Deutsch, 1987], 224). The essays in this section denounced Joyce, Pound, and Stein, among others.

20. Jameson, 130.

21. Ibid.

22. Eliot, *Complete Poems and Plays*, 49.

23. The prime example is Robert Browning's *Agamemnon*. Browning described it as "literal at every cost save that of absolute violence to our language." Thomas Carlyle, who had encouraged the undertaking, is reported to have said of the finished product: "*Can you understand it, at all?* I went carefully into some parts of it and for my soul's salvation (laughs) couldn't make out the meaning. If any one tells me this is because the thing is so remote from us—I say things far remoter from our minds and experiences have been well translated into English" (William Clyde DeVane, *A Browning Handbook*, 2d ed. [New York: Crofts, 1955], 416, 418).

24. An almost identical argument has been made by Christopher Lasch in a chapter of *The Culture of Narcissism* (New York: Norton, 1978) entitled "The Banality of Pseudo-Self-Awareness."

25. Originally, Eliot lay the blame for this "dissociation of sensibility" squarely upon the shoulders of Milton and Dryden. Later on, however, he found this explanation too simplistic, adding: "All we can say is, that something like [dissociation] did happen; that it had something to do with the Civil War; that it would even be unwise to say it was caused by the Civil War, but that it is a consequence of the same causes which brought about the Civil War; that we must seek the causes in Europe, not in England alone, and for what these causes were, we may dig and dig until we get to a depth at which words and concepts fail us" (*Prose*, 266).

26. Theologian Mark Taylor (*Erring*, 21) describes this religious revolution as follows:

> "The conclusion of [Luther's] quest for salvation is summarized succinctly in the theological doctrine implied by the phrase *pro nobis*. The significance of Christ, Luther argued, lies in the 'fact' that he lived and died '*for us.*' Luther himself never lost sight of the overriding ascendancy of the divine purpose. Moreover, he always insisted that a person never really possesses faith. Belief and doubt continually contend with each other for the mind and heart of the individual. For many people who were less dialectical than Luther, however, the notion that Christ is always *pro nobis* signaled a significant shift toward the centrality of the self. From this point of view, the emphasis on individual salvation suggested that *human* concerns lie at the center of divine, and therefore of cosmic, purpose. As will become increasingly apparent, this anthropological preoccupation grew considerably in the years following the Reformation."

27. Friedrich Nietzsche, *The Birth of Tragedy and the Genealogy of Morals*, trans. Francis Golfing (Garden City, N.Y.: Doubleday, 1956), 282–83.

28. To cite one amusing instance, Nietzsche uses Luther's words to the council at Worms, "Hier stehe ich; ich kann nicht anders," when apologizing for the critical taste that causes him to despise the New Testament (*Nietzsche Werke: Kritische Gesamtausgabe*, ed. Giorgio Colli and Mazzino Montinari [Berlin: Walter de Gruyter, 1967–], vol. 6, pt. 2: 411).

29. Meyers, *Enemy*, 277–78.

30. Jameson, 5.

31. Meyers, *Enemy*, 16; see also D. G. Bridson, *The Filibuster: A Study of the Political Ideas of Wyndham Lewis* (London: Cassell, 1972), 63.

32. M. C. D'Arcy, *The Nature of Belief* (London: Sheed and Ward, 1931), 23.

33. Ibid., 24.

34. Ibid., 23.

35. Sorel also found a champion in T. E. Hulme, who translated *Reflections on Violence*.

36. Georges Sorel, *Reflections on Violence*, trans. T. E. Hulme and J. Roth (New York: Collier, 1961), 161.

37. Ibid., 268.

38. Ibid., 272.

39. Ibid., 271.

40. Toward the end of his life, Lewis wrote a prospectus for a historical novel about an artist, modeled on Leonardo da Vinci, who gains effective control of a city-state. (See also the discussion of Pullman and Sammael in chapter six.)

The last page of a scrapbook in the Lewis archive at Cornell, preserving newspaper and magazine clippings of world events from the late 1940s and early 1950s, displays an engraving of the romantics' great hero-legislator: Napoléon.

41. This attitude appears, for example, in Achilles's speech to Priam at the end of the *Iliad* (trans. Robert Fitzgerald [New York: Anchor-Doubleday, 1974], 585):

> At the door of Zeus
> are those two urns of good and evil gifts
> that he may choose for us; and one for whom
> the lightning's joyous king dips in both urns
> will have by turns bad luck and good. But one
> to whom he sends all evil—that man goes
> contemptible by the will of Zeus; ravenous
> hunger drives him over the wondrous earth,
> unresting, without honor from gods or men.

Achilles's words leave us with the impression that Zeus makes his choices quite arbitrarily, without concerning himself about the justice of his actions.

42. Jorge Luis Borges, *A Universal History of Infamy*, trans. Norman Thomas Di Giovanni (New York: Dutton, 1979), 84.

5. *The Childermass*: Modernist Apocalypse

1. See, for example, *Bagdad*, in Michel, *Paintings and Drawings*, 109. Richard Cork (*Wyndham Lewis: The Twenties* [London: Anthony d'Offay, 1984], 42) has described this picture in words equally appropriate to our occasional glimpses of the Heavenly City in *The Childermass*:

Unlike the urban structures he created in his Vorticist pictures, which conveyed the clangour, energy and vertiginous power of the machine age metropolis, this city seems hushed and peaceful. Apart from a hint of almost Surrealist foreboding, which helps to explain why Lewis viewed de Chirico's work with favour, nothing threatens to disturb the profound calm. Although vestiges of figures can be discerned in the painting, most of the city is silent and uninhabited. . . . *Bagdad* is an eerie union of past and future, historical fantasy and clear-eyed prophecy.

2. "On 3 February 1928 Lewis contracted with Chatto and Windus to write and submit Parts II and III of *The Childermass*. . . . Chatto and Windus entered a formal claim for damages against Lewis for breach of contract on 8 November 1932 because he had not submitted Parts II and III of *The Childermass*" (Omar S. Pound and Philip Grover, *Wyndham Lewis: A Descriptive Bibliography* [Folkestone: Archon-Dawson, 1978], 19).

3. I. A. Richards, "A Talk on *The Childermass*," *Agenda* 7–8 (Autumn-Winter 1969–70): 16.

4. In fact, Lewis would turn forty in about *two* years. This adjustment was necessary, he felt, to compensate for time lost during the war—time that those who did not go to the front used to advance their careers.

5. Hannah Arendt, *The Origins of Totalitarianism* (New York: Harcourt Brace, 1951), 328.

6. Because Lewis worked on the components of "The Man of the World" more or less simultaneously, publication dates are not a foolproof guide to dates of composition. We can safely assume that most of *Time and Western Man* was written after *The Art of Being Ruled*, since Lewis cites *ABR* several times in *TWM* and at one point discusses the latter book as a kind of sequel to the former (*TWM* 119). The situation with *The Childermass* and *The Apes of God* is more complicated. Although *AG* appeared in book form two years after the completed *CM*, Lewis seems to have begun work on *AG* earlier—certainly by 1923. (Two sections of the novel, later revised, were published in T. S. Eliot's journal, *The Criterion*, in 1924.) At all events, Lewis considered *The Childermass* an unfinished work until he went back to it in the 1950s, and certainly in this sense we can say that it follows *AG*.

7. Cited in J. R. Hammond, *An H. G. Wells Companion: A Guide to the Novels, Romances, and Short Stories* (New York: Barnes and Noble, 1979), 95.

8. The relationship between *The Childermass* and *Finnegans Wake* is detailed by Geoffrey Wagner in *Wyndham Lewis: A Portrait of the Artist as the Enemy* (New Haven, Conn.: Yale University Press, 1957), 168–88.

9. James Joyce, *Finnegans Wake* (1939; New York: Viking-Penguin, 1971), 415, 419.

10. Ibid., 8.

11. Eliot, "Ulysses, Order and Myth," in *Prose*, 177–78.

12. See Hugh Kenner, "The Devil and Wyndham Lewis," in *Gnomon: Essays in*

Contemporary Literature (New York: McDowell, Obolensky, 1958), 215.

13. Jameson, 79.

14. Cited in Jameson, 79.

15. Christopher Hill, *Milton and the English Revolution* (New York: Viking, 1978), 398.

16. Ibid., 382.

17. Jonathan Swift, *Gulliver's Travels and Other Writings* (New York: Modern Library-Random House, 1958), 55.

18. Hugh Kenner, *Joyce's Voices* (Berkeley: University of California Press, 1978), 4–5.

19. Swift, 17.

20. Ibid.

21. Peter Laslett, *The World We Have Lost: Further Explored* (New York: Scribner's, 1984), 1–21.

22. See Michael Bell's discussion of the paradox that as science became more aware of its "creative dimension," literature began to seek "the scientific model of detachment," in *The Context of English Literature, 1900–1930*, ed. Michael Bell (New York: Holmes and Meier, 1980), 36–43.

23. Hulme, "The Philosophy of Intensive Manifolds," in *Speculations*, 173ff.

24. Jameson, 21.

25. Ibid., 117.

26. Actually, Lewis's characters represent a parody of Pound's romantic image, which appears at the end of Canto 74. Carroll F. Terrell (*A Companion to the Cantos of Ezra Pound*, vol. 2 [Berkeley: University of California Press, 1984], 388) glosses "rose in the steel dust" as follows:

> A pattern formed under magnetic influence. A graphic image of divine order operating in the material world—a miracle which can be seen occasionally in such a thing as the "down" of a swan. Allen Upward [*The New Word*, 222] had written: "He who has watched the iron crumbs drawn into patterns by the magnet, or who in the frostwork on the window pane has apprehended the unknown beauty of the crystal's law, seems to me to have an idea more wholesome to our frail imaginings of the meaning of the Mystery of Life."

27. Jameson, 123.

28. Arendt, 327.

29. Cited in Jameson, 180.

30. William Butler Yeats, *A Vision* (1925, 1937; reprint, New York: Collier-Macmillan, 1966), 177.

31. Ibid., 179.

32. Ibid., 178.

33. Hill, 366.

34. Nietzsche, *Genealogy of Morals*, 231.

35. Cited in Meyers, *Enemy*, 29.

36. Michel, *Paintings and Drawings*, plate 74.

6. *The Human Age*: Favoring the Divine

1. "A few extremists talked of creating an alternative, quasi-Soviet authority; this was far from the spirit of the general council. The strike of 1926 was no repetition of the threat which had prevented war against Soviet Russia in 1920. That threat had been a deliberate political act, and the union leaders had recognized that they might have to take over the running of the country. In 1926 their sole object was to ease the government into negotiations over the coal industry. When they failed in this, they had inevitably to retreat" (A. J. P. Taylor, *English History 1914–1945* [New York: Oxford University Press, 1965], 246).

2. Jameson, 145.

3. Meyers, *Enemy*, 21–23.

4. Valerie Parker, "Enemies of the Absolute: Lewis, Art and Women," in Meyers, *Wyndham Lewis*, 217.

5. These sentimental figures who later emerge as heroines include April Mallow in *The Vulgar Streak*, Hester Harding in *Self Condemned*, and Mary Card in *The Red Priest*, who actually serves as the novel's central consciousness.

6. Ezra Pound, *The Cantos* (New York: New Directions, 1972), 81 / 521.

7. Jameson, 150.

8. Ibid.

9. Lewis seems to have conceived the third volume of *The Human Age* as essentially a repetition of the second, with the difference that the theological stakes were higher in the later work. In August 1955, he wrote to Hugh Kenner: " 'Monstre Gai' shows [Pullman] entrapped by the Bailiff, in whose power he reluctantly remains. . . . Then the same situation is repeated in Malign Fiesta, only even more tragically, and the figure in that case is Divine, though Diabolic" (*L* 562).

10. Jameson, 150.

11. See Michel, *Paintings and Drawings*, plates xv, 154.

12. The narrator of *Monstre Gai* remarks of Pullman: " He was not for the Right wing, he was for the Left wing, there was nothing to influence him in one direction rather than the other. But about one thing there was no question whatever: for a writer of his experimental sort it was to the Left wing that he must look, for sympathy, interest, and patronage. It had been like that in his earthly life: and in his unearthly life it was apparently just the same, only more so" (*MG* 146).

13. Eliot, "Note on *Monstre Gai*," 524.

14. Albert Camus, *The Plague*, trans. Stuart Gilbert (New York: Vintage, 1972), 23.

15. Ibid., 25.

16. Ibid., 123.
17. Ibid., 236–37.
18. Ibid., 237.
19. Ibid., 235–36.
20. Ibid., 237.
21. Ibid.
22. Ibid., 269.

Epilogue

1. Friedrich Nietzsche, *The Gay Science*, trans. Walter Kaufmann (New York: Vintage-Random House, 1974), 336–37.

Select Bibliography

Works by Wyndham Lewis

The Apes of God. 1930. Santa Barbara: Black Sparrow, 1981.

The Art of Being Ruled. 1926. Ed. Reed Way Dasenbrock. Santa Rosa: Black Sparrow, 1989.

BLAST 1. 1914. Santa Barbara: Black Sparrow, 1981.

BLAST 2. 1915. Santa Barbara: Black Sparrow, 1981.

Blasting and Bombardiering. 1937. London: John Calder, 1982.

The Caliph's Design: Architects! Where Is Your Vortex? 1919. Ed. Paul Edwards. Santa Barbara: Black Sparrow, 1986.

The Childermass. 1928. London: John Calder, 1965.

Collected Poems and Plays. Ed. Alan Munton. New York: Persea Books, 1979.

The Complete Wild Body. Ed. Bernard Lafourcade. Santa Barbara: Black Sparrow, 1982.

The Diabolical Principle and the Dithyrambic Spectator. London: Chatto and Windus, 1931.

The Enemy: A Review of Art and Literature. 1927–29. New York: Kraus Reprint, 1967.

The Letters of Wyndham Lewis. Ed. W. K. Rose. Norfolk, Conn.: New Directions, 1963.

The Lion and the Fox: The Rôle of the Hero in the Plays of Shakespeare. 1927. London: Methuen, 1951.

Malign Fiesta. 1955. London: Calder and Boyars, 1966.

Men without Art. 1934. Ed. Seamus Cooney. Santa Rosa: Black Sparrow, 1987.

Monstre Gai. 1955. London: John Calder, 1965.

Mrs. Dukes' Million. Toronto: Coach House, 1977.

The Red Priest. London: Methuen, 1956.

The Revenge for Love. 1937. Chicago: Henry Regnery, 1952.

Rude Assignment. 1950. Ed. Toby Foshay. Santa Barbara: Black Sparrow, 1984.

Satire and Fiction. London: Arthur, 1931.

Self Condemned. 1954. Santa Barbara: Black Sparrow, 1983.

Snooty Baronet. 1932. Ed. Bernard Lafourcade. Santa Barbara: Black Sparrow, 1984.

Tarr. 1918. Ed. Paul O'Keefe. Santa Rosa: Black Sparrow, 1990.

Tarr. 1928. Harmondsworth: Penguin, 1982.

Time and Western Man. 1927. Boston: Beacon, 1957.

The Vulgar Streak. 1941. Ed. Paul Edwards. Santa Barbara: Black Sparrow, 1985.

The Writer and the Absolute. London: Methuen, 1952.

Wyndham Lewis the Artist: From 'Blast' to Burlington House. 1939. New York: Haskell House, 1971.

Secondary Sources

Abrams, M. H. *Natural Supernaturalism: Tradition and Revolution in Romantic Literature.* New York: Norton, 1971.

Allen, Walter. *The Modern Novel in Britain and the United States.* New York: Dutton, 1964.

Altick, Richard D. *The English Common Reader: A Social History of the Mass Reading Public 1800–1900.* Chicago: University of Chicago Press, 1957.

Altizer, Thomas J. J. "History as Apocalypse." In *Deconstruction and Theology,* 147–77. New York: Crossroad, 1982.

Altizer, Thomas J. J., et al. *Deconstruction and Theology.* New York: Crossroad, 1982.

Arendt, Hannah. *The Origins of Totalitarianism.* New York: Harcourt Brace, 1951.

Asmussen, Jes P. *Manichaean Literature: Representative Texts Chiefly from Middle Persian and Parthian Writings.* Delmar, N.Y.: Scholars Facsimiles, 1975.

Babbitt, Irving. *The New Laokoön: An Essay on the Confusion of the Arts.* Boston: Houghton Mifflin, 1910.

Bedell, George C. *Kierkegaard and Faulkner: Modalities of Existence.* Baton Rouge: Louisiana State University Press, 1972.

Bell, Michael, ed. *The Context of English Literature, 1900–1930.* New York: Holmes and Meier, 1980.

Benda, Julien. *The Treason of the Intellectuals.* Trans. Richard Aldington. New York: Norton, 1969.

Bergonzi, Bernard. *Heroes' Twilight: A Study of the Literature of the Great War*. New York: Coward-McCann, 1966.

———. *The Myth of Modernism and Twentieth Century Literature*. Sussex: Harvester, 1986.

Bergson, Henri. *An Introduction to Metaphysics*. Trans. T. E. Hulme. New York: Putnam, 1912.

———. *Laughter: An Essay on the Meaning of the Comic*. Trans. Cloudesley Brereton and Fred Rothwell. New York: Macmillan, 1928.

Berman, Marshall. *All That Is Solid Melts into Air: The Experience of Modernity*. New York: Simon and Schuster, 1982.

Binion, Rudolph. *After Christianity: Christian Survivals in Post-Christian Culture*. Durango, Col.: Logbridge-Rhodes, 1986.

Borges, Jorge Luis. *A Universal History of Infamy*. Trans. Norman Thomas Di Giovanni. New York: Dutton, 1979.

Bridson, D. G. *The Filibuster: A Study of the Political Ideas of Wyndham Lewis*. London: Cassell, 1972.

Buchloh, Benjamin H. D., et al., eds. *Modernism and Modernity: The Vancouver Conference Papers*. Halifax: Press of the Nova Scotia College of Art and Design, 1983.

Bultmann, Rudolf. *New Testament and Mythology and Other Basic Writings*. Trans. and ed. Schubert M. Ogden. Philadelphia: Fortress, 1984.

Calinescu, Matei. *Faces of Modernity: Avant-Garde, Decadence, Kitsch*. Bloomington: Indiana University Press, 1977.

Cameron, Kenneth Neill, ed. *Shelley and His Circle: 1773–1822*. Cambridge: Harvard University Press, 1961.

Campbell, SueEllen. *The Enemy Opposite: The Outlaw Criticism of Wyndham Lewis*. Athens: Ohio University Press, 1988.

Camus, Albert. *The Plague*. Trans. Stuart Gilbert. New York: Vintage, 1972.

Caracciolo, Peter. "'Demavend! recalling Zendavesta': Ancient Iranian Myths in *The Human Age*." *Enemy News* 15–23 (1982–86): 12–15.

Chapman, Robert T. *Wyndham Lewis: Fictions and Satires*. New York: Barnes and Noble, 1973.

Clark, David Lee, ed. *Shelley's Prose, or The Trumpet of a Prophecy*. Albuquerque: University of New Mexico Press, 1954.

Cockshut, A. O. J. *The Unbelievers: English Agnostic Thought 1840–1890*. London: Collins, 1964.

Cork, Richard. *Vorticism and Abstract Art in the First Machine Age*. Berkeley: University of California Press, 1976.

———. *Wyndham Lewis: The Twenties*. London: Anthony d'Offay, 1984.

Currie, Robert. *Genius: An Ideology in Literature*. New York: Shocken, 1974.

Daniels, Mary F., ed. *Wyndham Lewis: A Descriptive Catalogue of the Manuscript*

Material in the Department of Rare Books Cornell University Library. Ithaca, N.Y.: Cornell University Library, 1972.

D'Arcy, M. C. *The Nature of Belief.* London: Sheed and Ward, 1931.

Dasenbrock, Reed Way. *The Literary Vorticism of Ezra Pound and Wyndham Lewis: Towards the Condition of Painting.* Baltimore: Johns Hopkins University Press, 1985.

Davie, Donald. *Ezra Pound.* New York: Viking, 1975.

DeVane, William Clyde. *A Browning Handbook.* 2d ed. New York: Crofts, 1955.

Edelstein, Arthur, ed. *Images and Ideas in American Culture: The Functions of Criticism.* Hanover, N.H.: University Press of New England, 1979.

Eliot, T. S. *After Strange Gods: A Primer of Modern Heresy.* New York: Harcourt Brace, 1934.

———. *The Complete Poems and Plays 1909–1950.* New York: Harcourt Brace, 1971.

———. "A Note on *Monstre Gai.*" *Hudson Review* 7, no. 4 (Winter 1955): 522–26.

———. *Selected Prose of T. S. Eliot.* Ed. Frank Kermode. New York: Harcourt Brace Jovanovich, 1975.

Elliott, Robert C. *The Power of Satire: Magic Ritual Art.* Princeton: Princeton University Press, 1960.

Ellmann, Richard. *James Joyce.* New York: Oxford University Press, 1959.

Erlich, Victor. *Russian Formalism: History–Doctrine.* 4th ed. The Hague: Mouton, 1980.

Fish, Stanley E. *Self-Consuming Artifacts: The Experience of Seventeenth-Century Literature.* Berkeley: University of California Press, 1972.

Frye, Northrop. *The Great Code: The Bible and Literature.* New York: Harcourt Brace, 1982.

Frascina, Francis, and Charles Harrison, eds. *Modern Art and Modernism: A Critical Anthology.* London: Harper and Row, 1982.

Gamache, Lawrence B., and Ian S. MacNiven, eds. *The Modernists: Studies in a Literary Phenomenon.* Rutherford: Fairleigh Dickinson University Press, 1987.

The Gathas of Zarathustra: From the Zend-Avesta. London: Concord Grove Press, 1983.

Girard, René. *Violence and the Sacred.* Trans. Patrick Gregory. Baltimore: Johns Hopkins University Press, 1977.

Grabo, Carl. *Prometheus Unbound: An Interpretation.* 1935. Reprint. New York: Gordian Press, 1968.

Green, Christopher. *Leger and the Avant-Garde.* New Haven: Yale University Press, 1976.

Grigson, Geoffrey. *A Master of Our Time: A Study of Wyndham Lewis.* 1951. New York: Haskell House, 1972.

Gwynn, Frederick L. *Sturge Moore and the Life of Art.* Lawrence: University of Kansas Press, 1951.

Hagstrum, Jean H. *William Blake, Poet and Painter: An Introduction to the Illuminated Verse.* Chicago: University of Chicago Press, 1964.

Hammond, J. R. *An H. G. Wells Companion: A Guide to the Novels, Romances, and Short Stories.* New York: Barnes and Noble, 1979.

Handley-Read, Charles. *The Art of Wyndham Lewis.* London: Faber and Faber, 1951.

Hansen, Miriam. "T. E. Hulme, Mercenary of Modernism, or, Fragments of Avantgarde Sensibility in Pre–World War I Britain." *ELH* 47 (Summer 1980), 355–85.

Harrison, Jane Ellen. *Ancient Art and Ritual.* New York: Henry Holt, 1913.

Haug, Martin. *Essays on the Sacred Language, Writings, and Religion of the Parsis.* London: Kegan Paul, 1884.

Herf, Jeffrey. *Reactionary Modernism: Technology, Culture, and Politics in Weimar and the Third Reich.* Cambridge: Cambridge University Press, 1984.

Hill, Christopher. *Milton and the English Revolution.* New York: Viking, 1978.

Hilton, Nelson. *Literal Imagination: Blake's Vision of Words.* Berkeley: University of California Press, 1983.

Hulme, T. E. *Further Speculations.* Ed. Sam Hynes. Lincoln: Bison–University of Nebraska Press, 1962.

———. *Speculations: Essays on Humanism and the Philosophy of Art.* Ed. Herbert Read. 2d ed. London: Routledge and Kegan Paul, 1936.

Hynes, Samuel. *Edwardian Occasions: Essays on English Writing in the Early Twentieth Century.* New York: Oxford University Press, 1972.

———. *The Edwardian Turn of Mind.* Princeton: Princeton University Press, 1968.

Isaak, Jo Anna. *The Ruin of Representation in Modernist Art and Texts.* Ann Arbor: UMI Research, 1986.

Jackson, A. V. Williams. *Researches in Manichaeism with Special Reference to the Turfan Fragments.* 1932. Reprint. New York: AMS Press, 1965.

Jameson, Fredric. *Fables of Aggression: Wyndham Lewis, the Modernist as Fascist.* Berkeley: University of California Press, 1979.

Josipovici, Gabriel, ed. *The Modern English Novel: The Reader, the Writer, and the Work.* London: Open Books, 1976.

———. *The World and the Book: A Study of Modern Fiction.* Stanford: Stanford University Press, 1971.

Joyce, James. *Finnegans Wake.* 1939. New York: Viking-Penguin, 1971.

———. *A Portrait of the Artist as a Young Man.* 1916. Ed. C. G. Anderson. New York: Viking Press, 1964.

———. *Ulysses.* 1922. Ed. Hans Walter Gabler. New York: Random House, 1986.

Kandinsky, Wassily. *Concerning the Spiritual in Art.* 1914. Reprint. Trans. M. T. H. Sadler. New York: Dover, 1977.

———. *Kandinsky: Complete Writings on Art.* 2 vols. Ed. Kenneth C. Lindsay and Peter Vergo. Boston: G. K. Hall, 1982.

Kantra, Robert A. *All Things Vain: Religious Satirists and Their Art*. University Park, Penn.: Penn State University Press, 1984.

Kaufmann, Walter. *Nietzsche: Philosopher, Psychologist, Antichrist*. 3d ed. Princeton: Princeton University Press, 1968.

Kenner, Hugh. *Gnomon: Essays in Contemporary Literature*. New York: McDowell, Obolensky, 1958.

————. *Joyce's Voices*. Berkeley: University of California Press, 1978.

————. *The Pound Era*. Berkeley: University of California Press, 1971.

————. *Wyndham Lewis*. Norfolk, Conn.: New Directions, 1954.

Kern, Stephen. *The Culture of Time and Space 1880–1918*. Cambridge: Harvard University Press, 1983.

Klancher, Jon. *The Making of English Reading Audiences, 1790–1832*. Madison: University of Wisconsin Press, 1987.

Klonsky, Milton. *William Blake: The Seer and His Visions*. New York: Harmony Books, 1977.

Krieger, Murray. "The Ambiguous Anti-Romanticism of T. E. Hulme." *ELH* 20 (1953): 300–314.

Kush, Thomas. *Wyndham Lewis's Pictoral Integer*. Ann Arbor: UMI Research, 1981.

Langbaum, Robert. *The Mystery of Identity*. Chicago: University of Chicago Press, 1982.

Langer, Susanne K. *Problems of Art: Ten Philosophical Lectures*. New York: Scribner's, 1957.

Lasch, Christopher. *The Culture of Narcissism*. New York: Norton, 1978.

Laslett, Peter. *The World We Have Lost: Further Explored*. New York: Scribner's, 1984.

Leavis, Q. D. *Fiction and the Reading Public*. London: Chatto and Windus, 1939.

Lemon, Lee T., and Marion J. Reis, trans. and eds. *Russian Formalist Criticism: Four Essays*. Lincoln: Bison–University of Nebraska Press, 1965.

Levenson, Michael H. *A Genealogy of Modernism: A Study of English Literary Doctrine 1908–1922*. Cambridge: Cambridge University Press, 1984.

MacCabe, Colin, ed. *James Joyce: New Perspectives*. Sussex: Harvester, 1982.

Marcuse, Herbert. *One-Dimensional Man: Studies in the Ideology of Advanced Industrial Society*. Boston: Beacon, 1964.

Malandra, William W. *An Introduction to Ancient Iranian Religion: Readings from the Avesta and Achaemenid Inscriptions*. Minneapolis: University of Minnesota Press, 1983.

Mason, John Hope, ed. *The Indispensable Rousseau*. London: Quartet Books, 1979.

Materer, Timothy. "Lewis and the Patriarchs: Augustus John, W. B. Yeats, T. Sturge Moore." In *Wyndham Lewis: A Revaluation*, ed. Jeffrey Meyers. Montreal: McGill-Queen's University Press, 1980.

————. *Vortex: Pound, Eliot, and Lewis*. Ithaca: Cornell University Press, 1979.

————. *Wyndham Lewis the Novelist*. Detroit: Wayne State University Press, 1976.

Mellor, Anne Kostelanetz. *Blake's Human Form Divine*. Berkeley: University of California Press, 1974.

Meyers, Jeffrey. *The Enemy: A Biography of Wyndham Lewis*. London: Routledge and Kegan Paul, 1980.

————. *Painting and the Novel*. Manchester: Manchester University Press, 1975.

————, ed. *Wyndham Lewis: A Revaluation*. Montreal: McGill-Queen's University Press, 1980.

Michel, Walter. *Wyndham Lewis: Paintings and Drawings*. Berkeley: University of California Press, 1971.

Michel, Walter, and C. J. Fox, eds. *Wyndham Lewis on Art: Collected Writings 1913–1956*. London: Thames and Hudson, 1969.

Mill, John Stuart. *Principles of Political Economy with Some of Their Applications to Social Philosophy*. 1848. Ed. J. M. Robson. Toronto: University of Toronto Press, 1965.

Miller, J. Hillis. *The Disappearance of God: Five Nineteenth-Century Writers*. Cambridge: Harvard University Press, 1963.

Morrow, Bradford, and Bernard Lafourcade. *A Bibliography of the Writings of Wyndham Lewis*. Santa Barbara: Black Sparrow, 1978.

Mukarovsky, Jan. *The Word and Verbal Art: Selected Essays by Jan Mukarovsky*. Trans. and ed. John Burbank and Peter Steiner. New Haven: Yale University Press, 1977.

Nietzsche, Friedrich. *The Birth of Tragedy* and *The Genealogy of Morals*. Trans. Francis Golfing. Garden City, N.Y.: Doubleday, 1956.

————. *The Gay Science*. Trans. Walter Kaufmann. Vintage–Random House, 1974.

Pater, Walter. *Selected Writings*. Ed. Harold Bloom. New York: Signet, 1974.

Patterson, David. *Affirming Flame: Religion, Language, Literature*. Norman: Oklahoma University Press, 1988.

Peckham, Morse. *The Triumph of Romanticism*. Columbia, S.C.: University of South Carolina Press, 1970.

Perl, Jeffrey M. *The Tradition of Return: The Implicit History of Modern Literature*. Princeton, N.J.: Princeton University Press, 1984.

Perloff, Marjorie. *The Futurist Moment: Avant-Garde, Avant Guerre, and the Language of Rupture*. Chicago: University of Chicago Press, 1986.

Pike, Christopher, ed. *The Futurists, the Formalists, and the Marxist Critique*. London: Ink Links, 1979.

Poggioli, Renato. *The Theory of the Avant-Garde*. Trans. Gerald Fitzgerald. Cambridge: Belknap–Harvard University Press, 1968.

Porteus, Hugh Gordon. *Wyndham Lewis: A Discursive Exposition*. London: Desmond Harmsworth, 1932.

Pound, Ezra. *The Cantos*. New York: New Directions, 1972.

————. *Literary Essays of Ezra Pound*. Ed. T. S. Eliot. New York: New Directions, 1968.

————. *Pound/Lewis: The Letters of Ezra Pound and Wyndham Lewis*. Ed. Timothy Materer. New York: New Directions, 1985.

————. *Selected Prose*. Ed. William Cookson. New York: New Directions, 1973.

Pound, Omar S., and Philip Grover. *Wyndham Lewis: A Descriptive Bibliography*. Folkestone: Archon-Dawson, 1978.

Pritchard, William H. *Wyndham Lewis*. New York: Twayne, 1968.

Proudhon, P.-J. *Selected Writings*. Trans. Elizabeth Fraser. Ed. Stewart Edwards. Garden City, N.Y.: Doubleday, 1969.

Quinones, Ricardo. *Mapping Literary Modernism: Time and Development*. Princeton: Princeton University Press, 1985.

Richards, I. A. "A Talk on *The Childermass*." *Agenda* 7–8 (Autumn–Winter 1969–70): 16–21.

Riquelme, John Paul. *Teller and Tale in Joyce's Fiction: Oscillating Perspectives*. Baltimore: Johns Hopkins University Press, 1983.

Robinson, Alan. *Symbol to Vortex: Poetry, Painting, and Ideas, 1885–1914*. New York: St. Martin's, 1985.

Rosenberg, D. M. *Oaten Reeds and Trumpets: Pastoral and Epic in Virgil, Spenser, and Milton*. Lewisburg, Pa.: Bucknell University Press, 1981.

Russell, Charles. *Poets, Prophets, and Revolutionaries: The Literary Avant-Garde from Rimbaud through Postmodernism*. New York: Oxford University Press, 1985.

Scharf, Aaron. *Art and Photography*. London: Allen Lane, 1968.

Schneidau, Herbert N. *Sacred Discontent: The Bible and Western Tradition*. Berkeley: University of California Press, 1977.

Schwartz, Sanford. *The Matrix of Modernism: Pound, Eliot, and Early Twentieth-Century Thought*. Princeton: Princeton University Press, 1985.

Seidel, Michael. *Satiric Inheritance: Rabelais to Sterne*. Princeton: Princeton University Press, 1979.

Sorel, Georges. *Reflections on Violence*. Trans. T. E. Hulme and J. Roth. New York: Collier, 1961.

Stableford, Brian. *Scientific Romance in Britain 1890–1950*. New York: St. Martin's, 1985.

Steiner, Wendy. *The Colors of Rhetoric: Problems in the Relation between Modern Literature and Painting*. Chicago: University of Chicago Press, 1982.

Swift, Jonathan. *Gulliver's Travels and Other Writings*. New York: Modern Library–Random House, 1958.

Symons, Julian. *Makers of the New: The Revolution in Modern Literature 1912–1939*. London: Andre Deutsch, 1987.

Taylor, A. J. P. *English History 1914–1945*. New York: Oxford University Press, 1965.

Taylor, Mark C. *Erring: A Postmodern A/theology.* Chicago: University of Chicago Press, 1984.

———. *Kierkegaard's Pseudonymous Authorship: A Study of Time and the Self.* Princeton: Princeton University Press, 1975.

Terrell, Carroll F. *A Companion to the Cantos of Ezra Pound.* 2 vols. Berkeley: University of California Press, 1984.

Tomlin, E. W. F. *Wyndham Lewis: An Anthology of His Prose.* London: Methuen, 1969.

Wagner, Geoffrey. *Wyndham Lewis: A Portrait of the Artist as the Enemy.* New Haven, Conn.: Yale University Press, 1957.

Walch, Peter, and Thomas F. Barrow, eds. *Perspectives on Photography: Essays in Honor of Beaumont Newhall.* Albuquerque: University of New Mexico Press, 1986.

Wees, William C. *Vorticism and the English Avant-Garde.* Toronto: University of Toronto Press, 1972.

Whitehead, Kate. *The Third Programme: A Literary History.* New York: Oxford University Press, 1989.

Wilson, Simon. *British Art from Holbein to the Present Day.* London: The Tate Gallery and Barron's, 1979.

Worringer, Wilhelm. *Abstraction and Empathy: A Contribution to the Psychology of Style.* Trans. Michael Bullock. New York: International Universities Press, 1953.

Wright, T. R. *Theology and Literature.* New York: Basil Blackwood, 1988.

Yeats, William Butler. *Essays and Introductions.* New York: Collier, 1961.

———. *A Vision.* 1925, 1937. Reprint. New York: Collier-Macmillan, 1966.

Index

All titles in italics or quotation marks, unless otherwise noted, refer to works by Wyndham Lewis.

Abraham, 94
abstract art, 8, 45, 66, 172–73, 196 (n. 14)
Abstraction and Empathy (Worringer), 33–34
Action française, 35, 119
Aeschylus, 114
aestheticism, 21, 23–24, 27, 28, 35, 84, 137, 196 (n. 15); philosophical division within, 30
Agamemnon (Browning, translator), 203 (n. 23)
Ahrimanes (Peacock), 202 (n. 6)
Amos, 2
anti-Semitism, 119
Apes of God, The, 12, 18, 67, 70–83, 86, 107, 113, 122, 130, 148, 152, 160, 175, 201 (n. 5); style, 87, 114, 115; relationship to "The Man of the World," 129; relationship to *The Childermass*, 132–34
Apuleius, 158
architecture, 62
Arghol (character), 96–98, 111
Arnold, Matthew, 15, 112, 113, 130, 141
"Art as Technique" (Shklovsky), 36
Art of Being Ruled, The, 73–74, 83, 85, 91, 103–4, 107, 116, 119, 130, 134, 151, 153, 155; relationship to *The Apes of God*, 81; relationship to Catholicism, 118; relationship to "The Man of the World," 129, 205 (n. 6); relationship to *Time and Western Man*, 131–32

Art of Spiritual Harmony, The (Kandinsky), 8
Arts and Letters (periodical), 67, 70
atomic bomb, 170
Auden, W. H., 6
Auschwitz, 176
Austen, Jane, 86
Avesta, 106

Babbitt, Irving, 196 (n. 15)
Bacchus, 150
Bagdad (painting), 204–5 (n. 1)
Bailiff, the (character), 101, 111, 127, 128, 133, 136, 137, 141, 146–47, 148–58, 168–71, 175, 190, 191
Balla, Giacomo, 65
Balzac, Honoré de, 28
Barrie, J. M., 74
Baudelaire, Charles, 199 (n. 3)
Beckett, Samuel, 42, 115
behaviorism, 86, 89–90, 109, 131
Bell, Vanessa, 74
Benda, Julien, 202 (n. 12)
Bergson, Henri, 34, 35, 50, 83, 121, 146–47, 155; quoted, 95–96
Berkeley, Bishop, 111, 123
Bible, 2, 10, 106, 113, 122, 139
Blake, William, 2, 6, 38, 74, 78, 102, 105, 107, 109, 113, 129, 137, 140, 150, 182, 186
BLAST, 5, 27, 43, 47, 48, 59–61, 65, 140, 141, 159
Blasting and Bombardiering, 19, 39–40, 48, 128, 148, 159

Bloomsbury, 67, 74, 75
Boleyn, Dan (character), 72, 73, 76, 80, 81, 83, 133
Bomberg, David, 32
Borges, Jorge Luis, 122, 130
Bradley, F. H., 112
British Broadcasting Corporation (BBC), 168
Brittany, 4, 7; Lewis's opinion of, 50, 67
"Brobdingnag," 96–98
Brobdingnag (character), 95–98, 175
Browning, Robert, 203 (n. 23)
Buffalo, New York, 6
Bultmann, Rudolf, 197 (n. 32)
Bunyan, John, 141
Burke, Edmund, 88
Byron, Lord, 2, 30, 121, 129
Byzantine art, 33, 35

Caliph's Design, The, 61–64, 131, 159
Calvinism, 110–11, 112, 114, 115, 124
Campbell, Roy, 92
Camus, Albert, 186, 187–91
Canada, 6, 167
Canadian Gun Pit, A (painting), 66
Canadian War Memorials project, 65
"Cantleman's Spring Mate," 165
Cantos (Pound), 106, 129, 167–68
Caracciolo, Peter: quoted, 103
Card, Father Augustine (character), 184–85
Carlyle, Thomas, 203 (n. 23)
Catholicism, 17, 98, 115–25, 168, 171
Cézanne, Paul, 8
Chamber Music (Joyce), 18
Chaplin, Charlie, 150
Chesterton, G. K., 56, 125
Childermass, The, 9, 18, 78, 103, 106, 107, 126–58,
159, 160, 168, 169, 182, 204–5 (n. 1); relation-
ship to The Apes of God, 132–34; absence of
women in, 164; original plan for sequels, 205
(n. 2); relationship to "The Man of the
World," 205 (n. 6); relationship to Finnegans
Wake, 205 (n. 8)
Chirico, Giorgio de, x, 204–5 (n. 1)
Christianity, 16, 98, 102, 141, 155, 169, 171;
Nietzsche's contempt for, 102; relation to
Hegelianism, 105; asceticism,106; Lewis re-
invents, 184
Cold War, 169
Coleridge, Samuel Taylor, 45, 151
communism, 152, 171; Lewis's relationship to,
104
Conan Doyle, Arthur, 18
Confucius, 106
Conrad, Joseph, 111
Criterion, The (periodical), 128, 205 (n. 6)

Critique of Pure Reason (Kant), 129
Cromwell, Oliver, 178
cubism, 5, 27, 61, 63, 84, 172
"cult of the child," 73

Dachau, 176
Daily Mail (periodical), 58
Dante, 125, 130, 138, 177
D'Arcy, M. C., 119
Darwin, Charles, x, 10, 77
"Death of the Ankou, The," 7, 98–101, 106; com-
position of, 201 (n. 5)
Deussen, Paul, 103
Devil, the. See Sammael, Lord
Dickens, Charles, 15, 81
Dionysus, 81
"Dithyrambic Spectator, The," 124
Divine Comedy, The (Dante), 137, 176–77
Dostoevsky, Fyodor, 4, 113, 161
Dryden, John, 203 (n. 25)
Durkheim, Émile, 50

Edwards, Paul: quoted, 70
Egoist, The, 4
Egyptian art, 35, 95
Einstein, Albert, 77, 139, 146, 147
Elijah, 2
Eliot, T. S., x, 3, 16, 21, 69, 104, 112, 128, 139, 151,
194, 203 (n. 25); on The Childermass and
Monstre Gai, 9, 182; mythical method, 11,
136–37; religious ideas compared with
Lewis's, 115–16
Elliott, Robert C.: quoted, 79, 93
empiricism, 144
Endymion (Keats), 93, 158
Enemy, the (Lewis's persona), x, 2, 110, 157
Enemy, The (periodical), 118
Enemy of the Stars, The, 18, 43, 44, 96–97, 101,
122, 126, 137, 140; relationship to audience,
114; nature of characters, 149
English Review (periodical), 50, 55
Epstein, Jacob, 32
Erlich, Victor: quoted, 36–37
existentialism, 186
expressionism, 61
Ezekiel, 108

Fabianism, 56
Fane, Hercules (character), 23, 24, 25, 26, 27, 28,
30
fascism, 82–83, 152, 167, 171; Lewis's understanding of, 104; Sorel's relationship to, 119
Finnegans Wake, 18, 105, 129; relationship to The
Childermass, 136–38, 205 (n. 8); how main

character resembles the Bailiff, 149
Finnian-Shaw, Lord Osmund (character), 72
Fish, Stanley: quoted, 82
Flaubert, Gustave, 3, 85
Folklore in the Old Testament (Frazer), 103
Ford, Ford Madox, 3, 6, 21, 42, 43, 49, 50, 151;
    account of first meeting with Lewis, 55
Frazer, James G., 103
French Revolution, 14, 74, 101, 111, 143, 150
Freud, Sigmund, 3, 10, 83
Fry, Roger, 58, 67
Frye, Northrop: quoted, 106
futurism, 5, 38, 69, 70; Italian, 39, 65

Gargantua and Pantagruel (Rabelais), 129
Gaudier-Brzeska, Henri, 59
Gauguin, Paul, 4
Gay Science, The (Nietzsche), 102, 193; Lewis's
    reading of, 199 (n. 42)
Genealogy of Morals, The (Nietzsche), 116–17, 155
General Strike of 1926, 71, 149, 159, 207 (n. 1)
George V, 140
Girard, Rene, 91
Golden Ass, The (Apuleius), 158
Greene, Graham, 168
Group X, 149
Gulliver's Travels (Swift), 77, 154, relationship to
    The Apes of God, 76; relationship to *The
    Childermass*, 142–48, 153
Guns (art exhibition), 66, 173

Handley-Read, Charles, 173
Hanp (character), 97
Hansen, Miriam: quoted, 56
Hardcaster, Percy (character), 160–61, 163–64,
    165
Harding, Hester, 166, 207 (n. 5)
Harding, René (character), 165–68, 174, 180,
    185–86
Hegel, G. W. F., 105
Herod, 126
Hesse, Hermann, 104
Hill, Christopher: quoted, 139
Hitchcock, Alfred, 88
Hitler, Adolf, 5–6, 152, 153
Hobbes, Thomas, 144
Hogarth, William, 67
Homer, 130, 138, 204 (n. 41)
House of Lords, 35
Hulme, T. E., 32–36, 38, 39, 85, 122, 146, 172,
    193; "Critique of Satisfaction," 12–14; on
    religion, 15–16; on Original Sin, 16–17, 56
Human Age, The, ix, 18, 26, 95, 103, 127, 168, 169,
    174, 182, 186, 190–91, relationship to *The

Red Priest*, 185; similarities with *The Plague*,
    188; relationship between second and third
    volumes of, 207 (n. 9)
humanism, 12, 15, 95, 115, 117, 119, 172–73; rela-
    tionship to the divine, 167
Hume, David, 144
Hyperides (character), 127, 136, 155, 156–57

Ibsen, Henrik, 150
"If So the Man You Are," 1
Iliad (Homer), 204 (n. 41)
imagism, 122
imperialism, 60
impressionism, 30
"Inferior Religions," 84–85, 96, 101; Lewis de-
    fines "wild body," 95
Ingres, Jean Auguste Dominique, 173
Isherwood, Christopher, 6

James, Henry, 44, 87
James, William, 121
Jameson, Fredric: quoted, 18, 105, 111, 118, 138,
    149, 169, 171–72
Japanese language, 37
Jehovah the Thunderer (painting), 173–174
Jeremiah, 108, 122
John, Augustus, 65, 109–10, 118
John, Henry, 118
Johnson, Samuel, 111
Jonson, Ben, 10, 156
Joyce, James, x, 2, 3, 4, 16, 17, 42, 85, 87, 111, 128,
    130, 131, 139, 190, 194; mythical method, 11;
    satirized in *The Apes of God*, 12; artistic de-
    velopment, 17, 44; romantic tendencies in,
    76; naturalistic method, 107; technical inter-
    est in language, 113; affinities between his
    work and Lewis's, 136–38
Jupiter, 102
Justice in the Revolution and the Church
    (Proudhon), 105
Juvenal, 80

Kafka, Franz, 52, 55, 133
Kandinsky, Wassily, 8
Keats, John, 25, 92, 158
Kell-Imrie, Sir, Michael (character), 86–93, 101,
    164, 176
Kenner, Hugh, 138, 183, 207 (n. 9); quoted, 3, 9,
    90, 106, 129, 143, 185
Kern, Stephen: quoted, 10
Ker-Orr (character), 99–101, 175
Kierkegaard, Søren, x, 113, 188; aesthetic, ethi-
    cal, and religious stages, 17, 94, 197 (n. 34)
King Lear (Shakespeare), 12, 108

Kreisler, Otto (character), 28, 29, 40–42, 44–46, 111, 149, 161, 163, 175

Lafourcade, Bernard, 67; quoted, 87
Langer, Susanne K., 196 (n. 15)
Lasch, Christopher, 203 (n. 24)
Laslett, Peter, 145
Lasserre, Pierre, 35
Lawrence, D. H., 3, 4, 57; style parodied in *Snooty Baronet*, 106; attitude toward women, 165
Lawrence, T. E., 106
League of Nations, 5
Lenin, V. I., 83, 153
Leonardo da Vinci, 204 (n. 40)
Les Demoiselles d'Avignon (Picasso), 11
"Les Saltimbanques," 50–55, 64, 70, 78, 108, 153, 156, 159, 201–2 (n. 5)
Leviathan (Hobbes), 144
Lévy-Bruhl, Lucien, 50
liberalism, 56, 171
Lion and the Fox, The, 90, 186–87; relationship to "The Man of the World," 129
Literature and Dogma (Arnold), 112
Locke, John, 78, 115
Lolita (Nabokov), 87, 130
Lost Generation, 16
"Love Song of J. Alfred Prufrock, The" (Eliot), 21, 71, 115
Ludo (character), 99–101
Lunken, Bertha (character), 28, 42, 161
Luther, Martin, 108, 116–17, 124, 203 (nn. 26, 28)

Macbeth (Shakespeare), 22
Machiavelli, Niccolò, 2, 90, 131, 180, 186–87
Maeterlinck, Maurice, 22
Malevich, Kasimir, 45
Malign Fiesta, 127, 168, 169, 170, 175–84, 190; relationship to *Monstre Gai*, 207 (n. 9)
Manicheism, 102, 105
"Man of the World, The," 128–30, 159, 186; composition of, 205 (n. 6)
Marinetti, F. T., 39
Maritain, Jacques, 125
Marx, Karl, 10, 78, 119; Lewis's opinion of, 104
Marxism: Lewis's opposition to, 105
Materer, Timothy, 87
Matthew, Gospel of, 126
Maurras, Charles, 119
Melville, Herman, 88
Men without Art, 159
Mill, John Stuart: quoted, 14–15
Miller, J. Hillis: quoted, 15
Milton (Blake), 107

Milton, John, 2, 113, 125, 138–41, 155, 186, 203 (n. 25)
Mithraism, 86, 87, 91
Moby Dick (Melville), 88, 89
modernism, 4, 59, 70, 172; definition, 84; importance of the text, 113
monotheism, 122
Monstre Gai, 9, 127, 168, 169–72, 174, 181, 190; relationship to *Malign Fiesta*, 207 (n. 9)
Montessori, Maria, 78
Moore, T. Sturge, 26, 30, 56; remembered by Lewis, 19–20; opinion of Lewis's poems, 21
Morris, William, 58
Mr. Wyndham Lewis as a Tyro (painting), 67, 158
Mrs. Dukes' Million, 18, 22–27, 30, 39, 49, 50, 84, 176
Mussolini, Benito, 83, 153, 167

Nabokov, Vladimir, 87
Napoléon, 23, 150, 204 (n. 40)
Nashe, Thomas, 129
naturalism, 30, 45, 196 (n. 14)
Nature of Belief, The (D'Arcy), 119
Neoplatonism, 202 (n. 8)
New Age, The (periodical), 56, 104, 200 (n. 5)
New English Art Club, 30
Newton, Isaac, 78, 146, 147, 180
Newton, J. F., 202 (n. 6)
Nietzsche, Friedrich, x, 2, 10, 36, 52, 61, 89, 97, 136, 137, 140, 155, 161, 190, 194; on truth and rhetoric, 11; Lewis's opinion of, 44, 199 (n. 42); on Zoroastrianism, 102–3; Luther, 116–17, 203 (n. 28); on the will to power, 149, 150
Not-self, the, 111–13, 115, 124, 172
nouvelle roman, 115

"Ode to Psyche" (Keats), 25
Oedipus the King (Sophocles), 12, 101
Omega Workshop, 58, 59
Orage, A. R., 56, 57, 200 (n. 5)
Origins of the Aryans, The (Taylor), 103
"Our Wild Body," 56–58

paganism, 122, 124
Paine, Thomas, 143
painting, x, 58, 62, 172–73; relationship to writing in Lewis's career, 7–8, 67, 122; in the post–World War I period, 63, 126
pantheism, 123
Paradise Lost (Milton), 102, 116; relationship to *The Childermass*, 139–40
Paris, 79
Parker, Valerie: quoted, 162
pastoralism, 160

Pater, Walter, 20, 196 (n. 15)
Peacock, Thomas Love, 102, 201–2 (n. 5)
Perloff, Marjorie, 39; quoted, 59
Persia, 86, 87, 92
Peter, Saint, 99, 127
Peter Pan (Barrie), 74
Petersburg University, 36
Philosophy of Style (Spencer), 36
photography, 8
picaresque, 76, 142
Picasso, Pablo, 11, 64, 199 (n. 3)
Pierpoint (character), 76–89 passim, 101, 111,
 132, 133, 152, 175
Plague, The (Camus), 187–91
Planck, Max, 180
Plato, 10, 122
Play (Beckett), 42
Ploumilliau, 99
Poe, Edgar Allan, 26, 113
Poggioli, Renato, 59, 75; quoted, 199 (n. 3)
Poirier, Richard, 38
Pope, Alexander, 26, 76, 78
Portrait of the Artist as a Young Man, A (Joyce),
 12, 18, 26, 27, 29, 42, 71, 114
Potebnya, Alexander, 36
Pound, Dorothy, 188
Pound, Ezra, x, 16, 29, 66, 94, 118, 128, 130, 139,
 150, 167–68, 188, 194, 206 (n. 26); opinion of
 Lewis, 2, 3, 4–5; aestheticism, 21; opinion of
 Ford, 42; on *The Apes of God*, 71; as transla-
 tor, 114; interest in paganism, 122
Prince, The (Machiavelli), 90
Prometheus, 102
Prometheus Unbound (Shelley), 102, 202 (n. 8)
Protestantism, 17, 107–14, 117
Proudhon, Pierre-Joseph, 104; critique of
 Hegelianism, 105; Sorel's relationship to,
 120
Pullman, James (character), 127, 133, 134, 136,
 140, 142, 147, 148, 150, 157, 168–72, 174–86
 passim, 190–91; political sympathies, 207
 (n. 9)
Puritanism, 116, 178

Quinn, John, 61, 65, 71, 128

Raza Khan (character) 22, 24, 25, 26, 31, 176
Read, Herbert, 66
Rebel Art Centre, 58–59
Red Priest, The, 184–85, 207 (n. 5)
Reflections on Violence (Sorel), 120
Reformation, 108, 116; Lewis's understanding
 of, 121
Renaissance, 11, 13, 33, 147, 155, 172

Renaissance, The (Pater), 20
Revenge for Love, The, 159, 160–65, 182
Richards, I. A.: quoted, 127
Rieux, Bernard (character), 188–90
Rights of Man, The (Paine), 143
Rilke, Ranier Maria, 199 (n. 3)
Robinson, Alan: quoted, 20
Robinson Crusoe (Defoe), 144
romanticism, 44, 74, 82, 108, 115, 129, 140, 143,
 187; T. Sturge Moore's relationship to, 20;
 German, 60, 196 (n. 15); the hero in, 101;
 Lewis's dislike of, 105, 130, 147; Lewis as ro-
 mantic mythmaker, 153
Rosebery, Earl of, 88
Rossetti, Dante Gabriel, 6
Rousseau, Jean-Jacques, 14, 115, 129
Rowlandson, Thomas, 142
Royal, Evan (character), 23, 24, 25, 26, 27, 28, 30,
 31, 49, 84
Rude Assignment, 65, 130, 161, 173, 186–87, 199
 (n. 42)
Rugby School, 4, 127
Ruskin, John, 162, 165

Sammael, Lord (character), 101, 111, 169–70,
 175–83, 191
Sartre, Jean-Paul, 186, 187–88, 190
satire, 70, 174–75; conventional assumptions
 about, 72; absence in the twentieth century,
 75; in seventeenth and eighteenth century,
 76; Lewis's departures from conventional
 assumptions about, 78; and moralism, 79–
 80; non-moral, 80, 178
Satire and Fiction, 76, 79, 135
Satters. *See* Satterthwaite
Satterthwaite (character), 127, 133, 134, 140, 142,
 147, 148, 168, 181
Saussure, Ferdinand de, 137
science, 8, 143; non-impersonality of, 84–86; as
 basis of modernity, 134; in *Gulliver's Travels*,
 145; early twentieth-century conception of,
 146, 206 (n. 22); praised by the Bailiff, 150,
 155
sculpture, 21, 62
Seidel, Michael: quoted, 91, 93
Self Condemned, 140, 165–68, 175, 185–86, 207
 (n. 5)
Severini, Gino, 65
Shakespear, Olivia, 153
Shakespeare, William, 20, 76, 90, 101, 108,
 186–87
Shan Van Vocht, 92–93, 164
Shelley, Percy Bysshe, 47, 49, 74, 81, 121, 129,
 141, 181; on Zoroastrianism and

Manicheism, 102, 202 (nn. 6, 8)
Shklovsky, Victor, 32, 36–39
"Sigismund," 67–70, 78
Sitwell family, 75
Slade School of Art, 4, 7
Small Crucifixion Series I–IV (painting), 174
Snooty Baronet, 18, 67, 86–93, 106, 158, 159, 175, 176, 179; feminine voice in, 164
Snooty Baronet, the (character). *See* Kell-Imrie, Sir Michael
socialism, 131
Sophists, 10–11
Sorel, Georges, 119–21, 159
Southern Agrarians, 16
Spencer, Herbert, 36
Spengler, Oswald: criticized by Lewis, 111–12, 196 (n. 15)
Stamp, Margot (character), 160, 162, 163–64, 165, 174
Stamp, Victor (character), 160, 162, 163–64, 165, 174
Starr-Smith (character), 82–83
Stein, Gertrude, 131; satirized in *The Childermass*, 136
Stendhal, 150
Strindberg, Frida, 58
suffragette movement, 60
surrealism, 204–5 (n. 1)
Swift, Jonathan, 76, 77, 78, 91, 138, 141–48
symbolism, 36–37
Symons, Arthur, 30
Symons, Julian: quoted, 202 (n. 19)
syndicalism, 56, 120; Lewis's understanding of, 104
System of Economic Contradictions (Proudhon), 105

Tarr, 2, 4, 18, 19, 22, 27–32, 39–48, 55, 58, 71, 95, 112, 113, 115, 118, 122, 129, 137, 149, 165, 176; Rousseau's ideas critiqued, 14; relationship to *The Childermass*, 127; contrasted with *The Revenge for Love*, 161–63
Tarr, Frederick (character), 27, 28 31, 32, 40, 41, 42, 44, 46, 47, 161, 163, 175; as self-portrait of Lewis, 162
Tarrou, Jean (character), 188–91
Taylor, Isaac, 103
Taylor, Mark C., 11–12; quoted, 203 (n. 26)
Teiresias, 101
Theatre Manager, The (painting), 27, 65, 84
Thus Spake Zarathustra (Nietzsche), 102, 103
Time and Western Man, 18, 77, 107, 108, 111, 112, 113, 119, 121–24, 136, 153, 155, 187, 193–94, 196 (n. 15), 202 (n. 19); relationship to "The Man of the World," 129, 205 (n. 6); as de-

fense of western civilization, 130; relationship to *The Art of Being Ruled*, 131–32
Timon of Athens (Shakespeare): Lewis's illustrations for, 67
Tolstoy, Leo: quoted, 38
totalitarianism, 129
Trial of Man, The, 183–85
Tristram Shandy (Sterne), 87
Tyros and Portraits (art exhibition), 66, 75

Ulysses (Joyce), 2, 12, 71, 76–77, 87, 130; Lewis's opinion of, 107, 112–13, 128; idea of history in, 136–37
Uncle Tom's Cabin, 74
Unnameable, The (Beckett), 115
Upanishads, 106
Upward, Allen, 206 (n. 26)

Van Gogh, Vincent, 160
Vasek, Anastasya (character), 28, 31, 42
Victorian period, 14–15, 18, 19–21, 25, 30, 114, 203 (n. 23)
Villon, François, 1, 2
Virgil, x, 94, 132, 138
Vision, A (Yeats), 153–54
vorticism, 59, 61, 65, 140, 204–5 (n. 1)
Vulgar Streak, The, 159, 207 (n. 5)

Wagner, Richard, 9, 196 (n. 15)
Warhol, Andy, 53
Waste Land, The (Eliot), 68–69, 71, 104, 112, 151
Watson, James B., 78, 109
Wells, H. G., 3, 4, 40, 134–38, 147
West, Rebecca, 3
When the Sleeper Wakes (Wells), 134, 135
Whistler, James McNeill, 8
Whittingdon, Dick (character), 73, 74
Wild Body, The, 98, 101, 201 (n. 5)
Wilde, Oscar, 36, 65
Windham, William, 88
Winters, Yvor: on T. Sturge Moore's poetry, 20
women: in Lewis's fiction, 164–65; in *The Human Age*, 179
Woolf, Virginia, 77, 162
Wordsworth, William, 14, 15, 129, 162
World of William Clissold, The (Wells), 135
World War I, x, 5, 16, 44, 47, 49, 60, 74, 109, 126, 142; effect on Lewis, 64, 65, 83, 120–21, 136, 139, 172; and "human engineering" (Yerkes), 77; Lewis's religious position during, 118
World War II, x, 17, 118, 165–67, 169
Worringer, Wilhelm, 33–35
Writer and the Absolute, The, 187

Yeats, W. B., 3, 16, 20, 30, 36, 148, 155, 156; aes-
    theticism, 27, 31; praises *The Childermass*,
    141–42; notes similarities between *The
    Childermass* and *A Vision*, 153–54
Yerkes, R. M., 77, 109

Zagreus, Horace (character), 71–83 passim, 85,
    111, 132, 133, 134, 175; explains "impersonal-
    ity" of science, 86
Zoroastrianism, 102–7, 202 (nn. 6, 8)

About the Author

Daniel Schenker is Associate Professor of English at The University of Alabama in Huntsville. He received his bachelor's degree from Brandeis University and his master's degree and doctorate from Johns Hopkins University.